George Fiske

Profits in poultry

Useful and ornamental breeds and their profitable management

George Fiske

Profits in poultry
Useful and ornamental breeds and their profitable management

ISBN/EAN: 9783337146870

Printed in Europe, USA, Canada, Australia, Japan

Cover: Foto ©Lupo / pixelio.de

More available books at **www.hansebooks.com**

Profits in... Poultry

USEFUL AND
ORNAMENTAL BREEDS
AND THEIR
PROFITABLE
MANAGEMENT

PROFUSELY ILLUSTRATED

NEW YORK
ORANGE JUDD COMPANY
1900

COPYRIGHT 1893 BY
ORANGE JUDD COMPANY

FRED'K SCHOLES

PUBLISHERS' PREFACE.

As denoted by the title of the book, the editors have given most prominence to the side of poultry keeping which returns an income. The ways and means by which eggs or poultry can be grown at a profit are discussed in great detail. So many questions are constantly asked about the various breeds and also concerning diseases and their treatment, that these topics have been quite fully considered. The turkey department has been made as complete as possible on account of the increasing interest in that branch of poultry keeping.

Incubators, care of chicks, feeding and care for eggs, or for meat, building coops and houses, caponizing, marketing, warfare against pests, raising waterfowl and ornamental poultry, are described at length. The reference matter and tables are a special feature of the book. The present volume is nearly one-third larger than any previous edition.

Experience of breeders and poultry farmers has been drawn upon freely, resulting in that breadth of view which can be obtained only by comparison of successful methods in actual practice. Among those who have directly assisted in furnishing the new matter are many of the foremost poultry experts and specialists of the present time. The entire material has been carefully prepared by Mr. George B. Fiske, poultry editor American Agriculturist. About 100 pages and many illustrations have been added to the new and enlarged edition, but without any increase in the price of this useful book.

CONTENTS.

	PAGE
PUBLISHERS' PREFACE	3

CHAPTER I.
Poultry Raising.. 7

CHAPTER II.
Convenient and Good Poultry Houses..................... 13

CHAPTER III.
Special Purpose Poultry House............................. 25

CHAPTER IV.
Poultry House Conveniences................................ 31

CHAPTER V.
Natural Incubation... 46

CHAPTER VI.
Care of Chickens—Coops for them........................ 54

CHAPTER VII.
Artificial Incubation.. 65

CHAPTER VIII.
Preparing for Market.. 80

CHAPTER IX.
Eggs for Market... 86

CHAPTER X.
Caponizing—How it is done................................. 93

CHAPTER XI.
Poultry Keeping as a Business.............................. 98

CHAPTER XII.
Hints about Management.................................... 101

CONTENTS.

CHAPTER XIII.
Some Popular Breeds.. 121

CHAPTER XIV.
Asiatic Breeds.. 123

CHAPTER XV.
European Breeds... 136

CHAPTER XVI.
American Breeds... 168

CHAPTER XVII.
Diseases of Poultry... 178

CHAPTER XVIII.
Parasites upon Poultry.. 189

CHAPTER XIX.
Raising Turkeys... 193

CHAPTER XX.
Raising Geese... 210

CHAPTER XXI.
Raising Ducks... 218

CHAPTER XXII.
Ornamental Poultry.. 235

CHAPTER XXIII.
Breeding and Cross Breeding... 247

CHAPTER XXIV.
Feeding for Growth.. 261

CHAPTER XXV.
Feeding for Eggs.. 273

CHAPTER XXVI.
Turkeys on the Farm... 288

CHAPTER XXVII.
Diseases and Pests.. 317

CHAPTER XXVIII.
Poultry Dictionary and Calendar....................................... 335

Index—Alphabetical.. 350

PROFITS IN POULTRY.

CHAPTER I.

POULTRY RAISING.

No other business connected with agricultural pursuits, seems so attractive as poultry farming. Even those who fail in the business and retire from it, aver that they are certain they could succeed in a new trial. At the start, the general idea is that the business consists of throwing out corn to a flock of hens with one hand, and gathering eggs with the other. But while this may be true in some cases, it is very different in others. The expert poultry raiser may perhaps meet with no difficulty, and all may go on smoothly, but the novice is in trouble from the first; the eggs are few, and the chicks die. One may easily keep ten or twelve fowls with profit, who could not double or treble this number successfully, because with a large number all the difficulties which arise, such as want of cleanliness, the presence of vermin, impure air, and risk of infection, increase in a much larger ratio than does the number in the flock. But if one has succeeded with a small flock, there is no reason why he should not be able to do so with several flocks, if each is kept in just the same manner as the original one. Afterwards the flocks may be enlarged, but as this is the very point on which most of the younger poultry raisers fail, the greatest caution should be observed in adding to the number of fowls kept in each coop or house, or yard.

THE BEST BREED FOR MARKET PURPOSES.

What follows in this chapter is from E. A. Samuels of Massachusetts: I find it very difficult to answer the question: "Which breed of fowls do you recommend as being the best for market purposes?" for it is almost impossible to lay down as a guide any rule, or name any particular breed, or cross, or variety which will net the best results in *every* market. A great deal depends upon the locality where the breeder is situated, and it also depends upon whether the breeder desires "broilers," or early or late "roasters."

In the Philadelphia, Baltimore and New York markets, as well as among the Paris and London dealers, chickens with white or light skin are preferred to those with yellow skin, and consequently the Dorkings, Black Spanish, Houdans, and other white skinned varieties or their crosses always bring the best prices, and are in the quickest demand, while in the Boston and the other New England cities, and in Chicago, and perhaps some of the other large western cities, where any decided preference has been expressed, the yellow-skinned birds are in the greater demand.

In the Boston markets and hotels a lot of bright, yellow-skinned chickens will always command a better price than will a lot of white-skinned birds, although the two lots may have been fed precisely alike, and be in equally as good condition; this I have proved repeatedly, so that, as I before stated, a great deal depends upon the intended market.

Many persons believe that the color of the chicken's skin is governed largely by the kind of food the birds are provided with; believing that yellow Indian corn will produce a yellow-skinned chick, while wheat or oats will cause the skin to be white. Although there may be some little reason for this belief, I think that it cannot be regarded as of much importance, for a lot of chickens of different varieties, if fed and reared in the same pen, will exhibit all shades of color in the skin from yellow to white. It seems natural to some breeds to secrete a fat that is yellow, while other breeds secrete a fat that has but little tint.

A great deal has been written in regard to the merits of different breeds of fowls, and people are, generally, pretty well acquainted with the characteristics of each, so that it would seem almost an act of supererogation here for me to dwell upon this topic, did not my experience in a measure differ from that of many writers. From extended and careful observation, I have arrived at the following conclusions :

If a breeder intends to raise chickens for the Philadelphia and other first-named series of markets, a cross of Plymouth Rock cock, one year old, on a two-year-old Light Brahma hen, produces the most desirable early "roasters;" a pure-blood Plymouth Rock mating gives the best "broilers" and late "roasters." In fact for my own table I prefer Plymouth Rock chickens, either as broilers or roasters, to all others. Of course, at present, Langshans and Wyandottes are too valuable to be taken into account as table fowls.

Next to the above matings, for the markets named, a cross between a yearling Black-breasted Game and White or Buff Cochin, makes desirable broilers, but not so quick selling as those first named.

In my experience, the principal objection to Plymouth Rocks and their crosses lies in their dark pin-feathers, which abound in the skin of broilers, and are very difficult to be removed, and when they are taken out thoroughly the skin is often badly broken and marred by the picker.

For the Boston and other markets named in the second list, I find that for broilers a cross between a yearling White Leghorn cock, on a two-year-old Light Brahma hen, is by all odds most desirable. The chicks mature very rapidly; they are plump and full-breasted at nine to twelve weeks old; they have a bright, yellow skin, and no dark pin-feathers.

I prefer a two-year-old hen to breed from for the reason that her chickens are larger and more vigorous than are those of a yearling, and they mature much more quickly.

Next in value for broilers in these markets to this cross, in the succession they are named, are the pure-blood Light Brahma, Plymouth Rock, White or Buff Cochin, and cross of Brown Leghorn on Partridge Cochin, all of the age of from ten to twelve weeks old if hatched in January or February, or nine to eleven weeks old if hatched in March or April, they growing a little more rapidly then than the earlier hatched birds. For early roasters, for these markets, I prefer a cross of Plymouth Rock yearling cock on Light Brahma hen, the latter furnishing the large frame-work on which the blood of the former builds a full-breasted, quick-maturing fine-meated bird. Light Brahma cockerels, nine to twelve months old, make good and marketable roasters, but they are not so profitable to raise as the cross I have named.

MANAGEMENT AND FEED.

As much depends on the management of the chickens, however, as on the characteristics of the different breeds. A good poultryman may, with poor stock, succeed better than would a bad manager with the best of stock.

It is of great importance, in raising chickens, that they should be well supplied with a variety of food. "Short commons" does not pay in chicken raising. The common custom is to keep a dish of "Indian meal dough" mixed up, and three times a day a lot is thrown down to the chickens. If they eat it, well and good; if not, and the chances are they will not, having become tired of one single article of diet set before them day after day, it stands and sours. If a quantity is thus found uneaten, the next meal is likely to be a light one, and the chickens, driven by hunger, finally devour the sour stuff. The result is cholera or some other fatal disease sets in and their owner wonders why his chickens are dying off. In my own practice I find that small quantities of varied food, if given to the chickens often, produce vastly better results than any other method of feeding.

On no account, do I permit young chickens to be fed with Indian meal dough. For the first morning meal I give all my young stock boiled potatoes mashed up fine and mixed with an equal quantity of Indian meal and shorts. I find nothing so good and acceptable as this food, and I use only small unmarketable potatoes; they prove more profitable than anything else I can employ.

I have had many hundreds of chickens at one time in my houses, varying in size from those but a few days old to others large enough for the table, and positively no other article of "soft food" was ever given to them; and I venture to say a more healthy and thrifty lot of chickens could not be found. When, in days gone by, I used to feed to the young stock the traditional "dough," I always counted on losing a large percentage, and the numbers that died from cholera, diarrhœa and kindred diseases, were great. Now a sick chicken is a rarity in my yards. After the potato mash is disposed of I give my chickens all the *fine* cracked corn they will eat up clean. Of course large chickens, those which are ten or twelve weeks old, can be fed with corn coarser cracked, but the young birds want it very fine. In about two hours after the cracked corn is eaten, I give all the wheat screenings the chicken will eat, and in another two hours, some oats. For supper they have all the cracked corn and wheat they can eat. It is of the utmost importance that the young birds should, at the close of the day, have full crops; for the nights in the winter and early spring are long, and as soon as the chickens have digested all their food they stop growing for the time being. I always make it a point to feed them as late in the afternoon as they can see, and as early in the morning.

By the above described system of feeding, the chickens are constantly tempted by a variety of healthy food, and the result is a rapid growth and perfect immunity from disease. If abundance of grass is not accessible to them, young chickens should have fed to them at least one meal a day of grass and clover chopped fine with a pair of scissors. In winter I give my chickens cabbages, throwing in whole heads for the birds to pick at.

CHAPTER II.

CONVENIENT AND GOOD POULTRY HOUSES.

A VERY CHEAP HEN HOUSE.

Experience has proved that twenty fowls, properly housed, provided with suitable food, pure water, clean nest boxes, plenty of dust, lime in some form, and gravel, will return more clear profit than fifty, kept as they generally are upon farms. Suggest a good poultry house to the average farmer, and frequently there arises in his mind the image of an elaborate affair costing one hundred, to one hundred and fifty dollars. Not being able to spare that amount for such a purpose, he goes without, and his poultry, exposed to the inclemencies of the

Fig. 1.—A CHEAP HEN HOUSE.

weather, are a dead expense fully two-thirds of the year, eating valuable food constantly and yielding nothing in return. A poultry house large enough to properly shelter twenty fowls can be erected at a very small cost. We give an engraving of one, all the materials of which, with the exception of the sash, cost three dollars and eighty-five cents. The sash was taken from a hot-bed that is used for sprouting sweet potatoes late in the spring. When the sash is required for the hot-bed the season is mild and the opening is covered with boards. This structure is nine feet wide, twelve feet long, and five feet high in the center. The short side of the roof is two feet long, and the long side, which fronts south and comes to within eighteen inches of the ground, is seven feet. At the further end the roof boards extend over an opening made for the fowls to pass in and out. The perches are one foot above the floor and extend along the north side of the interior. The bottom board on that side is hung with hinges so it can be raised, and the droppings under the perches scraped out. The nest boxes are ranged along the low side, the dust box is placed in the sunniest spot, and the feed and water troughs near the door. One pane of glass in the sash is loose so that it may be moved down for ventilation. The floor should be covered with sand when obtainable, if not, with straw, chaff, or other similar material that can be raked out when soiled. The whole interior should be given a coat of fresh lime whitewash at least four times a year, and the perches swabbed with kerosene. Hens kept in this house lay steadily all winter. The poultry house here described is easily cleaned, and answers the purpose nearly as well as one costing twenty times as much.

A WARM FOWL HOUSE.

Eggs in winter are what we all want. To secure them we must have for our hens a warm, snug house, easily kept clean, with provision for dusting, feed, water and exercise. To consider these requirements in the order named, we have first warmth as an important desideratum. Artificial heat has rarely been found profitable, hence we will not consider it. The fowls must depend for their warmth upon the sun, the natural heat of the earth, and the temperature of their own bodies. If we notice a flock of chickens, we shall see that they warm themselves by huddling together, by crowding on their roosts, by sitting flat upon the ground, and by standing or sitting in the sun. We must therefore employ all these ways to secure that warmth, without which we shall have few eggs, with no less or even greater expense for food.

Fowls suffer most from cold at night. In fact, nights are almost always colder than the days, and it is fortunate that by night when it is cold, we have less wind. A poultry house to be warm, must be close and tightly made, yet with good ventilation, for if warm and ill-ventilated, the birds may be suffocated. This has not un-

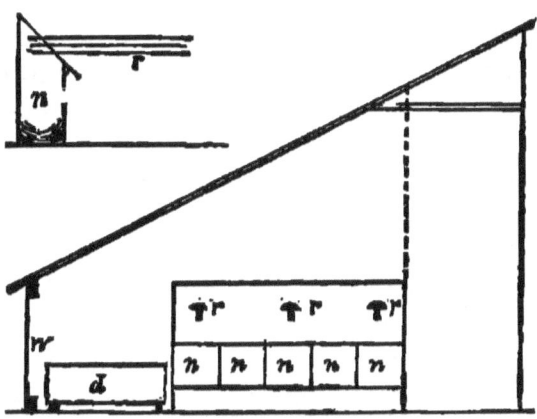

Figs. 2 and 3.—SECTIONS OF ROOSTING ROOM.

frequently occurred. By the accompanying section and plans (figs. 3 and 4), we secure warmth from every source. Too much sunlight is often disadvantageous, hence the low roof without windows. The windows (w), admit sunlight upon the floor and dust box. The house is twelve feet square, divided by a partition of boards. This leaves the two apartments each six feet wide. It is intended for less than twenty to thirty adult fowls. The perches (r), are five feet long each, so that thirty fowls will be pretty well crowded upon them. The full hight of the house is nine feet, in order to give the roof a good pitch, but within a ceiling is placed at the hight five and a half to six feet. This may be of slats, or plastering lath, placed the width of a lath apart, and in the winter the space above may be filled loosely with straw. Thus, with ventilating doors above, there can be no direct draft upon the fowls. In such a room there will always be a circulation of air. The air warmed by the bodily heat and the breadth of the fowls, rises into the upper part of the room. There is a constant current of cool air flowing down against every window, and this causes a circulation —up through the roosts, down by the window. After a while the air may become charged with carbonic acid gas from the breath of the fowls. This is heavier than the air, hence would, after being chilled by the window, not be likely to rise, but would in part flow off into the other compartment, through the passage for the fowls near the window. The closeness of the quarters for the number of fowls stated, will secure a high temperature at night, provided the walls and roof are reasonably tight, without danger. Perhaps the best way to secure a warm roof is the following: lay first a roof of hemlock boards, laid with the slope; upon these, shingling laths, and shingles. This secures an air space an inch thick under the shingles, in addition to the board roof. So constructed, no rafters would be needed, but one scantling, set edgeways and supported by posts in the middle of each side, and in the partition, to make the roof stiff.

The roosting-room is supplied with a large dust-box, always well filled, and two ranges of nest boxes, with sloping tops, as shown in figure 2. The chickens can not stand on these tops, and being set on each side of the room, they are made to support the roosts, which should not be higher than two feet, or two and a half feet from the floor. The best form of roost is made by taking two straight grained, smooth pine sticks, two inches wide and one inch thick, and nailing them together T-fashion.

If the top edges of the cap piece are rounded off by a plane, the result will be a stiff, strong perch, which will not disfigure the breast-bones of fowls, and which will keep their feet warm.

This apartment should be cleaned out every morning. To do this the perches are taken up, cleaned off with a wooden knife or scraper, and set in one corner. The roofs of the nest boxes are cleaned off with the same implement, and after scattering a little of a mixture of road-dust and plaster over the floor, all is swept up and put

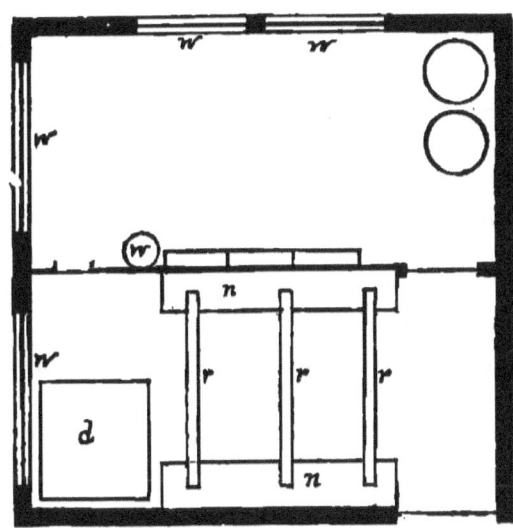

Fig. 4.—PLAN OF FOWL HOUSE.

in a barrel. Then a small layer of dust is scattered over the floor under the roosts, which however are not replaced until evening, or say three or four o'clock, when the last gathering of eggs is made.

We have considered the matter of warmth, and incidentally that of dusting, and in part of cleanliness. The day compartment is as light as we can conveniently make it. It ought to have a cement, or hard clay floor, well pounded down. Cement is preferable. The water fountain (w) should be cleaned and filled daily. If there is danger of its freezing, the water may be thrown out as soon as the fowls are on the roosts, and refilled with tepid water at daylight in the winter mornings. Three feed boxes are sufficient, one for soft feed, one for ground oyster shells, and one for ground bone. Grain should be fed upon the floor, and preferably at evening. This brings us to consider the last of our list of requirements, namely, exercise. To secure this, cover the floor with chopped straw to the depth of three inches, and scatter the grain upon this. Feed at such an hour that the chickens will not have time to find it all before it is dark, and this will be an inducement for them to get up early and go to scratching. Some provision of this kind is very important when fowls can not have much range and out-of-door exercise on account of snow and rain. In winter a dry outside run is very important. It is best provided by a long, low, lean-to roof, on the south side of an east and west fence. The sun should, even at noon, reach all the ground under the shed. If such a house as we have indicated, be built against a hillside, somewhat sunken perhaps; and earth banked up against the sides, except where windows come, will add greatly to its warmth.

CONVENIENT AND CHEAP POULTRY HOUSE.

Those who need a cheap building, and can do the greater part of the work themselves, will find the following plan excellent. The center of the building (see fig. 5), is 10x10 feet, and is six feet to the eaves. The wings are each 8x6x4 feet. Either of the three parts may be built first, and the others may be added from time to time. No posts are used in building it. The sills, 3x4 inches, and 10 feet long, and are mortised and put together in place; the plates, 3x4 inches, and 10 feet long, are put

CONVENIENT AND GOOD POULTRY HOUSES. 19

on the sills; then eight boards are cut six feet long, four of them with the angle at the top to correspond with the pitch of the roof. These are nailed to the sills, and

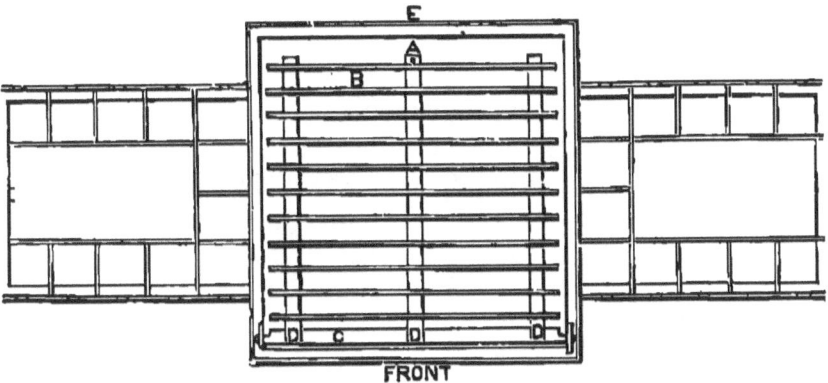

Fig. 5.—GROUND PLAN OF POULTRY HOUSE.

those in front and back nailed to the edges of those on the ends. Then four sticks are cut each five feet six inches long, the plate is raised up, a stick put under it

Fig. 6.—FRONT ELEVATION OF POULTRY HOUSE.

on the sill, in each corner: the boards are then nailed to it, and the frame is raised; boarded, and battened, and it is strong enough. The roosts are arranged as in figure 5; the piece, *C*, rests on the plates, and is held in place by cleats, and acts as a hinge. The pieces, *D*, are secured to it, and the roosts, *B*, to them. At *A* is a ring bolt, and overhead a hook. When the house is to be cleaned out, the roosts are raised and hooked up, and are six feet high, so there is no trouble in working under them. The door, *E*, is 6x3 feet. In each wing there are two rows of nests, each nest 18x18x12 inches, 12 in a row, 24 in each wing, and 48 in all ; the bottom of the lower row is two feet from the ground, and under it are five coops on each side, in each wing, twenty in all, (18x18x20 inches). These are closed inside with slats, and each one is inde-

Fig. 7.—END ELEVATION.

Fig. 8.—SECTION.

pendent, and entered from the outside, as shown in figures 6 and 7. The entrances to the nest-rooms are in the doors, as in figure 7. Figure 8 is an inside view of one of the wings, showing the interior arrangement of one side. The two windows in front, one in each wing, three doors, and twenty-three entrances for the fowls, will give sufficient ventilation, but if more is needed, small doors or windows, 18x18 inches, can be put above the plates, in the ends of the center building. The cupola is not necessary, but it allows the foul air to escape ; it costs about a day's work for a handy man, and is built of scraps. The roof need not, of necessity, be shingled.

CHAPTER III.

SPECIAL-PURPOSE POULTRY HOUSES.

A VERY COMPLETE POULTRY HOUSE.

The very complete yet simple plan for a poultry house on the following pages was submitted by Charles H. Colburn, of New Hampshire, in competition for prizes offered by the publishers, and received the highest award. It is built with the windows to the south. Fig. 9, a, is a door eighteen inches square for putting in coal; b is a place for early chickens; c, boxes for oyster shells and ground bone; d, movable coops for hens with chickens. The inside doors are at e, e, e, e; boxes for soft feed at g, g, and bins for grain are at h, h. A scuttle for the droppings is placed at i, in the passage-way, under which is a receiving box, and a track laid to the door j. This door is hung with T-hinges, and opened only for the passage of the box. A ventilating hole is left in the door. The nests for setting hens are at k; lobby for the hens at l, and small ten by twelve-inch openings through the wall for hens to enter the yards, are shown at m. Other similar openings for hens pass from yard to yard are at n. A small coal stove, o, is used to cook feed and for heating rooms in the coldest weather. Lead pipes, p, boxed up and packed with sawdust, run under the floor of the passage-way from the water tank to the end pens, where a faucet is attached and regulated that water will fall into dishes. The windows are at g, nine by twelve-inch glass; each sash is arranged to raise. The roosts, r, are one and a half by three inches, and rounded on the edge. The platform, s, under the roosts, is three feet wide, with a two-inch strip on the front; the whole may be covered with zinc if desired. There are two rows of nests, *t*, under the roosts, made with movable bottoms and sides, and may be taken out and cleaned from the passage-way. There are eight doors opening into the passage-way, that eggs may be gathered without going into the pens. Two long doors (one by seven and a half feet), hung with T-hinges, open upward, through which droppings can be easily removed. A water tank, *u*, holding a few gallons, is boxed up and packed in sawdust. There is a ventila-

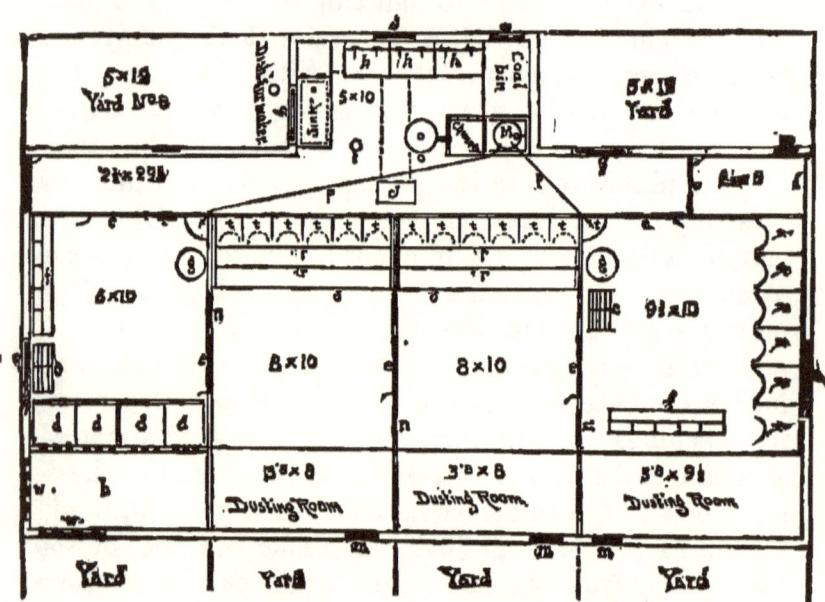

Fig. 9.—PLAN OF THE POULTRY HOUSE.

tor in the center of the roof that can be opened or closed by a cord from the passage-way. A double set of drawers, *v*, for holding eggs, may be made over the grain bins. A lattice door, *w*, is built in the wall for chickens, with a tight door in the outside that can be fastened up or down as desired. Small chickens may be fed from the outside by sliding the window, and from inside by letting down a board over the coops, or by opening a small door in the back of the coop. Over the sink, *x*, is a board (eighteen by thirty-six inches) with hinges, to be raised up as a side table for holding fowls while being dressed. A cupboard

Fig. 10.—THE SOUTH SIDE OF THE POULTRY HOUSE.

under the sink holds the knives, lantern, etc. At one end of the cupboard is a box for oyster shells and ground bone. A pail is set at *y* to catch the blood when fowls are killed. Over this pail, screwed into the rafter, is a hook with cord attached, to hang up the poultry by the legs, and a cord with a loop in it and a window weight,

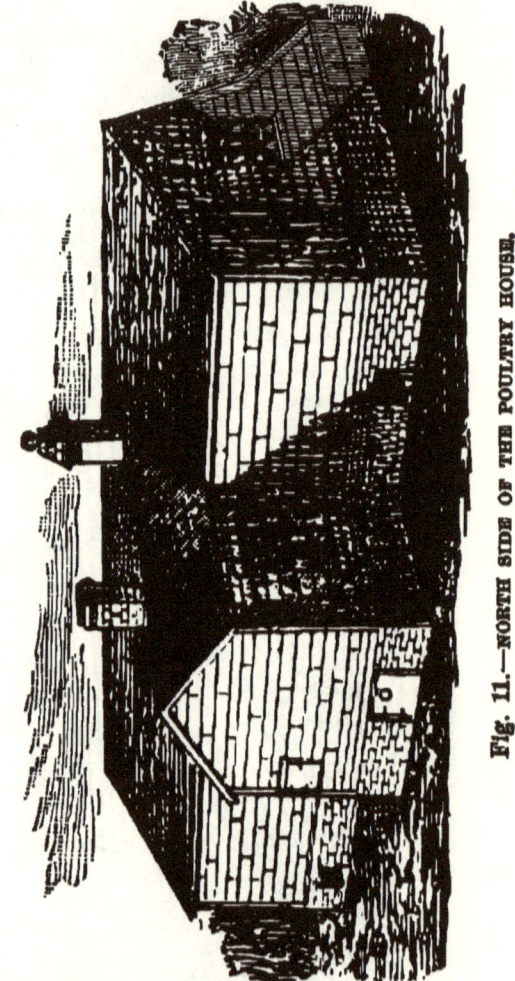

Fig. 11.—NORTH SIDE OF THE POULTRY HOUSE.

to be put over the fowl's neck before being struck with an axe. A small passage under the walk, is for fowls to enter the yard.

This poultry house can be built for $165.70, and when lathed and plastered will cost twenty-five dollars more.

It may be constructed for $130 by having the studding and rafters 22 inches apart, instead of 16 inches, and by setting it on posts and planked up two feet, in place of brick underpinning. The following are the estimates of material:

1 M Square Edge Boards for outside	$12.00
150 ft. Matched Spruce for entry floor	2.25
400 ft. Pine Sheathing for partitions, platforms, and doors	7.20
100 pieces 1¼ by ⅜ Pine for open work of partitions and caps	50
480 Chimney Brick	2.40
Lime and laying brick	2.00
400 Spruce Clap-boards, laid 4 inches to weather	7.00
3¼ M Shingles	7.70
Outside Door and Frame, 2¼ by 6¼	2.25
8 Windows and Frames, 9 by 13, glass	16.00
4 Sashes over Dusting Room	8.00
30 ft. of Capping	30
Hardware, including zinc, nails, locks, hinges, cords, etc.	10.00
175 ft. Pine Boards for nests, boxes, etc.	3.75
1168 ft. Timber	16.25
Labor	20.00
Painting	10.00
4 M Brick	22.00
Lime, Cement, and laying brick	10.00
Iron Sink	1.25
155 ft. Pine Finish for outside	3.10
23 Matched and Grooved Boards over Dusting Room	1.75
Total	$165.70

HALF UNDERGROUND FOWL HOUSE.

The Poultry-House, Fig. 12, is intended to be four feet below the surface of the ground. In this case the bottom should be well drained, at least a foot in depth beneath the wall, and the house must be kept well ventilated, to avoid dampness, which is the most injurious thing possible for fowls. If perfectly dry such a house would be unobjectionable. As to interior arrangements, there should be an entrance as shown at *a*, fig. 13, opening on to a plank extending the whole length of the

Fig. 12.—EXTERIOR OF POULTRY-HOUSE.

building, from which the fowls can reach the roosting poles. Beneath the poles there should be a sloping partition, upon which the droppings may collect and slide down to the plank-walk already mentioned. From this they should be swept off every day, and carried away. To prevent the droppings from clinging to the partition, it should be well dusted every day with dry plaster, road dust, or sifted coal ashes. Beneath the plank walk let the partition extend to the floor, dividing the house into two apartments. At the front of the house a row of nest boxes, supported by braces, as seen at *b*, should be made. The rear partition may be devoted to hatching and rearing chickens, a door at the further end of it opening into the front apartment. This would make an excellent poultry house for a village lot, being cheap, plain, and including many conveniences under one roof. The sash in front sloping to the south, would keep the house

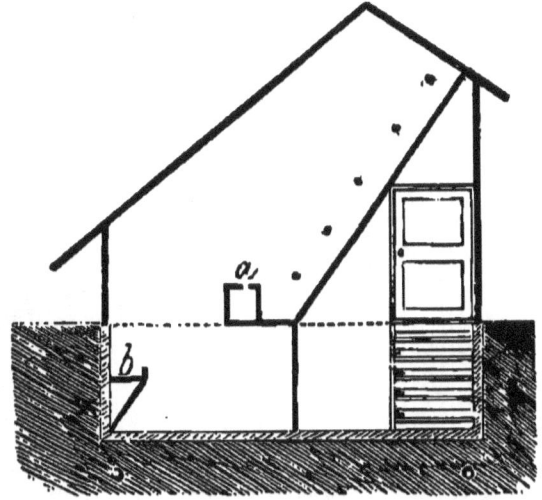

Fig. 13.—SECTION OF POULTRY HOUSE.

warm during winter, and with proper care to feed the fowls well, and keep the house perfectly clean, eggs might reasonably be expected all the winter.

PORTABLE POULTRY-HOUSE.

A movable poultry-house is by no means novel, it having been described and used years ago. Geyelin described one which was used in grain fields in France to gather the scattered grain after harvest. This was constructed something like one of those vans used in transporting animals kept in traveling menageries. It was 20 feet long, about 7 feet wide, and the same in height.

A set of steps was fixed at one end for the fowls to enter and leave, and nest-boxes and roosts were provided within. Several of these houses were drawn to the field, and one of them was furnished with a small apartment for the keeper who attended to the fowls. A large number of fowls could be accommodated in one of these houses, as they were intended to be cleaned daily, and the droppings scattered upon the ground around them as they were moved from place to place each day.

An excellent house of this kind was designed by R.

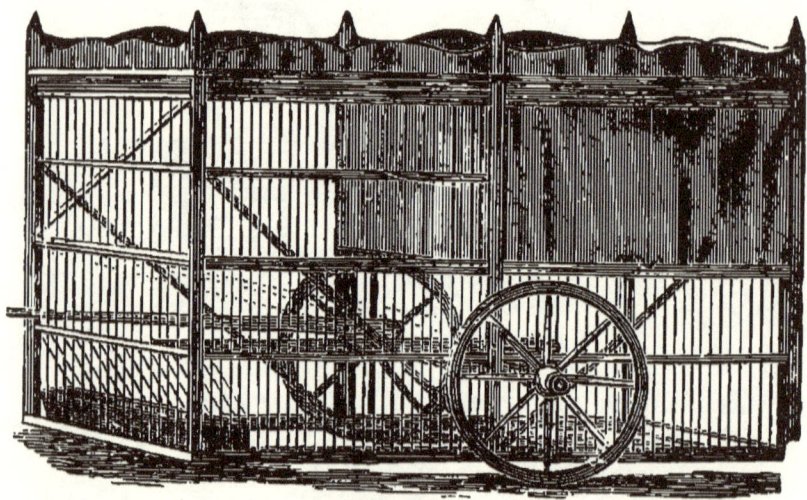

Fig. 14.

Sproule of Pennsylvania, and a view of it is given in figure 14. It is of wood, and as will be seen, is mounted upon an axle and a pair of wheels. By means of a pair of levers, raised to the position shown by the dotted lines, the house is lifted, and made to rest wholly upon the wheels, so that it can be moved from place to place as desired. Figure 15 shows the ground plan, with the boxes for feed, water, and gravel. These are secured to the sills and are kept clean by a sloping cover of small rods. The house is 10 feet long by 5 feet wide, and as high as may be necessary. The nest boxes, 16 inches square and 4 inches deep, are secured to the upper corners of the enclosure, a small door being provided for reaching the eggs. The roosting poles are so arranged that the fowls can easily climb from one to the other. The enclosure is

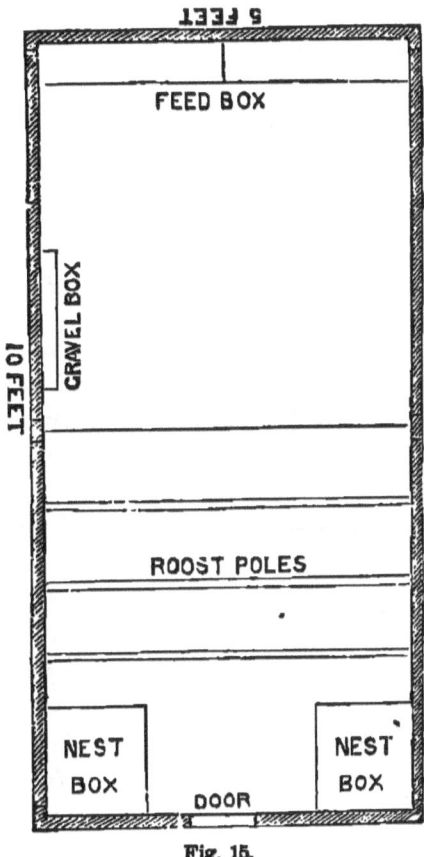

Fig. 15.

made of oak rods and rails which are bored to receive the rods. Any cheaper method of construction may be used.

The size of the house may be 5x10, or 4x8 feet, and 5 feet high to the eaves. The sills are made of 1¼x3 inch stuff, laid flat down, halved together at the corners, and nails driven through upward into the ends of the posts. The corner posts are 3x3 inches, the middle ones are 3x4 inches. Each is properly mortised to receive the rails of the open sections. A light cornice, or a 2½-inch band, is securely nailed around the top, a little above the eaves, leaving sufficient room for the roof boards to pass under between the band and the upper rail. To the back side of this band is nailed the balustrade, each piece having its ends toe-nailed to the posts. A light ridge pole is attached at each end to the balustrade near the top, which forms a double-pitch flat roof. This is made of one thickness of ⅝-inch boards, the same as the enclosed sides. The upper section at the end, over the feed trough, is hung with hinges for a door through which to place feed, etc. The levers have their fulcrum ends resting on the axle, and are bolted on it. About 12 inches from it, and opposite to it, and through the middle posts, are pivot bolts, on which the weight of the house hangs when the levers are pressed down. Narrow strips are used as braces for stiffening the frame lengthwise, which are placed inside, also bits of hoop iron should be used about the corners to strengthen the joints. With these appliances and proper tools, any skillful mechanic can complete the job. Its weight is about 300 pounds, and the house affords room for keeping from 12 to 24 fowls through the season. The advantages of such a house are that the fowls are under perfect control, and are kept quite as healthy as when running at large. Every morning when the house is moved, there is provided a clean, fresh apartment, with fresh earth and grass. Fowls become thoroughly domesticated by being thus treated. Those that are inclined to sit, are put outside; they will hang about and make an effort to get in, and the desire to sit soon passes away. The manure is all saved to the best advantage, being applied at once.

CHAPTER IV.
POULTRY-HOUSE CONVENIENCES.

Anything that will add to the ease of management of the poultry-yard is gladly welcomed. The practice among farmers of letting their poultry roost about the farm buildings upon harrows, plows, wagons, and farm machinery is growing less prevalent each year, as many of them are building suitable poultry-houses.

PERCHES, ETC.

At figure 16 is shown a neat and handy arrangement of perches; $r, r, r,$ are scantling, eight feet in

Fig. 16.

length, two inches thick, and three inches wide, made of some tough, light wood. The upper ends are hinged to the side of the building, four feet apart, and are con-

(31)

nected by means of roosts or perches made of octagonal strips nailed fast to the supports. Perches should be placed about eighteen inches apart. At any time when it is desired to gather up the droppings, the end of the frame-work is raised and fastened to the ceiling or roof by a hook at *n*, the whole arrangement being up out of the way for thorough cleaning. At the corner of the building, opposite the roost, is placed a box, *p*, containing ashes, road-dust, etc., that the fowls may dust themselves. The box should be two feet square and about one foot in height, and should be kept half filled with dusting material, both summer and winter. In the corner is placed a box, *e*, and should contain a supply of gravel and broken oyster-shells. The foregoing conveniences cost but little and will prove valuable additions to any poultry-house.

LOW ROOSTS.

For the large fowls low roosts should be used, as they cannot reach high ones without a ladder, and in dropping from them are very apt to injure themselves. A

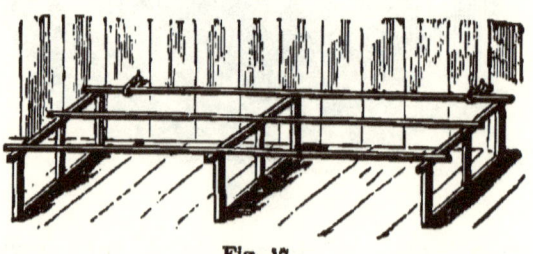

Fig. 17.

roosting-frame, made for Asiatic fowls, is shown at Fig. 17. It is made of chestnut strips two inches square, with the edges of the upper part rounded off to make them easy to the feet of the fowls. Three of these strips are fastened to frames made of the same material for supports. The whole is fastened to the wall by rings fixed in staples, so that it can be turned up and held against the wall by a hook. It is twelve feet long, three feet wide, and should stand eight inches from the wall and about one foot from the floor.

STOVE FOR A POULTRY-HOUSE.

A simple and safe method of warming a poultry-house in winter is as follows: With a few bricks and common mortar build a box five feet long and two and one-half feet wide, leaving an open space in the front about a foot wide. Lay upon this wall, when fourteen inches high, so as to cover the space within the wall except about six inches at the rear end, a plate of sheet-iron. Build up the wall a foot above the iron and then build in another plate of iron, covering the space inclosed all but a few inches at the front. Then turn an arch over the top and leave a hole at the end for a stove-pipe. A small fire made in the bottom at the front will then heat this stove very moderately; the heat passing back and forth, will warm the whole just sufficient to make the fowls comfortable, and there will be no danger of injury to their feet by flying up upon the top, as it will never be hot if a moderate fire only is kept. The stove will be perfectly safe, and may be closed by a few loose bricks laid up in front, through which sufficient air will pass to keep the fire burning slowly. Ordinarily a fire need only be made at night during the coldest weather.

NEST-BOXES.

Many farmers and other persons who keep poultry fail to provide nests for their hens, and then grumble because they seek their nests about and under the farm buildings in fence corners, under brush-heaps, and various out-of-the-way places. If clean boxes, provided with straw or other nesting material, had been put up at convenient points, the hens would have used them and would not "steal" their nests. A very good size for a nest-box is little more than one foot square and nine or ten inches in depth. They should be well made; and if planed and painted, all the better. Apply kerosene freely to the inside, where the boards are nailed together. This should be applied early in spring, and again about the first of July; it will kill hen-lice and also prevent their getting a foothold about the boxes.

Fig. 18.

Nest-boxes should never be permanently attached to buildings, but placed upon a floor, or hung upon the side of a hennery or other convenient place for both fowls and attendant. An excellent plan for thus securing the boxes is shown in Fig. 18. At one side of the box, near the top, is bored an inch hole, through which a wooden or iron pin driven in the side of the building passes loosely. Considerable annoyance is often experienced by laying hens interfering with those that are sitting; often a whole sitting of eggs is broken. This trouble is readily avoided by those who have a poultry-house with two rooms, by the use of sliding boxes, as shown in Fig. 19. A hole is cut through the partition about two feet from the floor, to the bottom of which is firmly nailed a shelf or platform, e, e, about two feet in length and nearly one foot in width. Upon this board rest the nest-boxes, made so that they can be easily slid back and forth. The ends are made one inch higher than the

Fig. 19.

sides, that they may not slide clear through or fall down. At *b* one box is shown pulled out in the room, while at *a* the box is seen pushed through into the adjoining room. As fast as the hens manifest a desire to sit, they may be furnished with eggs and put in the sitting-room, in which laying fowls are not allowed. As all do not

Fig. 20.

have poultry-houses, a box similar to the one shown in Fig. 20 may be adopted. A light frame-work of lath is placed over the box before moving.

A SET OF NEST-BOXES,

made without nails, which can be quickly taken apart for packing away, whitewashing, etc., may be made of any size to suit. The top and bottom boards have tenons on the ends passing through mortises in the end-boards, and held in place by wooden pins, as shown in the accompanying engraving, Fig. 21. The top and bottom boards have half-inch holes bored through them, which receive pins that pass into the corresponding

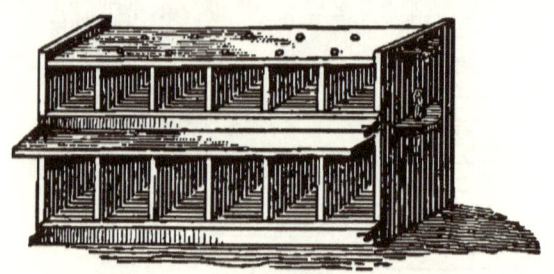

Fig. 21.

holes bored in the edges of the partition boards. As these partition pieces are all alike, they are easily put in place. There is a bar or step along the front of the nests to prevent any eggs from falling out; the bottom board of the upper tier may extend forward for a few inches to serve as a place upon which the fowls may alight.

A NEST FOR EGG-EATING HENS.

In the winter season hens frequently acquire the habit of eating eggs. Sometimes this vice becomes so confirmed that several hens may be seen waiting for another one to leave her nest, or to even drive her off, so that they may pounce upon the egg, the one that drops it being among the first to break it. In this state of affairs there is no remedy except to find some method of protecting the egg from the depredators. The easiest way of doing this is to contrive a nest in which the egg will drop out of reach. Such a nest is shown in the engraving. It consists of a box with two sloping floors; one of these being depressed below the other sufficiently to make a space through which the egg can roll down out of the way. An extension of the box with a lid affords a means by which the eggs can be removed. Upon the bottom board of the nest a wooden or other nest egg is

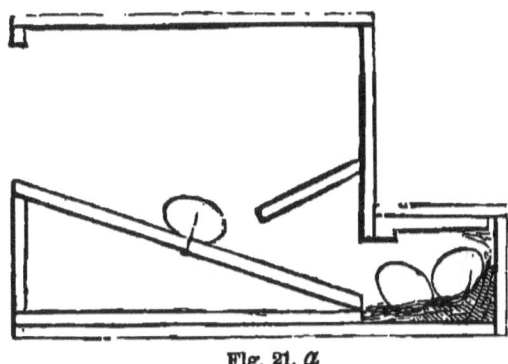

Fig. 21. *a*

fastened by a screw or by cement. The sloping floors may be covered with some coarse carpet or cloth, upon which it is well to quilt some straw or hay, and the bottom floor should be packed with chaff or moss, upon which the eggs may roll without danger of breaking. If the eggs do not roll down at once, they will be pushed down by the first attempt of a hen to pick at them.

A BARREL HEN'S NEST.

A hen's nest made of a whole barrel is vastly better than one in which the head is knocked out, and the hen is obliged to jump down from the top into her nest, and thus break the eggs. Two staves are cut through immediately above the hoops, and again eight inches above the first cut, the pieces cut out, leaving a hole large enough for the convenience of the hen. Barrels thus arranged are placed in quiet corners, where hens love to seclude themselves, and straw or other material is supplied for the nest.

WIRE NEST.

Figure 22 is an illustration of a good nest, which may be kept free from vermin. It is made of wire, or a similar one may be woven of willows or splints by any ingenious boy. A round piece of wood is fastened to the

Fig. 22.

front for the hen to alight upon, iron or wire hooks are fastened to it, by which it may be hung upon nails driven in the wall, and a piece of shingle planed smooth is fastened to the front, upon which the date when the hen

POULTRY-HOUSE CONVENIENCES. 39

commenced to sit may be written. When a wire nest needs cleaning, it is laid on the ground in the yard, the straw set on fire, and after that is consumed there will be no vermin left to infest the nest. A basket-nest may be drenched with boiling water and purified.

A LOCKED NEST-BOX.

It frequently happens that a nest-box that will lock up is desired. Such a box may be made 3 feet square and 18 inches deep, which will be large enough for two nests. The door is at *a*. At *b* is a partition extending half through the box, and at the inside of this are two

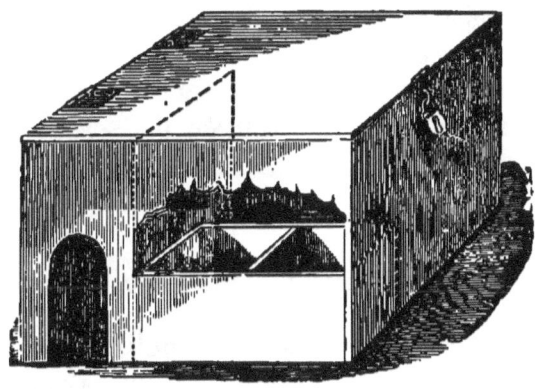

Fig. 23.

nests about 8 inches deep, 16 inches long, and 12 inches wide. These are seen through the side of the box, which is partly removed for this purpose. For small breeds of poultry the box may be made considerably smaller. Such a retired nest as this exactly meets the instincts of the hen, and it becomes very acceptable to her.

TIDY NESTS.

Hens often get the habit of sitting on the edge of their nests, and this results in the defilement of the nests and prevents other hens using them. A roller may be arranged at the front so that the fowls cannot roost upon

Fig. 24.

it, nor stand on it to fight other hens from them. The end partitions are raised 2 inches at the front above the others, and a roller or 8-sided rod, 2 inches thick, is fastened with a wooden pin at each end so that it will turn easily and a hen cannot roost upon it.

PNEUMATIC FOUNTAIN.

To prevent young chicks from fouling the water in the saucers in which it is given to them, take a common fruit can, remove the top, and cut or file but one (and that a triangular) notch, only $\frac{1}{4}$ inch high for a saucer or pan in which water will stand $\frac{3}{4}$ to 1 inch deep, as indicated in the engraving Fig. 25. Fill the can with water, place the saucer on top, and quickly reverse it, and you have a "pneumatic" fountain holding about one quart, which the chickens cannot foul. As the water is drunk or evaporates, more runs out of the can, keeping the saucer always full to the height of the notch.

FEED-TROUGH.

A device for keeping feed-troughs free from dirt, rain, or snow, is shown at figure 26. Supports are attached

Fig. 25.

to the trough, and extend equally above it, as at *E*, *E*, *H*, *H*, and should hold the trough six inches above the ground. When the trough is not in use, it may be tilted

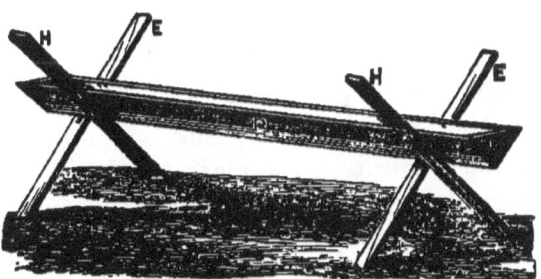

Fig. 26.

over so that it will be kept free from water, or rubbish, and always be in a proper condition whenever needed for use.

WINTER FOUNTAIN.

Poultry sometimes suffer greatly in winter through having their water supply cut off by freezing. There is some difficulty in keeping them constantly supplied with water in severe weather, but it can be done if one appreciates the necessity. A method is here illustrated which has proved of great value. A cask or flour-barrel is sawed in two, and one half used as the covering to the water-jug. An earthen jug is so fastened into the half-barrel by means of cross-pieces that its mouth will come near the bottom of the tub, upon one side—a piece of a stave being

Fig. 27.

removed at that point. The space around the jug is filled with fermenting horse-manure, and slats are nailed across when the "fountain" is ready for use. Fill the jug with water and cork it; then invert the tub, bringing the mouth of the jug over a basin, as shown in the engraving. When the cork is withdrawn the water will flow until the mouth of the jug is covered; it will then cease, and as the water is used, more will come from the jug, and so on, forming a continuous self-acting fountain. Such a contrivance will keep the water from freezing, except in the coldest winter weather. The jug should be emptied at night.

FOLDING SHIPPING-CRATE.

On farms, where chickens have full run of the yards, they pick up a great deal of food which would otherwise be wasted, and the cost of raising a limited number is comparatively small; but where they must be fed with grain, the profits are reduced to a fraction, and a very small fraction if they are sold to the storekeeper for "trade." One of the chief reasons why more farmers do not ship their own poultry is the lack of suitable shipping-crates. Express companies charge for *weight*, and unless the

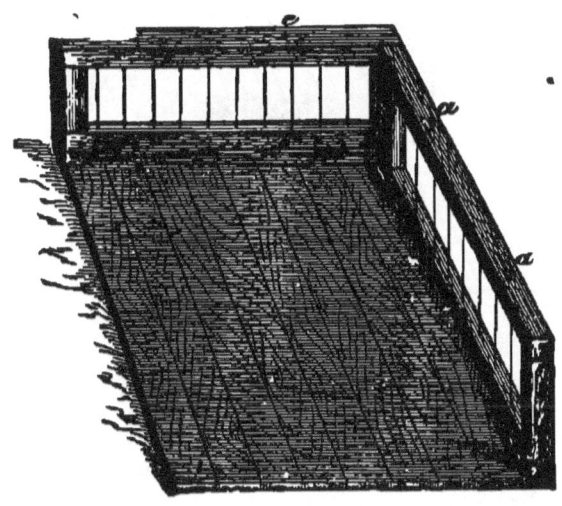

Fig. 28.

crates are light and well made, they object to returning them free. Poultry sells better in crates that are light, handsome, and airy.

An excellent folding-crate invented and used by Fred Grundy is thus described: The crate is exactly square. Figure 28 shows two sides and the bottom, or floor, as they are made and put together. Figure 29 shows the crate empty and folded, also the top, or cover, with its trap-door. The entire frame-work is of any tough wood —ash is best—one and a half to two inches square, according to size of crate. The bottom is half-inch pine. The wire used is common fence wire. The sides (Fig. 28) are hinged to the bottom, or floor, and when folded lie flat on the bottom. On the top of the side, two pins, *a, a,* iron or wood, fit into holes in frame of the cover. The sides are hinged to pieces which are screwed to the bottom, and when folded lie up on the sides. Through

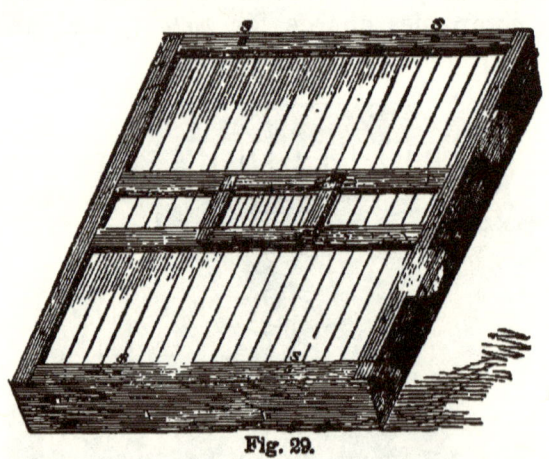

Fig. 29.

the top of the sides are two three-sixteenth-inch holes, *c, c,* into which bolts of the same size are passed, and, entering holes *s, s,* in the cover, hold it down. When the crate is folded these bolts are withdrawn from the holes *c, c,* and passed through the holes *e, e,* in the bottom piece of the same side, and then through holes in cover, and hold the whole crate solid and flat for shipping. Thumb-nuts should be put on these bolts, requiring no wrench.

The crate can be made of any size desired. A crate holding three to five dozen chickens is usually large enough. In shipping long distances care should be taken

POULTRY-HOUSE CONVENIENCES. 45

to not crowd the birds. Give plenty of room and it will pay in the end. Where the distance is short, ten or fifteen hours' travel, they will not hurt in this crate if crowded considerably, as they cannot become heated. When well made of good, seasoned wood, this crate will stand a large number of trips. It should be well washed after each shipment. The wood should be well oiled, but not painted. If thought desirable, the wires on the cover may be braced in one or two places with binding wire. Fasten one end to the frame, wrap it twice around each wire, and fasten to opposite side of frame.

CHAPTER V.

NATURAL INCUBATION

Although, in our opinion, there is greater skill required in caring for the little chicks than in getting them out well, a good deal of the success of the poultry crop depends upon the management of the hens while sitting. Those that steal their nests and follow their own instincts do very well if they are not disturbed, but frequently they get frightened or robbed, and the eggs are lost. As a rule, it is better to have all the sitting birds completely under your control, and make them follow your will rather than their own instincts. With a well-arranged poultry-house it takes but a little time daily to have all the birds come off for food and exercise. But without this we can manage to make the sitters regular in their habits. The best plan, usually, is to set the hens near together in a sheltered spot in boxes or barrels that we can cover, and thus perfectly protect them against enemies, and at the same time compel them to sit until the box is uncovered. Wherever they may lay, when they want to sit, remove them to a shed in an inclosed yard, by night, and put them securely upon a nest full of eggs. Every day about twelve o'clock remove the covers, and carefully take the hens from their nests for food and water. In pleasant weather they take from half to three-quarters of an hour to scratch in the dirt and take their dust-bath. Most of them return to their nests voluntarily before the time is up. Occasionally a bird will take to the wrong nest. It takes but a few minutes to see every bird in her place, and make her secure for the next twenty-four hours. As the hatching-time approaches, dip the eggs in tepid water every day to keep the pores open, and to facilitate the hatching. This moistening of the eggs will be found of special service in the hatching of the eggs of water-fowls set under hens. Following this method, good success with sitting hens is almost certain.

The selection of the eggs for hatching is an important matter. Some of our leading Asiatic fanciers make it a point to select eggs which have a particular cast of color. They claim that dark mahogany color in the shell of Brahma eggs alone indicates their absolute purity. While there are others of equal note as breeders who say it is all nonsense to regard the color of eggs that are deemed fit or unfit for hatching. But it is well, however, to look to shape and size, for it is clearly demonstrated that the regular, medium, well-formed oval eggs without extreme length, very small or very large ends, without wrinkles or furrows of any kind, are the best for hatching.

It is important, too, in the selection of eggs, to look to size. A happy medium must be secured in this as well as in some other things. In size they should be neither too large nor too small for the variety. When eggs of any kind are over-sized, they are usually double-yolked. and are, therefore, useless for hatching. And when they are under-sized, they are not so good as the average. Select from your best layers smooth, hard-surfaced eggs, without indentations, and of fair medium dimensions and proportions.

EGG-TESTERS.

A bad egg is never welcome, and any simple device that will quickly and satisfactorily detect the quality of an egg is important. A very simple method is shown in

Fig. 30. The egg is so held that the hand cuts off all direct rays of light from the eye, except those passing through the egg. The egg may be held toward the sun, or, better, toward the light from a lighted candle or lamp in a dark room. Egg-testers are made in which more than one egg may be examined at once. A small box, either of wood or pasteboard, is used, with a number of "egg-holes" cut in the cover. A mirror is placed within, set at a slant towards one side of the box, which is cut away for observation. If the interior of the box is painted black, the effect will be better. The quality of the eggs is determined by their degree of clearness. A fresh egg shows a clear, reddish, translucent light; an egg fit, perhaps, for cooking, but not for hatching, a less clear light.

Fig. 30.

The accompanying engraving (Fig. 31) represents a contrivance for testing the freshness or fertility of eggs, useful in the household or to the poultry-fancier. It consists of a small handle, with a cup in the end of it; around the cup is fastened a frame of sheet-tin or stiff card-board. This frame has a hole in the center, of the shape and size of an egg, and a strip of black ribbon or cloth is fastened around the frame, projecting a little beyond the inner edge. To test the egg, it is placed in the cup, so as to fill

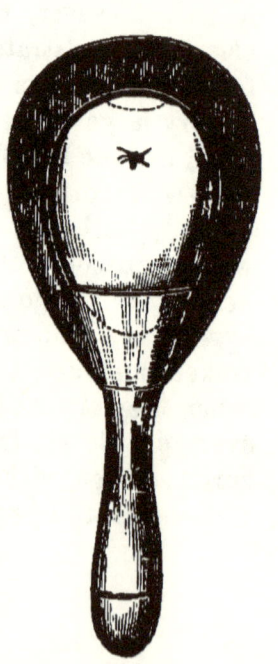

Fig. 31.

the space in the center of the frame, the edge of the black cloth or ribbon fitting close to the shell. When the egg is held close to a bright light, the light passes through the egg, and shows a fresh or infertile one to be perfectly clear, while a fertile one that has been sat upon, or that has been in the incubator two days, will show the embryo, as in the engraving, as a dark cloudy spot. Infertile eggs may then be taken from the nest or from the incubator on the third to the fifth day.

CARE OF SITTING HENS.

March is the month to set hens, for the earlier after this they are set, the better the chicks will prove. Of course every hen has been set that would stick to her nest during the past month; but as hens must lay out their clutches before the sitting fever takes possession of them, the larger number will not be ready for the nest before this month. Sell none but surplus eggs now, but crowd the hens by setting all that can be relied upon. When it comes to finding them all nests, much discretion is needed, that confusion does not cause trouble and loss. Of course, the simplest way to set them is in rows in the hen-house; but the hens will not all remember their own nests, and will crowd two or three on one nest, leaving their own eggs to become cold and perish. It is advisable to set the hens in different rooms and apart from one another; but if the nest rows must be used, then there must be careful watchfulness. A good rule is to keep the windows well darkened, so that the hens will not be tempted to leave their nests until noon. When you give the other chickens their noonday meal, and while they are feeding, go into the hen-house, take all the sitting hens off the nests, and make them go out to feed. While they are out, clear the nests of broken eggs, dirt, and feathers, loosen up the straw a little, and dust Persian insect-powder over the eggs. Now comes the critical time. Do not forget what you have done, and do not trust the hens, but within half an hour be sure to return, and see that each is on her own proper nest, or you will have trouble every time they come off. Hens are creatures of habit, and a little training goes a great way with them. If they can be made to keep the same nest three or four days, there will be little danger that they will make any mistake about it for the remainder of the time. That will save you the trouble of moving them, but not the responsibility of seeing that they return promptly to their nests after feeding. When all is right, darken the sitting-room again and leave them until the next day at feeding-time.

SECURE LAYING AND SITTING BOX FOR HENS.

There have been several devices, some of them patented, for accomplishing this end, which we here show how to do by a simple, home-made contrivance. Take or make a box three feet long by two feet wide (*a, a*). Take off one side, as shown in figure 32; tack on two cleats. and fit in a partition (*d*). Take out the partition, and cut a square hole, a little more than a foot square, near one end, and a notch an inch wide and six inches long on the opposite end. Make an opening for the hen to enter by (*b*), in the end of the box above the partition, and at the point where the notch is cut. The partition *d* forms the floor of the laying and sitting room. A box a foot square and eight inches deep is made to fit loosely in the opening in the floor. This is the nest, *e*. It

NATURAL INCUBATION.

is balanced on a hard-wood edge, upon the end of a broad lever, which works upon another edge of hardwood affixed to the bottom. A weight, h, placed near the end of the lever, counterbalances the nest as may be necessary, and a tin plate, g, attached to the end of the lever will rise and close the opening b, as a door, when the weight of the hen causes the nest to descend. The entire side, which is absent in the diagram, should be fastened on by screws so as to be easily removed, or attached by hinges to the bottom, so as to give access to the working parts. The sides of the nest must be

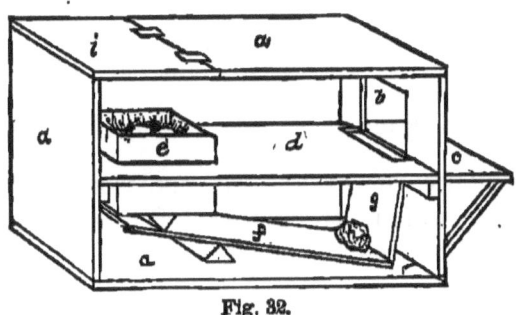

Fig. 32.

greased, and of course the tin door must move up and down without any catching. The counterbalancing of the nest should be so adjusted that the weight of sixteen average-sized eggs, say two pounds and a half, will bring it down. No laying hen weighs less than this, except Bantams, and perhaps some of the Hamburgs. So whenever a hen is on the nest the door will be closed. When she leaves it, the door will open. The advantages are that only one hen will occupy the nest at a time, and fighting over the eggs and breakage are thus prevented. Then, when a hen is set and is likely to be disturbed, the weight may be entirely removed, in which case the door will remain closed, whether she is upon or off the eggs. She may be let out towards evening, daily, after the other hens have laid, or food and water may be placed for her on the floor. In this case, a pane of seven by nine glass ought to be inserted in the top, or on the fixed side. At hatching-time she should be shut in until she brings off her brood. It is, moreover, important that a portion of the top (*i*) should be removable, or hinged on so that an attendant may have access to the interior at any time. Access to the nest by egg-eating dogs is by this method entirely prevented, unless the dogs are very small, in which case a board a little wider than the door, placed six inches in front of it, and nailed firmly both at top and bottom, will exclude even them.

A BROODING-PEN FOR HENS.

We have for several years used enclosed brooding-pens for hens with much satisfaction. Success with poultry depends wholly upon the convenient and effective man-

Fig. 33.—BROODING-PEN.

agement of the brood hens and the chicks. When hens cannot help it, they will do as their owners wish, and there are then peace and comfort and prosperity in the poultry-house. These pens are built around a part of the poultry-house, kept specially for the sitting hens. Each one is four by four, and three feet high; it has a hinged lid, which can be thrown back against the wall when it is desired, for attendance upon the hen. The front is covered with wire netting. The nest, shown by the removal of one side of a pen, is a box about sixteen inches square open in the front, and having a very low piece to keep the nest in it, and to permit the hen to step in and out. When it is necessary, the nest is closed by placing a piece of board in front of it. This is done for a day or two when the hen is restless, after having been put in the nest. When she is settled down, the board is removed. Each pen is supplied with a feeding-dish and water-cup, and is littered with sawdust. It is attended to every evening by lamp-light; the feed and water are renewed, and the droppings are removed, a pail and small shovel being kept in the house for this purpose. A pail of water and another of feed are carried to the house every evening. The hens are thus kept undisturbed during the day, although they are visited regularly to see that all is right. Each hen is separate and cannot see the others, and, the house being partly darkened and kept warm, the hens are quiet and comfortable, and mind their business satisfactorily.

CHAPTER VI.

CARE OF CHICKS—COOPS FOR THEM.

The foundation of the various poultry diseases is generally laid while the young chicks are in the coops. There they are crowded in a confined place, which is frequently damp and unclean. They are shut up close at night in these impure quarters, or they are allowed to

Fig. 34.

go out early in the morning, while the grass is wet with dew, and becomed chilled. Some die and some survive, to live unhealthily and die finally of roup or cholera. To prevent these troubles, the chickens, while young, should have the very best of care. The coops should be so made as to secure cleanliness, dryness, ventilation, safety, and to control the movements of the chickens. A coop of this character, which is very convenient in use, is shown in the accompanying illustrations. It is not costly, and

CARE OF CHICKS—COOPS FOR THEM.

it will pay to use it for common chickens. It is portable, having handles by which it can be lifted while closed, and moved to fresh clean ground. It therefore secures cleanliness, as ground that has been occupied by a number of chickens for a few days becomes foul and unwholesome. It is also provided with a floor-board or drawer, which can be withdrawn every day, and cleaned. If this is supplied with fresh sand or earth daily, the coop will be kept clean and sweet, and the manure

Fig. 35.

dropped may be preserved for use. It secures dryness, because it is raised from the ground by feet at the corners, and is covered with a broad sheltering roof. It has good ventilation, even when closed, by means of the wire gauze at the front, and by holes in the ends, which should also be covered with wire gauze. It is safe; no chickens can be killed in moving it; it is shut up at night, so that no rats or weasels can enter, and the chicks cannot roam abroad when the ground is wet. The movements of the hen and chickens can be controlled with facility, as the roof is hinged at the peak, and opens to admit or remove the hen. The door at the front is hinged, and, when opened, is let down to the ground, and makes a sloping platform upon which the chickens go in or out, and when closed is secured by a button. Twice in the season the coops should be whitewashed

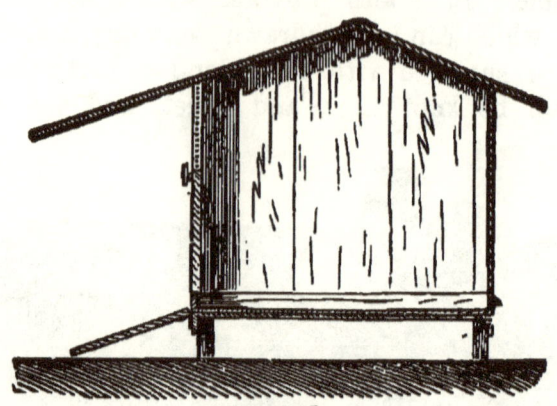

Fig. 35.

with hot fresh lime, which will keep them free from vermin. Fig. 34 shows a front view of the completed coop, arranged for two hens. Fig. 35 gives the rear view with the floor withdrawn, to be emptied and refilled, as well as the shape of the movable floor. In Fig. 36 is a sec-

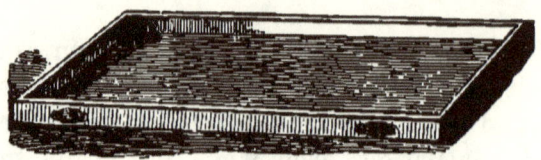

Fig. 37.

tion of the coop through the middle, showing the manner in which it is put together; and figure 37 is the drawer-floor board. There is economy in using such a coop as this, as one hen, when well cared for, may be made to bring up two or three broods together, and the hens discarded as mothers go to laying again.

BOX CHICKEN-COOP.

An ordinary dry-goods box may be used for a chicken-coop. To the open end a frame or lath is fastened, thus making a run or yard for the chickens when the box is placed upon the ground, as shown in figure 38.

Fig. 38.

The box furnishes a comfortable place for the hen and chickens during stormy weather, an escape from the hot sun, etc. When not in use the lath frame can be taken from the box, its three sides and ends separated, and stored away for use another season.

BARREL CHICKEN-COOPS.

Any old barrel that would otherwise be thrown away may be put to good use in making a comfortable place for a hen and chickens. Brace the barrel on the two sides with bricks or stones to keep it from rolling; raise the rear enough to bring the lower edge of the open end close to the ground; give a few stakes in front and

Fig. 39.

the coop is complete. It is best to put the barrel near a fence, that it may be all the more secure and out of

Fig. 40.

the way. Nests for turkeys may be made in the same way, in out-of-the-way places, omitting the stakes, and putting in a good supply of straw to make the nest.

CARE OF CHICKS—COOPS FOR THEM. 59

Very good chicken-coops may be made of old flour or fruit barrels. One way in which they may be made is by removing the hoops from one end, and putting them inside, in such a manner that the staves are forced apart on one side, as shown in Fig. 39. The barrel is set on the ground, with the open staves downward. On the other side of the barrel the staves should be kept close together, as a protection against the weather and vermin. Another way is to cut off the end of each alternate

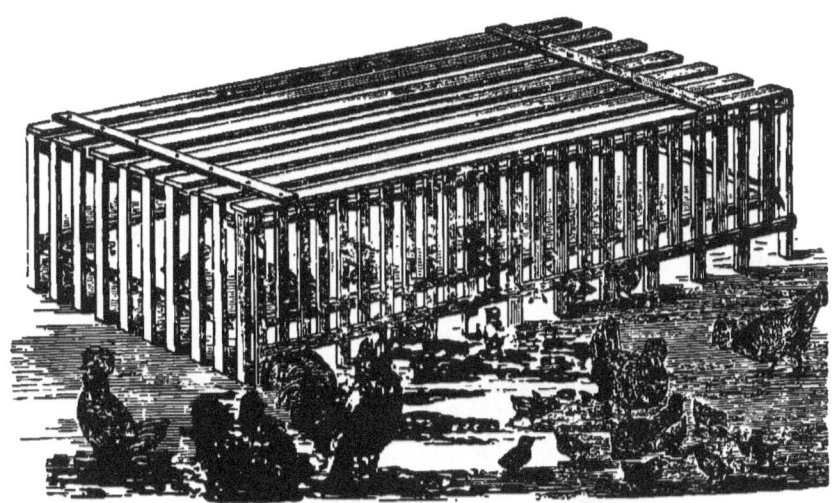

Fig. 41.—FEEDING-PEN FOR CHICKS.

stave, in lines, about three inches from each other. The halves of the barrels then taken apart, and set bottom upwards, make very good coops, as shown in Fig. 40. If a piece of leather is fastened upon the top of one of these coops, so as to form a handle, it may be lifted and moved to fresh ground very readily. Young chicks, that are permitted to range with the large fowls, may be fed without interference by the others, in an inclosure which may be made as shown in Fig. 41. Common laths are sawn into proper lengths and nailed to a frame, three inches space being left for the chicks to go in and out. On one side the laths are cut off six inches from the ground, and a strip, *A*, three inches wide, is secured so as to be raised as the chicks grow larger, to permit them to pass under it. If made ten feet long and five feet wide, it will be large enough to feed 200 chicks. The frames for the sides and ends may be attached to each other by pins, or hooks and staples, and when not in use they may be taken apart and packed away until again required.

REARING EARLY CHICKENS.

Warmth is the only requisite for rearing early chickens, which one finds it difficult to provide early in the season. But there is an easy way to furnish this for the early broods, where the other conveniences are con

Fig. 42.

sistent with it; that is, where the poultry-house is tight and warm, and is kept clean and free from vermin, and where the fowls are fed judiciously. The illustration (Fig. 42) represents an annex to a poultry-house, made at very little cost. It was built at the end of the poultry-house, and a door from this opened into it. It measures ten by twelve feet on the ground, and seven and a half feet high at the top of the roof. It required seven common hot-bed sashes, purchased for one dollar each (three of those are shown and the other four should be seen under the overhanging eaves), and the rest of the material cost about ten dollars. The floor was the ground, which was sandy and dry, and soon became quite warm under the heat of the sun even in January. When the hens wanted to brood, they were carried in the movable nest into this warm house, where they were fed and watered daily, and could enjoy a bath in the dry, warm, sandy floor. The droppings were gathered up daily in a pail, and carried out, and the house was kept as clean and sweet as possible. When the young chicks appeared, and had been nursed in the warm brooder, which has been previously described, they were given to the hen, who was put into a coop, and usually two broods were given to each, and sometimes three. A good, quiet Light Brahma or Plymouth Rock hen will take twenty-four or twenty-five chicks and rear them all safely when thus cared for, as the warm house greatly relieves her from the work of brooding the chicks and keeping them warm. The chicks are fed four times a day, the chief food at the first being crushed wheat and coarse oatmeal, with coarse cracked corn and clean water in a shallow plate, in the center of which an inverted tin fruit-can is placed, to prevent the chicks from running through it. The advantage of such a house as this is that chicks can be reared that are fit for market so early as to bring the highest price. An instance may be given of the income from a small flock of twenty light Brahma hens for a year, from January to December, which left a clear profit of a little over seven dollars per hen. It is quite possible to do this with a flock of one hundred hens which are good brooders, kept in one house and yard, and properly kept and cared for with such help as this, to secure early broiling chickens, as these bring a high price. A brood of eight chicks, which is a fair average for each hen, sold at seventy-five cents each, will make six dollars alone, and some of the cockerels in the case mentioned sold in the fall for eighteen cents a pound, and weighed nine pounds each, making one dollar and sixty-two cents each.

BROODERS FOR EARLY CHICKENS.

The greatest profit in poultry-keeping is from the early chickens. By good feeding and management some of the hens may be brooding in January, and all the chicks may be saved by the use of artificial brooders. Incubators are used by experts with success, but farmers and ordinary poultry-keepers are rarely successful with these machines. Brooders, however, may be used by any person, even a boy or girl, who will simply see that the heat is not excessive, and when the chicks open their mouths, give them fresh air. Eighty degrees is quite enough warmth for newly hatched chicks, which are taken from the nest as they come out, and are placed in the brooder until all the brood is out, when they may be removed to a warm, glazed coop, with the hen. Young chicks have been thus nursed until they were strong, which ran about in the snow in February with great pleasure and comfort, and not one was lost out of a lot of ninety, which were all hatched in January. All that is required is to have a warm part of the buildings or an attic room for the setting hens, and glazed coops set in a sunny place out of doors for the chicks when they come from the brooder. The brooder (fig. 43) is a box eighteen inches square or thereabouts, one end opening as a door and closing tight, lined with hair felt, or blanket cloth, and having a shelf in the middle, and a glass in the upper half of the door, so that the chicks may be seen. A tin heater having handles and a screw-opening to put in the hot water, fits into the lower part, which is also lined with the felt or double blanket. The heater is filled with boiling water and put in its place, wrapped in a piece of blanket to retain the heat and moderate it. A nest, covered with a sheet of paper, which can be removed when soiled, is put on the shelf. A pasteboard box, upon half-inch cleats, makes a good nest. A thermometer is kept in the nest, so that the

Fig. 43.

warmth may be regulated by putting more blanket over the heater, or by ventilating the brooder by holes in the door, closed by corks. Chipped eggs will be hatched in such a brooder; weak chicks may be saved, and all the losses by chicks being crushed in the nest are avoided. The heat is admitted to the nest by holes in the shelf.

Another brooder is shown at Fig. 44. This is a larger and shallower box, having a tray in the upper part with a slatted or wire gauze floor, upon which the heater rests; a lid is made to cover this tray. This heat descends through the floor of the tray into the lower part of the brooder, which is hung closely with short folds of flannels or woolen cloth for the chicks to nestle among. This is shown in the illustration. A glazed cover is put over the front of the brooder where the chicks are fed. Newly hatched chicks do not want feeding for twenty-four hours or more, but they will drink some water (or, better, *milk*) eagerly, and this should be supplied to them in a shallow plate. If one is taken in the hand and its beak is dipped in the water,

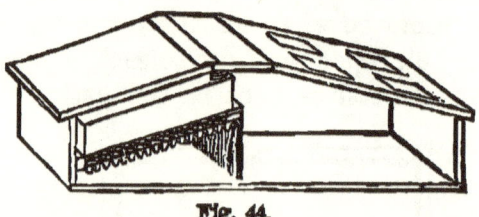

Fig. 44.

it learns to drink at once. Crumbs of corn bread or cracked wheat are good food for such young chicks while they are in the brooder. It will interest some persons to know that in some hospitals in Paris similar warm brooders have been used for weakly infants for many years, and the writer saw them there thirty years ago, used in almost precisely the same manner as is here described for the previously mentioned brooder for chicks (Fig. 43).

CHAPTER VII.

ARTIFICIAL INCUBATION

INCUBATORS AND BROODERS.

In endeavoring to lay before our readers something that may be to their advantage, I will avail myself of the opportunity of describing that which is in *practical operation*, and do not call upon others to assist me in solving theories. There are hundreds of methods of hatching chicks artificially, as nothing more is necessary than keeping the eggs for three weeks under certain conditions of heat and moisture. What are those conditions, and why do failures occur so often, even when every attention is given the process?

In the first place, there are a great many unforeseen difficulties in the way that are overlooked or not anticipated. An incubator cannot hatch every fertile egg, neither can the hen do so; yet there are some manufacturers who claim that the incubators made by them will hatch every fertile egg. To test the hatching of fertile eggs, I procured eggs from two different places. After placing them in the same incubator, and at the same time, I removed all clear eggs by the tenth day. Of the first lot of fifty eggs thirty-two were fertile, and of the second lot of fifty there were thirty-four fertile eggs. The eggs of the first lot hatched thirty chicks, while every chick of the second lot perished in the shell. Upon investigation, I found that the fowls from which the eggs of the first lot had been procured were in full health, and had plenty of exercise, a cockerel of about one year of age being mated with two-year old hens. The eggs of the second lot were from hens that were mated with a brother, and the flock had been bred in for three years. The consequence was that while there was life in each egg there was not sufficient vitality in the chick to enable it to break out.

There are numerous reasons for not expecting full hatches. Eggs from pullets do not always hatch, nor do those from hens that are very fat; yet such eggs may be fertile. Eggs that have been chilled will sometimes contain chicks that have advanced to the stage of ten days, when placed in an incubator; besides, frequent handling, or delay in placing them in the incubator, may also affect the result. Hence, the first and most important matter is to use eggs specially secured for the purpose. The hen that steals her nest, by running at large, and having all the privileges and advantages of exercise, hatches nearly all the eggs, for the reason that if one hatches all should do so, as they have the same parentage, while we are compelled to use eggs from different hens, but few of them being alike in any respect. The hen deposits her eggs where they are seldom disturbed, while we subject them to frequent handling and changeable temperatures. It is doubtful if any farmer would consider himself unlucky if he succeeded in raising seven chicks out of every ten hatched; yet this proportion is equal to a loss of thirty in every hundred. If, therefore, an incubator be used, this should be considered, and when the loss is apparently heavy, a comparison should be made with the work done by hens, which will, as a rule, be in favor of the incubator and brooder.

Having stated what the conditions should be, so far as the eggs are concerned, the next step is to consider the defects existing in many of the incubators that are placed upon the market; and as I am not a manufacturer, nor interested in the sale of incubators, I have no object in view other than a desire to correct some of the mistakes that have been made in the construction of incubators. The supposition that a constant stream of pure air must flow through an incubator is, in my opinion, an error. Not that there should not be plenty of pure air, but it should not pass through as a current. The hen on the nest airs the eggs, but she keeps the air still and motionless. The desire to regulate an incubator has caused incubators to be constructed that open and shut off the heat very easily; but an observer may notice that they will often open and close the valves every few minutes, thus causing the heat to change in as many times, and to allow of slow or fast currents according to the degree of frequency with which the valves open and shut. The best machines are those that *slowly* reach a point above or below the normal hatching point. Too much air passes into the incubators and not enough in the brooders, as a rule. A little chick does not require so large a volume of air as is usually allowed, and a hundred of them together will not consume so much as a small quadruped. If the air is admitted below the eggs, there will always enough escape to allow fresh air to enter for ventilation. We now hatch them, in our section, in incubators holding 400 eggs each, by closing the drawer, allowing no mode of ventilation other than to keep three or four one-inch tubes open at the bottom of the incubator, and the chicks remain thus shut up for twenty-four hours at a time without inconvenience. In fact, by leaving them in the drawer they are thoroughly dry and prepared for the brooder when taken out. A regulator should be a very simple arrangement. Some of them are so delicate in construction as to do more injury than good, and it is often the case that the *regulator* instead of the incubator must be watched. The majority of persons put too much *faith* in the regulator, relying upon it too implicitly, and often fail in consequence. Other incubators regulate the heat very well, but cannot do away with the work of watching the flame of the lamps. The flame must be regulated according to the temperature of the outside atmosphere. To be successful the operator must determine that he will do the work himself, and he must *watch* the incubator, whether it regulates or not. He who attempts to raise chickens artificially by using a self-regulating incubator without expecting to do anything except to trust to the machine, will always be of the opinion that incubators are humbugs. It means work and attention every time, but it is work that pays if well bestowed.

In Hammonton we do not use any self-regulators at all. Our incubators are simply tanks surrounded by sawdust, made by placing the sawdust between an inner and larger box, the tank being in the top of the inner box. The tank for a hundred egg incubator is 15x30 inches, 7 inches deep, and rests on strips around the edges, with half-inch rods under it every six inches to support the weight of water. The egg-drawer is 15x36 inches, 6 inches fitting in the space at the opening when the drawer is shut. This space in the front of the egg-drawer is also boxed off and filled with sawdust. The ventilator is six inches deep, the egg-drawer three inches deep inside. Two tin tubes, one inch in diameter, are placed at the bottom of the ventilator to admit air. Four inches of sawdust surround the inner box. A tube on top of the tank, which passes through the boxes, allows water to be poured in, while a spigot in front, over the egg-drawer, permits it to be drawn off. This tank is filled with *boiling water*. The eggs are hatched at 103 degrees. The heat is regulated by drawing off a bucket of water night and morning. The eggs are turned twice a day. Moisture is supplied with boxes of

ARTIFICIAL INCUBATION. 69

moist and under the egg-drawer, and by a few wet sponges in the egg-drawer.

These incubators do not require any *watching*. No one gets up in the night to look after them. The large body of sawdust absorbs heat, and gives it up to the egg-drawer as it begins to cool; hence, the heat varies very slowly. If a lamp is preferred, it may be attached by having two tubes, one above the other, extending to a small "boiler" outside, which is heated by a lamp, capable of accurate regulation, in the usual way.

HOW TO MAKE AN INCUBATOR.

To make this incubator, get your tinner to make you a tank fifteen inches wide, thirty inches long, and twelve inches deep, of galvanized iron or zinc, the iron being preferable. On the top should be a tube one inch in diameter and eight inches high. In front should be another tube, nine inches long, to which should be attached a spigot.

Having made your tank, have what is called the ventilator made, which is a wooden box with a bottom, but no top. The ventilator should be eight inches deep, and one inch smaller all around than the tank, as the tank must rest on inch boards, placed upright to support it, or on iron rods. In the ventilator should be two or three tin tubes, one half inch in diameter and six inches long. They should extend through the bottom, so as to admit air from below, and to within two inches of the top, or a little less.

Now make an egg-drawer, which is a frame of wood, three inches deep, having no top or bottom, except at the front, where it is boxed off and filled with sawdust, which is covered over afterward with a piece of muslin, boards, to keep the sawdust from spilling. Of course, the egg-drawer must be made longer than the tank and ventilator, in order to allow for this space which it fills in the opening, which is the packing all around the incubator. The bottom of the egg-drawer should be made by nailing a few slats lengthwise to the under side, or rather fitting them in nicely, and over the slats in the inside of the drawer a piece of thick, strong muslin should be tightly drawn. On this muslin the eggs are placed in the same position as if laid in a hen's nest. It allows the air to pass through to the eggs for ventilation.

Having prepared the tank, let it be covered with a close-fitting box, but the box must not have any bottom. This is to protect the tank against pressure of water on the sides, and to assist in retaining heat. Such being done, place your ventilator first, egg-drawer next, and tank last. Now place a support under the tank and the box, or have them rest on rods, and as the weight of water will be great in the centre, the iron rods should be placed crosswise under the tank every six inches. Now fasten the three apartments (ventilator, egg-drawer, and tank) together, with boards nailed to the sides and back and front (of course leaving the opening for the egg-drawer), care being taken to drive no nails in the egg-drawer, as it must move in and out, and should have a strong strip to rest on for that purpose. Having completed these preparations, make a larger box to go over all three, so that there will be a space on the sides, back, front, and on top, but as the ventilator must be filled with sawdust to within one inch of the top of the tubes, it serves for the bottom packing. Make the outer box so that there will be room for filling all around the inside box with sawdust, and also on top, being careful to let the tube for pouring in the water come through, as also the spigot in front. The front of the incubator must be packed also. The incubator should be raised from the floor about an inch, when completed, to allow the air to pass under and thence into the ventilator tubes.

The incubator being complete, the tank is filled with boiling water. It must remain untouched for twenty-four hours, as it requires time during which to heat completely through. As it will heat slowly, it will also cool slowly. Let it cool down to 110°; and then put in the eggs, or, what is better, run it without eggs for a day or two in order to learn it, and notice its variation. When the eggs are put in, the drawer will cool down some. All that is required then is to add about a bucket or so of hot water once or twice a day, but be careful about endeavoring to get up heat suddenly, as the heat does not rise for five hours after the additional bucket of water is added. The tank radiates the heat down on the eggs, there being nothing between the iron bottom of the tank and the eggs, for the wood over and around the tank does not extend across the *bottom* of the tank. The cool air comes from below in the ventilator pipes, passing through the muslin bottom of the egg-drawer to the eggs. The 15x30 inch tank incubator holds 100 eggs. Lay the eggs in, the same as in a nest, promiscuously.

In regard to the sawdust packing. The bottom board is wider than the ventilator. Each corner of this bottom board should be 2 x 3 well-fitted posts, the posts being six inches (or whatever height desired), higher than the three compartments (ventilator, egg-drawer, and tank) when the three are in position. To these posts fasten tongued and grooved boards, and you will then have the compartments enclosed with a larger box. Now fill in your sawdust (sides and top), covering the top sawdust with the same kinds of boards, first boring a hole for the tube on top, or fitting the boards around it by bringing two boards together on a line with the tube, each having a crescent cut into them thus ( ). Be sure and fasten up the compartments by nailing them together in such a manner that no sawdust can get in the egg-drawer, and be careful to drive no nails into the egg-drawer when fastening the three compartments. As the tank should be covered with wood, it is best to fasten

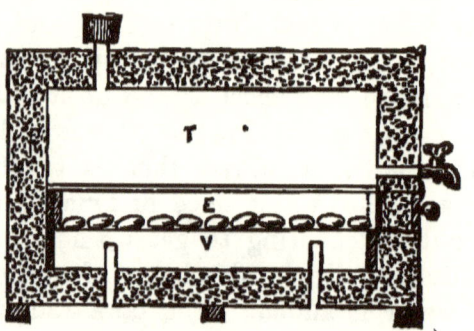

Fig. 45.—SECTION OF INCUBATOR.

the three parts together before making the *outer* box which holds the sawdust, by nailing upright strips closely together, fastening the top end to the wood surrounding the tank, and the bottom ends to the sides of the ventilator. We show in Fig. 45 a sectional view of the incubator.

DIRECTIONS.

To give the directions plainly, in order to avoid compelling our readers to write us, we will repeat them, and be as precise as possible:

The incubator should be filled with *boiling* water. It will take a large quantity, but once filled it will remain so. Let it remain shut up for twenty-four hours, in order to allow the heat to go all through it. Always look at the thermometer *as quickly as possible*, as it varies quickly. The drawer should be at 103 degrees, and if warmer than that leave the drawer out a little while until it cools down, always shutting it up first, in order to let the heat accumulate a moment or two before looking at the thermometer. Never try to cool it with cold water, for the heat is in the packing, and you can never tell what the effect will be for several hours. Should you add hot water, it will be from two to four hours before the increased heat appears. It is due to this fact that the incubator is so reliable, as the heating and cooling is gradual. When the thermometer reaches 110° put in the eggs. The eggs will cool the drawer, but do not be alarmed. Let them remain for an hour or two, and if the temperature is then below 100°, add a kettleful of water (nearly a bucketful), which will return the heat to about 103° in an hour or two. If the weather is moderate, once a day will only be necessary for adding water, but the better way to work the incubator is to divide the twenty-four hours into three periods of eight hours each, say 6 o'clock A.M., 2 P.M., and 10 P.M., when a gallon of water may be added at each time, and the eggs turned. This avoids late night work, and gives but little trouble.

Be sure and practice with the incubator for three or four days before putting in the eggs, for by so doing you will know just how much water to use.

The colder the weather the more hot water. All incubators do best in an even temperature.

Keep a pan of water in the ventilator, changing it to fresh water daily.

Keep the heat as near 103° as possible, and the last three days not over 102°.

Take the drawer out in the morning and let it remain out for the eggs to cool down to 70°. Then turn the eggs half way round, and place the drawer back. Make a mark on each side of the egg in order to be guided in knowing which side is up correctly. Turn them morning and night, but cool them down only once a day.

Always keep a few wet sponges in the egg-drawer, as they will indicate the moisture. Put the thermometer in among the centre of the eggs, the top of the bulb on a line with the top of the eggs, the upper end of the thermometer kept slightly raised.

Three weeks are required for hatching, and the temperature should not get below 98° nor over 105°. Should the eggs be over-heated, let them cool well, sprinkle them, and put them back. Heat as high as 108° for a *short time* is not necessarily fatal. Never sprinkle as long as the sponge keeps moist, and always sprinkle with tepid water.

BE SURE your thermometer is correct, as one half of them are incorrect, the low-priced ones being as true as the highest-priced ones. Place your thermometer next to a hen's body under the wing; shut down the wing closely upon it; let it remain so for a minute. Then quickly look at the thermometer, and it should be at 104°. It is best, however, to have it tested in a pan of warm water, by the side of one known to be correct.

Do not keep the incubator where there are any odors.

When the chicks hatch do not remove them until they are dry; then put them in the brooder. Keep the heat in the brooder at not less than 90°. Feed at first hard-boiled eggs for a day or two. No food should be given the first twenty-four hours. Then feed oat-meal and corn-meal, cooked and moistened with milk. Feed four or five times a day, at first, for a week. Keep fine screenings, cracked corn, fine gravel, fine-ground oyster-shells, pulverized charcoal, and clean water always where they can get at such, and keep everything *clean*. Give mashed potatoes, chopped onions, or cabbage, or anything that serves as a *variety*. Be sure and not *crowd*

ARTIFICIAL INCUBATION. 75

them. Divide them into small lots. Feed in little troughs.

An egg-drawer two feet wide and three feet long will hold one hundred and fifty eggs with an egg-turner. A drawer three feet wide and four feet long holds three hundred eggs. Only one drawer can be used to an incubator.

BROODERS.

The principal conditions necessary in a brooder are plenty of *fresh air* and sufficient heat to prevent the chicks from crowding. We have a building here, now in operation, divided into ten apartments, each apartment being five by seven feet and accommodating one hundred chicks. The building is fifty feet long and ten feet wide, and a passage way running its whole length, and taking up three feet of the ten, leaving the spaces for the chicks seven feet. The yards are sixteen feet long and five feet wide. The chicks are all brooded with a stove. To describe how it is done, we will explain that Fig. 46 is a box six inches deep, three feet wide, and fifty feet long. Two-inch iron pipes are arranged as shown in the illustration, the top of the box being removed to show the interior. The hot water may be supplied by an ordinary stove " water back," or by a coil of pipe in a stove. This is heated by a piece of pipe one inch in diameter, coiled in a stove, holes being cut in the stove for the purpose of admitting pipes. The hot water flows out and the cold water flows in. The floor of the box is made close, with tongued and grooved boards. The cold air enters through tubes reaching to the outside of the building. It is heated by coming in contact with the pipes, and enters into the tubes on the top of the floor, which are two and a half inches high. Over these tubes are little tables, one yard square and three inches high, with strips of cloth tacked around the edges.

The advantages of this brooder are, that it gives the heat from the top, as the warm air strikes the under side of the table (or brooder) and diffuses itself over the chicks, which cannot crowd easily, as there are no sides or corners. The warm air is pure, as it comes in fresh from the outside, and serves as heat and ventilation at the same time. Figs. 46 and 47 show the *ground* plan. The building has a window to each apartment, which is hung to a weight, so as to move up or down. Hence, when the window is up each apartment becomes a shed, open to the south. The chicks have a sand floor to scratch in, and are allowed to run in the yards when two weeks old.

This building, together with the heating arrangements, did not cost over one hundred dollars. The chicks are about ready for market, and are expected to realize six hundred dollars gross. The cost for feeding the chicks to the age of ten weeks is ten cents. The total cost, including the value of eggs, food, and other expenses is about nine cents per pound. They will average one and a half pounds when eight weeks old, and often bring fifty cents per pound. The building contains one thousand chicks, and as a new brood can be put in every ten weeks, it will hold five thousand in a year. The building and yards do not take up more than twenty-six by fifty feet of space, or less than one thirtieth of an acre.

The chicks are fed on hard-boiled eggs the second day, no food being given them the first day. Then milk and bread are allowed. On the fourth day they are fed on a mixture of one part corn meal, one part bran, and one part middlings, with a small quantity of bone meal and ground or finely chopped meat. They are fed five times a day till feathered, then four meals are given. Chopped cabbage, onions, and other green food are supplied. Skimmed milk may be used in the food, which should always be scalded or cooked. Plenty of water, gravel and dry earth are kept before them, a few screenings being scattered in the dirt to induce them to scratch. In giving water never allow them to become

Fig. 46.—INTERIOR OF BROODER BOX.
Showing hot-water pipes and cold-air pipes.

wet, as dampness is fatal. Avoid *bottom* heat in a brooder, as it causes leg weakness. It is always better to have too much heat in the brooder than too little, but the reverse is the case with an incubator.

A light, sandy soil is best for chicks. Hence, poor

Fig. 47.—TOP OF BROODER BOX.
Showing one of the brooder tables, and one space with table removed to show hot-air tube.

and unproductive locations can be thus used with advantage. Chicks require unceasing care, but by raising them in large numbers, labor may be economized. They need no care at night, other than to keep up the fire, which may be arranged so as to give sufficient heat till morning. They should be fed very *early* and *late*.

When ready for market correspond with a reliable commission merchant before shipping.

We have two or three large broiler establishments here. In one case two young ladies are hatching several thousand chicks annually, and they find it very profitable.

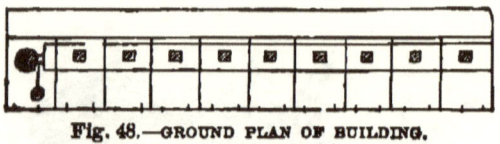

Fig. 48.—GROUND PLAN OF BUILDING.
Showing brooders, stove, and water-barrel.

As stated, nearly all the failures come from the *eggs*, and not the incubators, and until poultrymen realize this fact they will meet with disappointment. The loss does not exceed seven per cent, and that includes the weak chicks and all that die by accident. No gapes or lice effect them, as everything is kept very clean. As to what may

Fig. 49.—STOVE, WATER BARREL, AND END OF BROODER BOX.

be expected it may be stated that if fifty chicks are marketed from every one hundred eggs used, the result will be satisfactory, but this includes loss of bad eggs, dead chicks, and other causes. The chicks grow faster than when with hens, as they receive better care and can be counted at any time. They are safe from all enemies. My advice to beginners is to begin with a small incubator, and experiment the first year. Experience will be the best teacher. Do not expect too much, and do not expect to

Fig. 50.—BROODER HOUSE, WITH YARDS OMITTED.

raise chicks without work. Watching, care, and labor are essentials. No incubator or brooder, however well regulated, can be trusted. They are treacherous. But they will return a handsome profit if properly managed.

CHAPTER VIII.

PREPARING FOR MARKET.

FATTENING POULTRY.

No fowl over two years old should be kept in the poultry-yard except for some special reason. An extra good mother or a finely feathered bird that is desirable as a breeder may be preserved until ten years old with advantage, or at least so long as she is serviceable. But ordinary hens and cocks should be fattened at the end of the second year for market. When there is a room or shed that can be closed, the fowls may be confined there. The floor should be covered with two or three inches of fine sawdust, dry earth, sifted coal-ashes, or clean sand. The food should be given four times a day, and clean water be always before the fowls. A dozen or more fowls may be put at once in each apartment. One of the best foods for rapid fattening, for producing well-flavored flesh and rich fat, is buckwheat meal, mixed with sweet skimmed milk, into a thick mush. A teaspoonful of salt should be stirred in the food for a dozen fowls. Two weeks' feeding is sufficient to fatten the fowls, when they should be shipped for sale without delay and other lots put up for feeding. If the fattening-coop is kept dark and cool, as it should be, the fowls will fatten all the quicker for it.

WHEN TO MARKET.

Poultry which it is not intended to winter should be fattened before really severe weather comes on; otherwise money will be lost by them. They will barely hold their own in December on feed which caused them to increase rapidly in weight a month earlier. Those who have watched the market know that autumn prices usually are highest a little before and a little after Thanksgiving, say about the middle of November and soon after the first of December. The reason is that those who are fattening fowls keep them back for a short time before Thanksgiving-day and before Christmas-time, in order to get them in prime order for sale at those times. The result is usually an over-stocked market and plenty of cheap poultry. Soon after the first of January prices go up again; and well they may, for one or two months' feed has been consumed and very little weight added.

Capons grow rapidly, and their growth takes up the food, so that we have to wait until growth stops before they fatten. It is well, therefore, that this delicious class of poultry should not make its appearance before the first of February, when the game-laws prohibit venison, quail, and other choice game from being exposed for sale. At this time, consequently, fat capons and pullets meet a good market, and even during Lent, when a considerable portion of the Christian world abstain from meats, there is a sharp demand for the highest-prized meats to grace the table of the rich on Sundays. It is therefore well to have fine capons ready to supply this demand.

DRESSING AND SHIPPING.

The directions sent to their customers by Messrs. E. & O. Ward, 279 Washington Street, one of the oldest commission houses in New York City, though very brief and concise, give the results of an extensive experience and present all the essential points in dressing and shipping for that market. They say: "To insure highest market prices for poultry, they must be well fattened; crops empty when killed; nicely and well picked and skin not broken or torn; thoroughly cooled, but not frozen. Pack in boxes with a layer of clean straw (rye-straw the best) between the layers of poultry, in the same posture in which they roost. Mark each box, specifying what it contains. Send invoice by mail. Ship to reach us about the middle of the week —should never reach us so late in the week as on Saturday.

"There is the greatest demand for fine and fat turkeys for Thanksgiving; for prime and nice geese for Christmas; for extra large and nice turkeys for New-Year's-day. On all these occasions shipments should reach us two to five days in advance. If you cannot find any profit in sending poultry of *prime* quality and well prepared, you need not look for any in that of ordinary or poor qualities."

An ordinance adopted by the Board of Aldermen of New York City, and approved by the Mayor, is as follows:

"SECTION 1. That no turkeys or chickens be offered for sale in the city unless the crops of such turkeys and chickens are free from food or other substance and shrunken close to their bodies. That all fowls exposed for sale in violation of this ordinance shall be seized and condemned; such of them as shall be tainted shall, upon examination, be destroyed, and the rest which are fit for food shall be used in the public institutions in the city.

"SECTION 2. Every person exposing for sale any chicken or turkey in contravention of this ordinance shall be liable to a penalty of five dollars for each chicken or turkey so exposed for sale."

This ordinance took effect the first day of October, 1882.

DRESSING POULTRY—THE NEW ENGLAND METHOD.

While poultry for some markets is rarely, if ever, drawn, that for the Boston and other New England markets—at least that of the better class—always has the entrails drawn when the birds are killed. There is something in favor of both methods. In the former, no air being admitted into the cavity of the body, it keeps in good condition much longer than it would if opened. On the other hand, if the poultry is kept too long there is danger that any food which may be in the crop, etc., may ferment, even if nothing worse takes place, and impregnate the flesh unpleasantly. A poultry-raiser of Ayer, Mass., gives the following directions:

"First catch the chickens. Slide your hands carefully among their legs until you can grasp the desired one; hold quite still until the neck is grasped. Cut the throat near the under side of the bill quite deeply; then with the right hand upon the legs hold the wings over the back to avoid fluttering. Always drain the blood into the chicken's pail. If the fowl is wanted for immediate use, scald it for about half a minute, being careful to get the tail and wings under. Take out and strip the legs quickly from the feet towards the head. Hold a handful of feathers in the hand, pushing the feathers from tail to head. Scald three minutes in three quarts of water. Make a small slit behind and on the side of the crop, one chick after the other. Then take out entrails and crop and windpipe, carefully removing the liver from the gall. Take the gizzard to the pail and open and skin with another knife. Cut off the head and legs, putting these in a pile. When cold, cut them up and put them into the pail for your hens. This refuse thus disposed of is worth at least one cent per fowl. By scalding one can dress about six in an hour, while dry picking is much slower."

SAVE THE FEATHERS—FEATHER-BONE.

Few persons are aware that the coarse wing-feathers of turkeys and ducks, which cannot be used for dusters, and are generally a nuisance about the farm-yard, are of any value. Large poultry-raisers especially will be glad to learn that a recent invention of Mr. E. K. Warren of Michigan has created a demand for these hitherto worthless feathers, and that a company is now manufacturing, out of the quills of feathers, an excellent substitute for whalebone, which, by the way, is becoming scarce and dear.

The feathers are first stripped of their plumage by revolving shears, then the quill is divided into halves by delicate machinery, after which the pith is removed to be used as a fertilizer. Analysis has shown it to be rich in nitrogen, and therefore very valuable on the farm. The split quills are cut into narrow shreds and braided into strong strands by machinery. These strands are in turn combined until there is produced a firm elastic band so strong that great power would be required to break it. This is sewed lengthwise many times through with colored threads, the feather-bone taking various colors from the kind of thread used. Though the business is only a few months old, a hundred persons are employed, and it is daily increasing. Patents have been secured in the leading European countries, and large offers have been made for the right to use feather-bone in making whips, corsets, etc., but the inventor chooses to reserve his rights. One who has never given any attention to the subject scarcely comprehends the demand for a substitute for whalebone. This commodity is said to be even better for many purposes than the whalebone which it imitates.

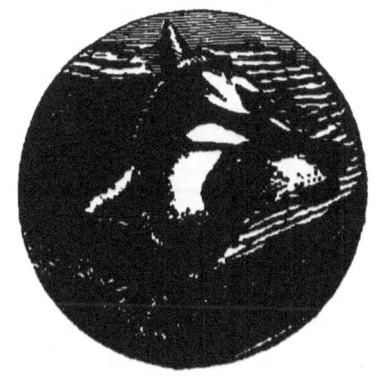

CHAPTER IX.

PRESERVING EGGS FOR MARKET.

To preserve eggs for a considerable time the pores of the shell must be stopped up, for two reasons: to prevent the entrance of the air, and consequent spoiling of the contents, and to prevent the evaporation of the moisture of the egg and a drying-up of the contents. There are two principal methods of doing this. One is, to smear the surface of the eggs with something that will close the pores, and then pack them in some material that will practically exclude the air. The eggs are smeared with lard, coated with linseed or cotton-seed oil, or with shellac varnish, and are afterwards packed in bran, dry sand, or other similar material. These methods will answer for home use; but whatever may be the coating material, the surface of the shells will have an unnatural appearance, which will prevent their ready sale in the markets. The only practical method to preserve eggs to be sold is to place them in milk of lime, which is another name for whitewash, and is prepared precisely as for whitewashing. The fresh eggs are packed in a barrel, and the lime-wash, well stirred and then strained, is poured over them. The eggs must be fresh when packed, and must be kept in a cool place. The eggs, according to the extent of the operations, are placed in barrels or in brick vats or tanks, built for the purpose. The dealers who handle large quantities of eggs have brick tanks built in a cool cellar. Any vessel, such as a but or barrel, will answer the purpose in a small way as well as the tanks. The eggs when sent to market are removed from the lime and thoroughly washed, and when dry are packed in barrels of cut straw, like other eggs. In the New York market they usually bring about five cents a dozen less than fresh eggs. When packing eggs for private use, it is well to wait until September, when the fowls, having had a good run on the stubble fields and about grain barns, begin to lay plentifully, and eggs become cheap. Take perfectly fresh eggs, and pack them in a butter firkin, or barrel, and pour over them milk of lime, or thick lime-wash, after it has cooled, and head up the keg; or pour over them the strongest brine; or smear the eggs with cottonseed or linseed oil, and pack them on their broad ends in wheat bran in a keg, barrel, or box, very tightly, and each week turn it over so as to reverse the position of the eggs. The last method has been found to be exceedingly satisfactory. Eggs packed in dry salt will not keep for any great length of time.

PACKING EGGS IN A BARREL.

A great number of eggs are lost every year through imperfect packing. The salable value of a package of eggs is measured by that of the poorest part of it; the good always have their value diminished by the bad; but the poor eggs are never raised in value by the good. If by poor packing any part is damaged, the whole is depreciated together. A badly packed barrel of eggs is a miserable thing to look at, and worse still to handle, especially when the weather is warm and a *very* few old nest eggs have been packed with the good ones, which does sometimes happen in spite of care, though not when only glass nest eggs, which never spoil, are used. The barrel should be a good one, clean, strong, and well hooped. At the bottom is placed three inches in depth of clean, dry, sweet rye or wheat straw, cut in a fodder-cutter into chaff not over half an inch in length. Upon this the first layer of eggs is placed on their sides, near together, but not touching. Some of the cut chaff is then scattered over the eggs, so that it falls between them and fills the spaces. Then one inch in depth of chaff is laid upon them, and another layer of eggs placed upon it. The number of eggs in each layer is marked upon a tally. An ordinary-sized flour-barrel will hold 70 dozen. It is not well to crowd more than this into a barrel. The chaff and eggs are placed in alternate layers in this way until the barrel is one-third full, when a piece of board is laid upon the chaff and pressed down carefully to make the mass solid. This is done again when the barrel is two-thirds full, and it is then shaken gently to settle the contents. When the last layer is packed, it is covered with three inches of chaff, which should project an inch or more above the chine of the barrel. When the head is pressed down steadily and slowly into its place with some shaking of the barrel, the eggs will be held so firmly that no shaking they may receive in the course of their journey will loosen them, and a severe jar will not break any of them. When they arrive at their destination they will be in good order, and bring the highest price, having cost no more to pack, except a little extra trouble, than the poorest barrel that may come to market. Musty or damp straw, or poor grain, will give a scent and flavor to the eggs which will injure them, notwithstanding it is generally supposed that an egg-shell is impervious to such influence. Cut wheat or oat straw is the best packing, wheat or oat chaff is the next; good sound oats are a good but expensive packing; hay is very poor material, and buckwheat bran the worst, as it so readily heats. When the barrel is packed, the number of eggs in it should be plainly marked upon the head.

PACKING EGGS FOR WINTER.

Of the various methods practised for preserving eggs for winter use, one of the most effective is that employed by the dealers who buy when the supply is large and prices low. This is as follows: Brick vats,

Fig. 51.—VAT FOR PICKLING EGGS.

or wooden tanks, are constructed in cool dry cellars, partly sunk below the level of the floor, as in Figure 51, the dotted lines showing the portion below the ground. These vats and tanks,—or casks, which may be used instead,—are partly filled with a preservative mixture of

Fig. 52.—EGG LADLE.

thick lime-water, or milk of lime, to which are sometimes added salt and a small quantity of cream of tartar (bi-tartrate of potash), and the eggs are placed in this mixture and kept covered. The eggs are placed in the tank by means of a peculiar dipper (Fig. 52), made of a round, shallow tin pan, with a long handle, the tin being perforated to drain off the liquid. The eggs are lowered to near the bottom, and gently rolled out, with little risk of breakage. Here they remain until required for sale. If they were fresh when packed away, they will come out after three or four months so little changed that few persons would be able to distinguish them from fresh ones. When wanted for sale they are taken out of the pickle with the dipper, and carefully placed in the crate, shown at Fig. 53. This is made of laths; but an open splint basket would answer the purpose as well.

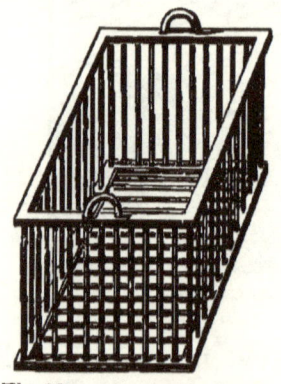

Fig. 53.—CRATE FOR IMMERSING EGGS.

Fig. 54.—TUB FOR DRAINING THE EGGS.

A large low tub, as half a hogshead, is provided, and two boards are placed across the top, as seen in Fig. 54. The crate of eggs is placed upon the boards, and water is run through it until all perceptible traces of lime are removed. In this method of preservation there is nothing that may not be done in a small way, and with any substituted apparatus which will answer the purpose. One thing is imperative—the eggs *must* be fresh when packed, or they cannot be kept in a good condition for several months.

THE MARKET FOR POULTRY AND EGGS.

The magnitude of this most important branch of agriculture is little appreciated by the casual reader, yet the millions of dollars represented in the annual product of poultry and eggs go far toward making up the farmers' profits of the year. In an investigation made not long ago by *American Agriculturist*, it was brought out that there is a permanent investment in this industry of about $340,000,000, comparing very favorably with some of the great cereals, and with various branches of live stock. A rapid growth has been made in recent years, particularly since the date of the last federal census, from which the figures of poultry and egg product were taken. Inasmuch as the census includes only poultry on farms, the business is really very much greater than indicated, counting in towns and villages.

By the census of 1890, there were 259,000,000 fowls, 11,000,000 turkeys, 8,440,000 geese, 7,544,000 ducks, in the United States, and the annual product of eggs was 819,728,000 dozen.

The production of poultry yards is all wanted at home, although exports of eggs, small at the best, have within the past year or so exceeded the imports. Practically no poultry is shipped abroad. The import movement is remarkable. Up to the imposition, in 1890, of a tariff of five cents per dozen, the foreign egg imports, chiefly from Canada, were enormous, approximating sixteen million dozen annually. The five cent duty cut imports rapidly, and they were less than two million dozen in 1894, increasing considerably the next year under a lower rate of three cents per dozen, but proving unimportant recently. The 1897 tariff resulted in a restoration of the old rate of five cents.

PROFITS IN POULTRY.

FOREIGN EGG TRADE, YEAR ENDED JUNE 30.

	Exports.		Imports.		
	Dozens.	Av. value.	Dozens.	Av. value.	Duty.
1897	1,300,183	13.9 cts.	579,681	8.2 cts.	3 cts.
1896	328,485	14.6	947,132	9.3	3
1895	151,007	16.7	2,705,502	11.7	3
1894	163,061	16.1	1,791,430	11.1	5
1893	143,489	23.1	3,318,011	11.8	5
1892	183,063	17.4	4,188,492	12.4	5
1891	363,116	17.6	8,233,043	10.8	5
1890	380,884	15.4	15,062,796	13.7	free
1889	548,750	13.8	15,918,809	15.2	"
1888	419,701	16.0	15,642,861	14.8	"
1887	372,772	16.3	13,936,054	14.1	"
1886	252,202	18.2	16,092,583	13.5	"
1885	240,768	21.5	16,098,450	15.4	"
1884	295,484	22.0	16,487,204	16.2	"
1883	360,023	20.8	15,279,065	17.4	"

EGG MOVEMENT AND MARKET: RECEIPTS AND PRICES AT LEADING POINTS.

	New York.				Chicago.				Boston.		
	Rec'pts Mil doz	Prices (in cents)			Rec'pts Mil doz	Prices (in cents)			Prices (in cents)		
		Apr.1	Sept.1	Dec.1		Apr.1	Sept.1	Dec.1	Apr.1	Sept 1	Dec.1
1897	83.1	11	19	25	*44.7	9½	13½	19	14	23	32
1896	77.8	12½	18	27	69.0	10½	11½	22	16	20	33
1895	68.5	14½	17	27	64.6	12	13	20	15	23	28
1894	69.7	12	19	27	63.2	10	15	21	13	22	30
1893	63.4	16	18	28	51.9	14½	14	21	18	22	30
1892	60.7	13½	22	32	64.6	13	17½	24	15	26	35
1891	56.0	20	19½	29½	41.8	17½	16½	26	22	23	35
1890	51.5	17	24	32	44.3	14	16½	25	18	24	35
1889		14½	16½	29	30.6	10½	14½	24	15	22	32
1888		22	20½	26	18.7	14	16	22	21	21	30
1887		13½	17½	26	13.5				16	21	30
1886		13	17	26	12.9				14½	18	29
1885		15½	16	28	11.4				17	18	28
1884	25.6	23	19	29					24	20	29
1883	21.0	20	23½	31½					21	24	32

*The year 1897 incomplete; express receipts missing. Earlier years include both freight and express receipts.

CHAPTER X.

CAPONIZING—HOW IT IS DONE.

Strange as it may seem, we have met with a number of ordinarily intelligent persons who supposed a capon to belong to a distinct race of fowls, as do Games, Bantams, etc. For fear that others may have a similar notion, it may be well to say that a capon is a castrated fowl. It bears the same relation to other male fowls that an ox does to a bull, and may be produced from any breed of fowls. A capon brings in market 50 per cent more than an ordinary fowl, and often double the price of a common male bird; besides, a capon will reach double the weight of a common fowl at the same age. As there is no difficulty whatever in caponizing, and the instruments cost very little, the practice might become very general.

Capon raising is a profitable branch of poultry culture which is not likely to be over done. The art of caponizing is easily learned. A neighbor of the writer learned to practice it a few years ago, and last year raised a large number of these delicious fowls. He informed me that he lost not more than two per cent, and that there is no need of losing any if the birds are empty of food, and the operator has sufficient light to do his work well. Good fat capons will bring fifty per cent more per pound than other fowls will sell for, and very large capons much more than that. The conditions for success are the possession of hens of a large breed, and the use of judicious crosses to produce quick growth with hardiness of constitution and aptitude to lay on flesh.

A poultry producer of large experience says: "Having practiced the operation for several years, the writer can truly say that by using no more care, and with no more skill, than is needed in operating upon a male pig, not more than one out of 30 or 40 fowls need be lost. For several years the writer has operated on from 12 to 30 fowls each year, and the loss during that time has not been more than five or six birds in all. The operation is best performed upon chickens about 3 months old, although it will succeed, if carefully done,

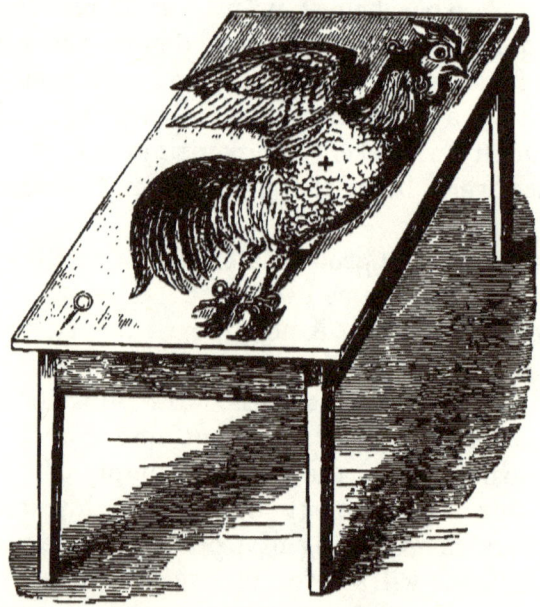

Fig. 55.—CAPONIZING TABLE.

with the majority of fowls when they are 10 or 12 months old. As with many other operations, this is one that can be learned most readily by seeing it done, and we advise those who would undertake it to procure instruction wherever it is available. Still, if one has a little confidence, he will meet with success if the directions here given are carefully followed. In the first place, a table is needed in which a few screw-eyes are inserted

CAPONIZING—HOW IT IS DONE. 95

at convenient places; these are furnished with broad tapes, by which the bird is securely held during the operation. The best plan for a novice is to kill a bird and operate upon that first, in order to learn the position of the parts. Lay the dead bird upon the table, dispose it as hereafter described, and then place the screw-eyes where they would be needed to secure a live fowl.

"One or two will be required to hold the wings, and one for each leg; six will be all that will ever be necessary. Place the bird upon the table and fasten it down upon its left side, as shown at Fig. 55, where the rings and tapes are seen. The spot where the opening is to be made is shown by the x. Here the feathers are plucked,

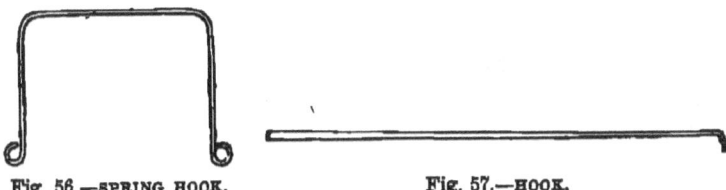

Fig. 56.—SPRING HOOK.   Fig. 57.—HOOK.

and an opening is made through the skin with a pair of shart-pointed, long-bladed scissors. We have found these better than a knife. The skin is drawn to one side and an opening is made with the scissors between the last two ribs for an inch and a half in length, great care being taken not to wound the intestines. The ribs are then separated by the spring hook (Fig. 56), so as to expose the inside. The intestines are gently moved out of the way with the handle of a teaspoon, and the glands or testicles will be seen attached to the back. The tissue which covers them is torn open with the hook (Fig. 57) aided by the tweezers (Fig. 58).

"The gland is then grasped with the forceps (Fig. 59) and the cord is held by the tweezers. The gland is then twisted off by turning the forceps; and when this has been done, the other one is removed in the same way. Care must be taken not to injure the blood-vessel which is connected with the organs, as this is the only seat of danger in the operation, and its rupture will generally be fatal. The hook is then removed, and if the skin has been drawn backward at the outset it will now slip

Fig. 58.—TWEEZERS.

forward and cover the inner skin which covers the intestines, and close the opening. No stitching is needed. A few feathers are drawn together on each side of the opening and plastered down upon the skin with the blood, where they will dry and form the best possible covering to the wound, which will begin to heal at once. The bird should be fed with a very little soft bread and milk for a few days after the operation, but should have

Fig. 59.—FORCEPS.

plenty of water. For two nights and one day before the operation no food nor water should be given to the birds; this will greatly facilitate the work and reduce the chances of loss. The operation, after a few successful trials, may be performed in less than one minute, and by the use of the rings and tapes, no assistance is needed. Capons may be made to earn their food by fostering young chicks, to which business they take very kindly.

CAPONIZING—HOW IT IS DONE.

To bring them to their full and most profitable size, they should be kept until the second year. By giving them corn-meal steeped in warm milk, and providing a warm house, they will grow during the whole winter, and their flesh will become very white, sweet, and juicy. A good capon of one of the large breeds will weigh 12 to 15 pounds at 22 months old, and will bring at the holiday season $2.50 to $3 each."

CHAPTER XI.

POULTRY-KEEPING AS A BUSINESS.

One newspaper correspondent asks how many fowls will support a family of six persons, as though it was a matter of figures, and only necessary to procure a certain number of fowls and a house, and start them laying eggs and producing chickens to secure a permanent income. Now it is quite safe to say that any person who knows so little about the trouble and risks of poultry-keeping as this would fail in it and lose his money, unless he should start with a dozen or two fowls, and go through an apprenticeship to the business. For a certain class of persons poultry-keeping is a very appropriate business, and may be made profitable. Those who are possessed of plenty of patience and perseverance, kindness and gentleness of disposition, a scrupulous love of order and cleanliness, a habit of close observation and quick perception, and a ready tact in finding out the cause when anything goes wrong, and in quickly remedying it, will generally succeed in keeping poultry, while those not so endowed will generally fail, and should never attempt it. Again, one must be able to justly appreciate either the difficulties or advantages of his location, such as the character of the land and its surroundings, the supply of food and the available markets. It would be folly to keep fowls on the borders of a forest or the margin of a swamp, on account of the vermin which such places shelter; it would be a great advantage to be located near a number of summer boarding-houses, where there is a good demand for eggs and chickens, or near a large city, where early plump chickens sell sometimes for 75 cents a pound, and where cheap food in the shape of various kinds of offal can be procured. A want of knowledge how to seize upon all the advantages that may offer, or to avoid the difficulties presented, will be fatal to success. Upon the character of the ground will depend greatly the kind of buildings needed. Buildings suitable for flocks of poultry kept for business and profit, where the available ground is of small extent, are shown in other chapters. The crops must be raised for food or shelter for the chickens, and to encourage the presence of insects, upon which the young chicks may feed. Sheltered by the rows of corn-stalks, or the stalks of rye or potatoes, the chicks are safe from hawks, which will not swoop down upon them except in clear ground. The coops are kept in or near this plot, being moved daily to fresh ground. The chickens are kept busy scratching in the loose ground, and there are few potatoes raised but what are scratched out and eaten by them. This furnishes them with employment and with some wholesome food, and it is for this purpose alone they are planted. If the owner of such a chicken farm is a gardener or florist, and his wife manages the poultry part of the business, producing every year two or three hundred pairs of chickens for market, besides eggs and old fowls, success may be deemed reasonably certain.

MONEY MADE BY POULTRY KEEPING.

It seems that the interest in poultry is increasing, and that more poultry keepers, instead of being absorbed by the insane idea that every one is going to get rich by selling fancy eggs at $3 a dozen, or poultry ready to lay at $3 to $5 a piece, are giving attention to raising eggs in winter, broilers in spring and summer, fat pullets in autumn, and capons in winter. In these products there is steady and sure profit. Of course a few will succeed as breeders of fancy fowls, but the number is limited, and they must have good judgment and perceptions, with persistence and perseverance.

ADVANTAGE OF CROSS BREEDING.

What breeds to cross is a problem which has not yet been solved. Asiatic fowls were bred pure, and also mated with Plymouth Rocks, which itself is a recognized cross-breed, but an established one. The result was that the cross-breed pullets and cockerels are several pounds heavier than the Asiatic pure-bred ones, which have had equally good care, feed, and other conditions of growth. Those cross-bred chickens, instead of making a great growth of *stilts* at first, and subsequently laying a modicum of flesh and fat upon them, are always ready for the table, and profitable to send to market, after they are as large as quails. The first cross makes, as a rule, the greatest improvement upon the parent breeds, and a number of practical questions come up, in regard to the subject of poultry raising, with the view simply to produce the largest amount of meat which will bring the highest price in the market. For instance, as in the crossing of Brahmas and Plymouth Rocks, or any Asiatics, with games, should the hens be of the larger breed, or the reverse? Which breeds crossed will develop the greatest early maturity? The greatest weight at the most profitable ages? The greatest weight and plumpness at the best market periods? Which makes the best capons? There have been a good many half-made efforts to solve these and kindred problems, but it can hardly be said that definite conclusions have been arrived at.

CHAPTER XII.

HINTS ABOUT MANAGEMENT.

COMMON SENSE IN THE POULTRY-YARD.

The "poultry" that everybody keeps are technically designated "Fowls," or "Barn-door Fowls." As a rule they are kept in small flocks, fed chiefly upon what no farmer misses. On most farms a flock of twelve to forty hens will pick up a living without receiving a particle of grain from May to October, including both months. Their food consists of insects, seeds, and grass or weeds; they need fresh water besides. What wonder is it that fowls thus kept are demonstrably more profitable than any class of stock, or any crop on the farm?

This is the best way to keep fowls, provided they can be induced to lay where their eggs can be found while fresh. To accomplish this a house of some kind is needed where the fowls may be shut in occasionally for a few days at a time, so as to make them roost and lay in convenient places. If fowls can roost in the trees, lay all over the farm, and "dust" themselves in the road, they will almost surely be healthy, lay a great many eggs, and keep in good condition. Besides, every now and then a hen will unexpectedly appear with a brood of ten or a dozen chicks, hatched under some bush where she had "stolen" her nest and done her hatching. That is all very well, so far as the hen is concerned, but no one wants it to happen. We wish the hens to lay and sit where we can put what eggs we please under them for hatching—and, what is still more important, we wish to be able to collect the eggs for use or for sale *daily*. A *fresh* egg is a joy, a delight, a good gift of Heaven—a *pretty good* egg is an abomination. An egg, to be fit to eat, or for sale, must be fresh beyond a peradventure, and utterly untainted with a suspicion of having been brooded or weathered. For this reason it is a most untidy thing to use natural nest-eggs. The nest-egg, after a while, is almost surely gathered, and of course is not "right."

The trouble about fowl-houses, even with liberal yards, is that fowls do not do well constantly confined. The number of eggs falls off, and the fowls become subject to disease, and especially to vermin—lice. All poultry-houses are liable to become thus infested, and the only cure and preventive is dust, and dustiness. It is best to provide extensive dusting-boxes—not out-of-doors somewhere, or under a cow-shed, where the fresh winds will carry off the stifling dust rendered disgusting by its "henny" smell; but in the house itself, so that the atmosphere of the entire establishment will become thus dust-laden and oppressive. Dust will settle everywhere, and one entering will need a white coat as much as does a miller. The hens will revel in the dust, however, and it will keep the lice down if not exterminate them.

The hens not only enjoy it, but dust is a necessity and a luxury to them, just as a morning bath is to civilized man. The dusting-box is their toilet-table—in fact, bath-tub, wash-bowl and pitcher, sponge and brushes and soap, and it gives health and long life as surely as the free use of water does to human beings.

As to feed—if fowls are confined they lose a great variety of food which must be, in some way, made up to them. When we depart from a close following after nature, we begin to complicate matters. Watch a hen as she trips picking about: now she takes a bit of grass or other greens; now she strips the seeds out of the seed-pod of some weed; now she makes a vigorous dive after an insect, and so on all day she scratches and forages. So a variety is essential to the health of fowls in confinement. They need grain and soft food, chopped scraps, or other flesh diet, and some grass, or other greens which they like—such as lettuce or cabbages. They must have plastering, oyster-shells pounded fine, or some other source of lime, besides fresh water constantly.

Better than all, they need an afternoon run, and a chance to scratch and pick in the door-yard, road, and barn-yard, if there be one. Here let us protest against hens being made use of as scavengers for picking up and cleaning up filth about the back-door. There is no better habit for farmer folks to cultivate in regard to poultry than on every occasion to drive them away from the kitchen door, and never to throw out anything that they can eat anywhere near the house. The practice of having a slop-hole—or spot near the back door where dish-water and other "slops," containing more or less that hens will eat, are thrown—is a filthy one at best. All such water should be thrown upon the dung-hill or compost heap. Here the hens may pick up many a crumb, and the manure will be greatly benefited.

In the matter of varieties the fancy breeds are best let alone by any one who does not make a business or a pastime of poultry-keeping. It is very pleasant for a person who keeps but a dozen or twenty hens to have them of some choice breed, and to take great pains with them; studying into their habits, their "points," and all that. But few persons have either the taste or inclination to be successful breeders; so, as a rule, it is best to keep common or mixed hens, but a full-blooded cock of one of the best breeds.

For general use most persons who have had experience will agree that the Plymouth Rock fowls are excellent, and either these or the Dominiques, or one of the Asiatic breeds, are to be recommended if a pure breed of fowls is desired for eggs, broilers, capons, and fat cockerels and pullets. For eggs alone, the White Leghorns are preferable; but they are neither economical for the table, nor are they to be depended upon as sitters and mothers. It is an excellent plan to use full-blooded cocks, making a change, not of cocks alone, but of the breed, every two years. Thus a recent writer, speaking of his own practice, says: "A stock of Light Brahmas were bred with a Dorking cock two years, then with Plymouth Rock cocks, and now I shall probably take a Brahma cross in the hope of effectually eradicating the tendency to throw pink-legged chicks, a relic of the Dorking cross, and black ones, which come from the Plymouth Rocks. After that I shall recur to the last-named variety, as I find it gives me earlier and better broilers, plenty of eggs, and fowls *always* fit for the table."

SALT IN THE RATION FOR POULTRY.

There is a prevalent notion that salt causes the feathers of fowls, or perhaps of the feathered tribes in general, to fall out. This, we believe is well founded. Certainly, excess of this condiment should be avoided. There appears to be some connection between salt and feathers. Feather-eating fowls are often cured of the tendency by adding salt to their food, and a small quantity of salt in the ration promotes, or is supposed to promote, the production of the new crop of feathers at moulting-time. This supposed effect may be simply the loosening of the old feathers. The result, as promotive of moulting, would be the same. Salt is a very important ingredient in the ration of pigeons, and where these birds are confined without it, they are never so thrifty. It is natural, then, to conclude that it is valuable in the food of other birds, and especially for barn-door fowls The earlier old fowls are out of their moult and in full

HINTS ABOUT MANAGEMENT. 105

plumage, the sooner will they begin to lay in the autumn. Pullets usually begin to lay as soon as they are completely plumed as adult fowls. It is worth while, therefore, to encourage moulting in every way, giving them exercise, insect food, or fish in their ration, with ground bone, ground oyster-shell, and sound grain. A tablespoonful of fine salt in the soft feed, given daily to a flock of twenty hens, will be a fair allowance. Fowls do not depend upon this for the salt which their bodies and feathers contain, for either the material itself, or the elements of which it is composed, exist to a greater or less extent in almost all the food they eat and the water they drink; and what we do by giving them salt is simply to increase the supply.

GREEN FOOD FOR FOWLS.

Fowls cannot be kept healthy without a good range, or a supply of green food in their yards. An excellent plan is, to have a roomy yard provided for them, and plant it with plum or dwarf pear trees. Plum-trees are very little troubled by curculios when planted in a chicken-yard, and good crops of fruit are secured, barring accidents of weather at the blooming season. The yard is divided into two parts; one is used for a month, while the other is growing up with some green crop, as turnips, oats, peas, rape, or mustard, which are very acceptable to the fowls. This yard is then used, and the other is plowed and immediately sown. This keeps the ground clean, provides suitable food, and avoids most effectively the troublesome disease known as gapes; the fatal cholera is also evaded by this management; the health being improved, more eggs will be laid.

CHARCOAL AND STIMULANTS.

Poultry in domestication are not in a natural condition. Their diet is more or less restricted in variety, and that which they have is frequently of a character to fatten rather than to promote growth or egg-laying. This may be in a measure counteracted by condimental food or stimulants. Before such measures are taken the poultry-raiser should provide everything else necessary or desirable—grain in variety, broken bones, oyster-shells or other form of lime, green food of some kind, cabbage or roots, gravel, and a dry-dusting box; besides, pure water; and if milk or buttermilk can be had, a trough for that should be provided.

Stimulants must be regarded not as food, but as medicine, used sparingly, and never daily. One mess of stimulating food once in two or three days is enough.

Charcoal should be a stand-by. It defends against disease, keeps up the tone of the system, aids digestion, and promotes laying. Feed it powdered, and mix it up with wheat bran and Indian meal. Add to this mixture a heaping table-spoonful of powdered Cayenne pepper for a dozen fowls, given every third day, or every second day in a cold snap, and continued for about ten days or two weeks, now and again, is promotive of laying and of health. This soft feed may be mixed with hot boiled potatoes, and fed either in the morning or at noon. Besides the hard grain fed at evening regularly, so that the fowls or other poultry may go to roost with full crops, and a little wheat scattered among leaves or straw to make them *scratch* for exercise, they will need little else.

Fig. 60.—GROUP OF BANTAM FOWLS.

SPECIAL FEED CROPS FOR POULTRY.

Every poultry-breeder understands the value of having a variety of food, and that it is essential for the health of the fowls and the production of fertile eggs from which he can expect strong, healthy chickens. One can imagine the result to a community who would try to live exclusively on corn; yet probably nine out of ten who raise poultry think their duty done when they have scattered before them their quart of corn and gathered the eggs. This treatment may appear to fulfill all necessary obligations when fowls can have unrestricted range through the summer season, as nature seems to provide means for sustaining life for feathered as well as human tramps. The necessity of providing corn, sometimes with wheat and oats for winter food, is generally understood; but if to these were added a supply of the other grains and vegetables of which fowls are fond, we would not hear so much complaint as now of stock "running out" and producing nothing but scallions.

As to the special grains, we may name buckwheat as one of the most valuable for the production of eggs. Sunflower-seeds should also be included in the bill of fare of all well-regulated poultry-yards. The large amount of oil they contain seems to be especialy valuable for young, growing chickens. They also give a gloss and brilliancy to the feathers probably unequaled by any other food. Even when fed in large quantities, no bad effects follow, as the husk or shell must be taken with the meat. An experiment was tried, one winter, by an observing poultryman with two flocks, one of five pullets and a cockerel of Plymouth Rocks, the other of twelve pullets and a cock of Light Brahmas, these latter having a well-appointed house, with all of the "modern improvements,"—sunlight, dust-bath, etc.

The former were in a small coop about four feet square, with a covered run formed by throwing cornstalks on some poles, and setting a hot-bed sash up against the south side. The food for the two coops was scalded Indian meal. They were both fed from the same dish, and in proportion according to their numbers. The Plymouth Rocks laid well, and gained in flesh all winter. The Brahmas "went back," both in eggs and in flesh. The reason was that the former had the strippings from the cornstalks to help in the assimilation of their food, which the latter did not have. This proved conclusively that some such coarse food must be provided if we would have the fowls thrive. Well-cured green cornstalks, and young, tender grass and clover should be provided for poultry as regularly as hay for other stock.

The soft or poor heads of cabbages, stored by themselves, probably are the cheapest and most easily obtained green food for poultry during winter. Two or three heads hung so that the fowls can easily reach them, around the sides of their coop, and renewed when necessary, will well repay the trouble. If one is going extensively into the raising of young chickens for an early market, it will pay to sow lettuce-seed in a box, and place it in a warm, sunny window. The young and tender leaves are easily grown, and will add greatly to the health and growth of the chickens. Onions should also be grown and kept for feeding. They are by many considered as a remedy for the chicken-cholera. If chopped moderately fine, they will be eagerly consumed by fowls. Tobacco should also be grown by every poultryman who wishes to keep his stock free from parasitic pests. Pull the plants before frost, and hang them in the barn or shed to dry. A handful of the leaves in the nests of sitting hens, particularly, will add a great deal to their comfort, and more to that of their young. It

Fig. 61.—WHITE SULTAN FOWLS.

(111)

makes no difference whether the tobacco is ripe or not before pull ng. Hemp-seed will be found useful for young and valuable chickens, b: t the sunflower is a go d substitute, and much more cheaply raised. Peppers are a most useful condiment during the winter months, helping greatly in the product.on of eggs through the cold weather. A sma l number of plants of the long)ed variety will produce a plentiful supply, much cheaper and purer than the ordinary ground cayenne of the stores. Use them in connection with potatoes and meal. Set the potato: s on the s ove after supper, and boil them until soft. Set them on again when the fire is started in the morning, and bring to a boil; pour off the water, add iu one or two chopped pepper-pods, and then add meal. meal and bran, or corn and oats ground together. Mush all together, and make a firm, a'most crumbly, mass. This is suitable for a morning meal, but not for night. Beans well cooked, either whole or ground, will help fill up the list of foods. Rape-seed is easily raised, and would be useful for choice young chickens. Seeds of the common millet, golden millet, sorghum, and broom-corn will make a va·iety in the list of good cheap foods. Egyptian corn, a kind of sorghum, is valuable for young or old fowls. It is raised as eas ly as corn, and will produce bountiful y. Barley, rye, and oats are well known to be a·cep'able to the inhabitants of the poultry-yard.

WINTERING FOWLS IN COLD LATITUDES.

Extreme care with poultry is necessary in cold latitudes to prevent many frozen feet, and even great loss of life during the cold weather, and it not unfrequently happens that entire flocks are frozen to death. Hence, keeping fowls in winter means simply keeping them alive and well until the spring; eggs are hardly expected.

First, prepare a warm place, well secured from cold winds and shifting snow. A corner in the stable is perhaps best, as the warmth of the stock in the stable is a great help to the chickens. But an independent fowlhouse may be made, by digging a cellar, say eight by ten feet, and three feet deep. Build a sod wall three feet thick and five or six feet high around the excavation, with a door in the east and a window in the south side. The window should be double, with one sash at the outside and another on the inside of the wall. Around the door, build an entry or vestibule of sod, with its door opening outward. Plaster all these walls upon the inside. The earth taken from the cellar, mixed with water, will answer to plaster with, and the whole can be done in a short time. The first coat will crack; the second coat should be very thin. The cover or roof may be made of poles and straw. If the poles are strong enough, some earth should be put over the straw, to make the roof warmer. The perches should be made low, and stationary strips arranged, so that the fowls can find their way to the perch, even during the dark, stormy weather. In the second place, the feed must be so arranged that each fowl can both find and eat it in the dark. To secure this end, take a board, one foot wide and four feet long; around this nail four strips three inches wide; two of these strips should be four feet long and the other two fourteen inches long, so as to form a box four feet long by twelve inches wide and two inches deep. Next, cut laths into three equal parts, and nail them perpendicularly around this box, two inches apart. Secure the tops by nailing around the outside of a similar board to the bottom, leaving an opening to put in the feed. The feed should always be placed in this box, and the box should always be kept in one position, so it may be as easily found during a storm as on a bright day. Plenty of food, such as the fowls can eat, without seeing it, should always be kept in the box. A vessel of milk-warm water should be set in the box each day, but removed before any ice is formed therein. A wire screen, or one made of slats, may be placed under the perch, to keep the fowls from walking in the droppings, as it is very essential that they keep their feet dry. When the weather is pleasant, let the chickens out into the fresh air awhile each day, but keep them out of the snow. Wheat and screenings may well be kept, say an inch deep, all the time at the bottom of the feed-box, whatever other kind of feed may be given extra.

SELECTING, SELLING, ETC.

Before a fowl is sold, a lot of the best pullets should be picked out, which, with the pullets kept the previous winter, will make up the regular flock. The two-year-old hens should be sold in the spring, as soon as eggs become cheap; they sell better at that time than at any other. A hen has seen her best laying days when she has completed her second year. If eggs are the chief object in view, the cockerels and surplus pullets should be sold as early as possible. The pullets kept for winter layers should be well fed and brought to maturity as rapidly as possible, and they will begin laying in October; and if they are cared for as herein advised, will lay steadily all winter.

EGGS IN WINTER.

Winter is the very time when eggs are worth the most, when hens want to lay as much or more than they do at any other time, and when they are not allowed to do so by most poultry-keepers. Folks think there is a great mystery about making hens lay in winter. There is none; anybody can do it; that is, the hens will lay if you let them. They bear a good deal of cold in the sunshine, and even freeze their combs and toes, and yet will not stop laying altogether if they can sleep warm. Now do not begin to plan setting up a stove in the hen-house, or introducing steam-pipes. Artificial heat is not poisonous perhaps, but very nearly so, to chickens. They are warm themselves, and need only to be crowded on their roosts, with the roosts all on one level. The ceiling of the roosting-room should be only a few feet above the fowls' heads, and provided with ventilation from the floor if possible. Give them very close quarters, with no draughts of cold air, and clean out under the roosts every morning, not excepting Sundays. The combs will then redden up, and eggs will be plenty on less feed than usual. It must not be corn, however, or only a small percentage of it, for this will make them too fat to lay well if they sleep warm.

A capital way to arrange a hen-house for winter is to make a ceiling of rails about six feet above the floor, covering the rails with salt hay, or coarse swamp hay of any kind. The roosts should be about three feet high above the floor, and movable, so that they may be kept perfectly clean. For small flocks of thirty to fifty hens, it is little trouble to take the roosts down every morning when the floor is cleaned, and replace them at night. It removes from lazy fowls the temptation to sit in idleness on the roost for half the day.

PREVENTION AGAINST LICE.

Almost all poultry are lousy, more or less. "A. B." says: good arrangements for dusting will always keep the lice in check. The small hen louse moves along the roosts and sides of the building several feet, and sometimes annoys cattle and horses, but the trouble to them is quite temporary. If the fowls are free from them, they will leave other stock at once. Roosts ought always to be removable, so that they can be scraped and washed with kerosene. I find kerosene or crude petroleum an excellent addition to whitewash. This treatment, with a good dusting-box for the fowls, in which there may be occasionally thrown a pailful of wood ashes and a pound of flowers of sulphur, will keep lice effectually in check. Horses and cattle in adjoining apartments, with only loose board partitions separating them from the poultry-house, will not be seriously troubled by the vermin.

A POULTRYMAN'S CROOK.

J. L. Cunningham, Gonzales Co., Texas, writes us: It is often troublesome to catch one out of a number of fowls in a coop. To save time and labor in such a case, I make use of an instrument like the one here figured. A small rod, three fourths of an inch in diam-

Fig. 61.—HOOK FOR CATCHING POULTRY.

eter and three or four feet long, is provided with a ferrule at one end. A stout, medium-sized wire, about one foot long, is bent at one end, and the long end of the wire inserted firmly into the ferruled end of the rod. Then by reaching into the coop of fowls with the rod, the one desired may be caught by the foot, and gently drawn within reach. I do not think the above invention has ever been patented, and it is too good to keep. By its use one person may handle a coop of fowls, which without it would require at least two or three persons to accomplish.

PASTURING POULTRY.

The farmer whose acres are broad can enclose his garden with a fence, and let the poultry run at will, but villagers and suburban residents, living on small lots, must enclose their chickens if they desire to cultivate either a garden or the good will of their neighbors. During the spring and summer months it is necessary that chickens have a supply of fresh, tender, green food, if kept in a healthy, growing condition. They cannot eat grass when it is tall enough to mow, and the refuse of the garden is little better than husks. A good plan is to pasture the chickens. Make a wire cage, put it on wheels having flanges, lay a track for the wheels to run on, and sow oats between. The frame is three feet high, six feet wide, and eight long. The upper part is 2 by 2-inch pine; the sills 2 by 4 inches. The wheels are sawed from 2-inch oak plank, and turn on 1-inch bolts. The flanges are 1-inch stuff, nailed to the wheels. The track is 2 by 2-inch stuff laid on the ground, the strips being thrown on top as the cage passes along. Wire half the thickness of fence wire is strong enough. The soil between the rails should be worked over, and sown with oats early in the spring and in successive sowings. When an inch high it will do to pasture. Have a small door in the poultry yard to match the one in the cage. Half an hour's pasturing each day will do the chickens more good than any amount of green stuff thrown to them. When the crop seems exhausted, let the fowls scratch it over; then sow again.

HOW TO GET LARGE BIRDS.

Many purchasers of fine stock, or of their immediate descendants, fail to secure as fine birds as the seller raises, and are unhappy. They hear of eighteen-pound light or dark Brahma cocks, and twelve-pound hens of some noted breeder, or of mammoth bronze turkeys weighing sixty or more pounds to the pair. They order the eggs or young birds of such stock, hand them over to some servant or neighbor, who is not skilled in breeding, feeds irregularly, or regularly stints them, and at the end of six months wonder that they have not first-class birds, equal to the advertisement. They think they have been cheated, and set down the breeder as a rogue. There are men, no doubt, in the poultry business who cannot be trusted, but there are also a large number of men who have brought capital, skill, and integrity to their business, and who would not knowingly let a poor fowl go from their yards. They sell, uniformly, stock true to name, but at so early an age that the development does not always answer expectations. A turkey does not get its full growth until the third year, but most of them are sold at from four to eight months. Ducks and hens are not fully developed until the second year, and yet most of them are sold under nine months old. While it is true that large stock is essential to the raising of large birds, another factor is quite as essential. This is abundant feed during the whole period of growth. The grand results obtained by our skillful breeders are reached by care and feed, after they have selected their stock. To make the most of a young bird, it should be fed with a variety of food at least five times a day, from daylight in the morning until the middle of the afternoon. It is well to omit late feeding, to give time for digestion. Slack or full feed will make a difference of six pounds in the weight of a turkey-gobbler at eight months old, which is the most of the difference between an ordinary and an extraordinary bird. Persons who buy thoroughbred young birds of good breeders should not expect to buy the skill of the breeder with his stock. That is a commodity that cannot be bought for money. It can only be gained by daily attention to the details of poultry breeding.

CHAPTER XIII.

SOME POPULAR BREEDS.

The agricultural interest owes much to poultry-fanciers. Those who devote their attention to fancy poultry are too often misunderstood by farmers as well as by others. As in many other cases where people devote themselves to some special pursuit—or hobby, as it is considered—the poultry-fanciers are generally looked upon as enthusiasts, who simply amuse themselves, without conferring any benefit upon the public; an error which does the poultry-breeder great injustice. In nearly every farmer's yard may be seen either some pure-bred or some crossed fowls that are much superior to the ordinary run of "barn-door" poultry. The common fowls may weigh three pounds at maturity, and may lay two or three dozen of eggs in the summer, and none in the winter. But the improved fowls, now kept by the majority of farmers, will reach an average weight of four pounds, and produce eggs, if not in the winter, at least very early in the spring, and continue late in the fall. The product of flesh and eggs is at least doubled. This result is due to the labors of poultry-fanciers, who have ransacked the world for new varieties, until perhaps there are none worth having that are not now to be found in this country.

No one can become a successful breeder of poultry—indeed one can hardly succeed in anything—unless he is an enthusiast; therefore enthusiasm, when usefully directed, is something to be commended rather than blamed. The profit derived by small farmers from poultry is usually an important item in their income.

We therefore advocate the improvement of poultry

by encouraging those who make it the business of their lives.

It is especially advisable that farmers should at least procure pure-bred cocks or cockerels for breeders, yet such a thing is the exception rather than the rule. In regard to this matter, Mr. Evans says: Many of the farmers can readily realize that it pays to use pure-bred bulls, or pure-bred rams, or pure-bred boars in their herds and flocks of cows, sheep, and swine; but they do not seem to realize that the same rule holds good with poultry, and also that the benefits are secured very quickly. This infusion of pure-bred blood amongst a flock of good common hens is sure to be of great benefit, as the constitutional vigor of the common stock intensifies the good qualities derived from the thoroughbreds, producing in point of early maturity, size, and laying qualities something both desirable and profitable, though these half-bloods cannot with anything like uniformity transmit these improved qualities to their offspring. First-class pure-bred cockerels can be bought at a moderate figure, and we do not see how farmers can afford to use the common ones in preference, no matter how good they may be. If large size is most desired, the Asiatics will be found to answer well, while for laying qualities principally we commend the Leghorns.

The popular breeds of the day may be classed among either the Asiatic, European, or American varieties.

CHAPTER XIV.

ASIATIC BREEDS.

The Brahmas, Cochins, and Langshans, which comprise the standard Asiatic breeds, have many desirable qualities. They are docile, not mischievous; fair layers, persistent sitters, and good mothers. As a class, there is little difference between the varieties; what may be said of one will generally apply to the others, the color of plumage being the chief point of preference that decides a choice.

LIGHT BRAHMAS.

The Light Brahma is now well known amongst breeders and fanciers, but is not yet nearly so popular amongst farmers, and those who rear poultry for market, as it should be. The small head, the lofty carriage, the broad full breast, the deep round body, the short, stout, well-feathered legs,—all mark the high-bred bird, and one producing a great amount of flesh with the least offal. This is one distinguishing feature of the Brahma fowl which renders it a profitable breed for the farmer. No other bird excels it as a winter layer; and as it is a good mother, the plentiful fluff about it serving to keep the chicks warm in the coldest weather, and as the chicks are hardy, it is easy to have very early birds. The young birds, as broilers, are remarkably juicy, well-flavored, and tender; and the young cockerels of four to six months, weighing, as they easily do, six to eight pounds, make most excellent roasters. As with all high-bred, pure races, the half-breed crosses of these, upon common stock, are nearly as good as the pure breed. To introduce one young cock for every twenty-five common hens would be to easily double the value of the farmer's yearly product.

From the time of its first introduction to American poultry-breeders, the breed has been held in the highest esteem. Other varieties have come up, the Plymouth Rock and Wyandottes, as market birds, and Leghorns in variety as egg-producers; still the Light Brahma has held its own as a family fowl among the lovers of choice poultry. Although quiet and unassuming in style, it has great dignity of carriage, and is really a majestic fowl. In excellent qualities for family use, it is hardly approached by any other. Its flesh is juicy and tender; and as it puts on flesh very fast, it remains a "chicken" until fully grown. The excellence of the hens as layers depends greatly on how they were bred, for some families are extraordinary egg-producers taken in comparison with other large-bodied fowls. They are layers of large, buff-colored eggs, which are very rich, and great favorites in the market. In disposition they are very kind and quiet. An ordinary picket-fence, three feet high, will restrain them; and if handled gently, they can be picked up at any time. The plumage is white with black points. The tail is black, as are also the flight feathers of the wings, which are not discernible when the wings are folded. There is also a fine penciling of black in the neck. It has a "pea," or triple comb, which, being small and set close to the head, is proof against all ordinary frost. They are easy to rear, very hardy, quick growers, and make very heavy fowls. On a well-kept lawn, there is nothing handsomer than a flock of Light Brahmas.

It is an interesting fact in connection with this breed that it is the only one of the Asiatic breeds not received through England. The original birds were brought

Fig. 62.—LIGHT BRAHMA COCK.

by a sailor to New York, obtained by a Connecticut breeder, the late Virgil Cornish of Hartford, bred and brought out by him.

DARK BRAHMAS.

In an article which recently appeared in a poultry journal, the writer says: "But few of the breeders are aware of the fact that this beautiful breed was perfected in the hands of our English breeders, out of a brood of chickens that were bred by mating a Black-red Shanghai cock with a Gray Shanghai (or, as then called, Chitegong) hen. But this is the fact. They were sent to England by an American breeder.

"There was no more heard from them, and the word Dark Brahmas, as a distinct breed of fowls, was not known in America till 1865, when the first importation was made. The assertion that the Dark and Light Brahmas were bred from the same original stock without crossing is not true. The first imported ones came with far more single-combs than Pea-combs. The breeding of Pea Comb Brahmas to Partridge Cochins produced new blood; and later we began to get them of less Cochin shape and in every way improved. Such was the early history of the breed.

"It is not a very flattering thought for home industry that we must send the crude material to a foreign country to be woven into a web of cloth, or perfected into a breed, and receive the same as a thoroughbred in only about a dozen years afterward. Be that as it may, our English brothers in this case have made for us a fine breed, and deserve much praise, and I for one would acknowledge the worth, and give the credit where it belongs.

"The earlier specimens were, more or less, bronzed

in the wing-coloring of the cocks, and the females bronze-gray in the ground-color, breeding more closely to the Partridge Cochin; but the introduction of Light Brahma cocks as an occasional cross secured the steel-gray color, which has become the standard color of America. These crosses have been so frequent that the reversion in color is prone to light, and we find English breeders indulging in the use of Partridge Cochin hens, occasionally, to retain the distinct barring of the feather in the females.

"My taste and knowledge of the breeds lead me to say that next to the Light Brahmas, among the Asiatics, the Dark Brahma must take rank in merit; yet I am compelled to acknowledge that the breed is fourth in the taste and demand of the public."

THE COCHINS.

The Cochin breed of fowls was introduced into this country about the year 1847, and to this was mainly due the celebrated "poultry mania" long to be remembered by breeders of domestic fowls. Men became almost wild after Partridge Cochins, and were willing to spend a small fortune for a trio of fine birds. The neck-hackles of the hens are bright gold, striped with black, the rest of the body being light brown, penciled with a darker shade of the same color. The hackles of the Partridge Cochin cock are bright-red, striped with black, the back being dark-red, with a bar of metallic green upon the wings. The breast and under part of the body are pure black. Some of the points of merit, as claimed by the breeders of these fowls, are as follows: they are hardier than any other breeds, except the Brahmas, and will thrive under conditions where most others would perish.

Fig. 68.—GROUP OF LIGHT BRAHMAS.

(129)

They are of large size, with a very gentle disposition, and the ease with which the Cochins are kept in confinement makes them favorites with many poultry-raisers. When full-grown the weight ranges from ten to fifteen pounds; they are too heavy to fly, and a fence two feet high will confine them. As sitters and mothers the hens are not surpassed, and are prolific layers, especially in winter, when eggs are scarce. The chickens grow rapidly, and at three months are large enough for eating.

It is true, they have some defects. The flesh is inferior, especially of old birds. The inclination to sit sometimes interferes with their greatest usefulness. This tendency is developed by over-feeding. As a breed the Cochins are most useful to supply the demands of a family for early chickens and a plenty of large, rich eggs. If the Cochins had done nothing more than to awaken a general interest in poultry-breeding, their introduction would still have been of benefit.

Besides the Partridge, which may be either of the single or Pea-comb variety, the principal sub-varieties of the Cochins are the White, Buff, and Black. With those who breed the White variety every feather must be pure, otherwise the fowl is looked upon with disfavor. The Buff Cochins may be of any shade, but the birds in a flock must correspond in color. With the Blacks, it is of the utmost importance that every feather should be solid black. In other respects than plumage, the several varieties of Cochins are very similar.

THE LANGSHAN FOWLS.

The Langshans are natives of the extreme northern part of China, where most of the fowls, both wild and domestic, are black, and where the winters are very severe. Mr. C. W. Gedney, of Bromley, Kent, England, resided for some years in that country, and professes to be well acquainted with the habits and character of these fowls, and we depend upon him for most of the information we have in regard to them in their native

Fig. 64.—LANGSHAN COCK.

country. They are entirely distinct from the Black Cochin, and their native home is 1000 miles distant from Cochin-China, whence the latter birds have been brought. These birds are erect in carriage, have larger combs, more feathered tails than the Black Cochins, an-

Fig. 65.—PAIR OF BUFF COCHINS.

(133)

are more active, hardy, and vigorous. A cockerel of this breed, seven months old, will weigh, if fattened, ten to twelve pounds; and a pullet of the same age, eight to nine pounds; the flesh is well-flavored and tender, and thickly laid upon the breast, the skin is clear white and transparent, and the bone very light and fine. The legs are of a bright slate color, and pink between the toes, and the plumage black with a vivid beetle-green reflection. These birds were first introduced into England in 1872 by an officer of the British army, Major Croad, of Sussex, who received them directly from a relative living in the northern part of China. Since then a second importation has been received in England, and Mr. Gedney states that the breed has been used to improve the Black Cochins. Since the opening of the Suez Canal, by which the voyage from China has been much shortened, the importation of fowls from that distant part of the world has been rendered much easier. Mr. Gedney sums up the merits of these fowls as follows: Extreme hardiness, rapid growth, great size combined with small bone, exquisitely white skin and flesh of the same purity of color, full breast, delicacy of flavor, and possessing none of that dryness so common to most of the large breeds. As prolific winter layers of large rich eggs, the Langshan hens will hold their own against all comers, whilst they lack that intense desire to sit which is so essentially a characteristic of the Cochin. In short, he considers that they " are the finest and most practically useful birds ever brought to England."

The Langshans were admitted to the American Standard of Excellence by the American Poultry Association at the meeting held at Worcester, Mass., 1883.

CHAPTER XV.

EUROPEAN BREEDS.

DORKINGS.

Speaking of this breed, a well-known authority says: Looking back into the dim past, to find any record of any pure-bred fowls is almost useless. But few peculiarities were noted in ancient records; perhaps the Dorking and Polish fowls are the only ones that can claim any great antiquity. In ancient paintings hens with crests are often seen resembling our Polish birds, and from which the latter are probably descended; and Columella, an old Roman writer, gives directions for the selecting of poultry to breed from, "such as five claws, square frames," etc. Such birds have been bred in England for centuries, but varying in color; the probability is that they were imported by the Romans while Britain was a Roman colony, for they took most of their luxuries along with them. At any rate, these fowls have been so long known in England that they are called an English breed; they have been bred mottled, gray, splashed, cuckoo or dominique colored, white, and silver-gray, which is the last fashion in color.

A fine Silver-gray Dorking cock is a well-shaped, noble bird, of about eight or nine pounds weight, with full silver hackle and graceful flowing tail; he certainly makes a show that few birds can match; his face and comb are bright-red, beak strongly arched; saddle, back, and hackle fine silvery white, wing coverts the same; breast, thighs, and tail black when complying with the Standard, but the thighs of young birds are nearly always a little grayish if the bird is any *size*, and birds

EUROPEAN BREEDS. 137

over one or two years old with me invariably have a little white on sickles. I have corresponded with many breeders of this breed, and they invariably tell the same experience. In "Lewis Wright's Illustrated Poultry Book,"

Fig. 66.—WHITE DORKING FOWLS.

the only portrait of a Silver-gray Dorking cock, which took cups at Crystal Palace, 1871; Dublin, 1872, and at all the principal English shows, has a white edge to the lower half of his sickle tail feathers. Hon. W. F.

Daniels, N. H., who carried the palm for his celebrated birds, states that he never had a bird worth breeding from that did not show white in his sickles at two years old; such birds are liable to be marked disqualified at any fair, as is sometimes done by judges who never kept and never knew anything about Dorkings, except from the Standard. The hen is a finely penciled steel-gray on back shoulders, and lower back part of body; the shafts of feathers on back form a fine white line, breast clear salmon color or light robin-red, shafts of feathers a lighter shade. The feet and legs of the hens, and also of

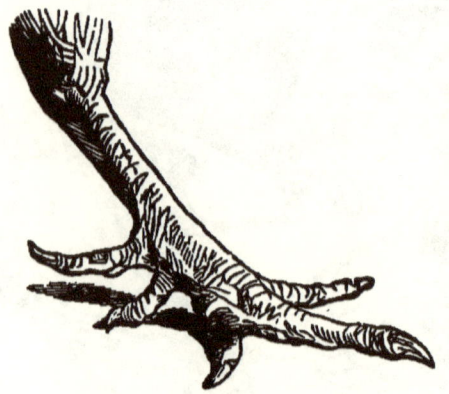

Fig. 67.—FOOT OF DORKING FOWL.

the cocks, pink or flesh colored, with five distinct toes, the fifth or upper toe well separated from the others, and slightly turned up. The neck is of a fine silvery-white color, with a black stripe down each feather. The disposition of this breed is very docile; no breed shows more intelligence; they are the best of mothers, taking care of their chicks for a much longer time than most fowls; they are good layers of fair-sized eggs, and lay well all through the summer; if not the best of winter layers, they commence early and keep it up till late in the season. One great advantage of this breed is, they are in their prime when most fowls are too old for use; they are long-lived. A hen has been known to bring up two broods in a season when she was six years old. They are most remarkable as foragers, being very active, industrious workers; if they do not improve your garden, they will find a good deal of their food on a farm or good run. As table fowl, their praises have been often sounded. They are second to none, and their cross with game produces a table fowl of absolutely supreme merit.

GAME FOWLS.

While the Asiatic, Leghorns, Hamburgs, Polands, and a host of other breeds, each have their champion advocates, each claiming for their particular favorites all the profitable good qualities; there are but few who advocate the cause of the Game fowl, and really but few who fully understand the superior qualities of this *Royal Bird*. The origin and nationality of the Game fowl have always been, and yet remain, a mooted question.

The record of Game fowls is as old as the oldest written history, wherein we find that the Persians, Greeks, Romans, and a host of other nations, each had their native Game fowls.

Games were known to the Britons, and cock-fighting was carried on in England prior to Cæsar's invasion, and hundreds of years prior to the Christian era, cock-fighting was an established insititution with the Greeks and Persians. China, Java, and the entire East Indies each had their native Game fowls.

Therefore, all theories advanced by naturalists as to the origin of the Game fowl are wholly speculative.

The Game fowl was regarded as sacred to the *gods* in ancient times, and was used in ancient military schools for teaching the youth, by practical illustration, courage and endurance in battle. They were used as emblems of ancient nationalities, being stamped on war banners, coins and shields; and, having withstood the decline of empires and witnessed the rise and fall of nations, they yet maintain to the present time their fame for gameness as of old, and are emphatically the kings of all domestic fowls.

But not alone for their antiquity and historic glory do the Game fowls stand at the head of their kind, as they possess useful qualities in a very high degree, being good layers of good-sized eggs, and the most devoted of mothers.

THE DUCK-WINGED GAME.

Of the varieties of Game fowls the Duck-winged is one of the most beautiful. Although its graceful form and dignified carriage are exceedingly attractive, its brilliantly colored plumage is still more so, and can only be truly shown by the painter's art. Its bright and varied colors are so beautifully blended together that it excites the admiration of those even who take no delight in breeding poultry, while to the fancier it is one of the first favorites. The face of the Duck-wing Game is a deep crimson; the head is covered with small silvery-white feathers; the hackle is white, slightly tinged with straw-yellow; the back is maroon, claret and straw-yellow; the saddle is slightly darker than the hackle, with fine short feathers hiding the points of the wings; the shoulders are bright brass-yellow from the butts up to the clear steel bar, and no light streak is admissible in a well-bred bird; the shoulder butts are black; the breast and tail are black, with a shade of bronze upon the sickle feathers; the eyes are red, and the legs yellow. The

Fig. 68.—BLACK-BREASTED RED GAME-COCK.

(141)

weight is from five to six pounds. The hen, when pure bred, has the head gray; comb and face bright red; hackle silvery gray, with dark stripes; the breast is bright salmon-red; the back and shoulder coverts should be slaty-gray, free from penciling; the tail is dark gray, so dark as to be nearly black; the fluff inside is a steel gray, and the legs yellow. In breeding Duck-wings for color, much care and skill is necessary; for the ordinary uses of poultry it is not necessary to do more than select the best birds, feed well, and keep them in the best and most vigorous health. Unfortunately for game poultry, their courage and endurance has been put to wrong uses, and through their enforced connection with the brutal and cruel sports of the cock-pit, they have in a measure come to be identified therewith, and are wrongly supposed to be good for nothing but fighting. On the contrary, the Game fowl is one of the most, if not the most, beautiful of our fowls. It is the best table fowl, so far as regards quality and flavor of flesh. Its eggs are exceedingly rich, and much desired for pastry or cakes. The cock is courageous, and will not hesitate to attack the hawk, and will defeat the intruder in every attempt to ravage the poultry yard. The hen is an excellent mother, and although somewhat nervous and excitable when brooding her chickens, yet with care and quiet, gentle treatment she may be handled with ease. While brooding, she is as courageous as the cock, and will defend her chickens from a hawk, and generally with success. A farmer whose grain fields, and those of his neighbors, offer a too tempting foraging ground for these active fowls, would be wise to choose some of the heavier bodied breeds; but where no damage of this kind can occur, any of the varieties of Game fowls might be chosen by those who fancy them, and wish for delicious eggs and flesh.

GAME FOWLS—A SENSIBLE GROWL.

It is a noticeable fact that the department of Games in our poultry exhibitions is the great center of attraction. Game fowls command higher prices than any of the old varieties, the eggs sell higher, and they are more extensively advertised in the poultry journals. The secret of this popularity lies mainly in the use to which these birds are put. The Game is unquestionably a good bird for eating, but is no better than some of the less quarrelsome varieties. They are prolific, but are surpassed by other varieties. They are quite handsome, but this is not what they are bred for. The only thing in which they excel all other domestic fowls is their capacity to fight until the last gasp. No doubt many breed them for their flesh and eggs. They are frequently crossed with other fowls, but their quarrelsome disposition does not make them favorites with the poultry men, who only want flesh and eggs. They are mostly bred for the pit, and there is unquestionably an increasing love of this cruel sport, principally among a certain class in our cities and villages. Cock fights are common, held in some places on the sly, in other places quite openly, and attended by the same rabble that run after prize fights in the ring, and for the same reason. They show courage, and draw blood, and offer opportunities for betting and gambling. Frequently a main is fought, and several cocks are pitted against a similar number upon the other side. It is expected in these contests that all the cocks upon one side will be killed. The worst passions are stirred by these brute contests, and there is the same objection to them that there is to other forms of gambling. The bull fights of Spain are no more bloody and cruel. They tend to harden the sensibilities, and so corrupt the morals. All the associations are low and degrading. There may be laws against these contests in some of the States, but they are seldom enforced, and do not remedy the evil. Our poultry societies have some responsibility in fostering the breeding of these birds. As a matter of fact, we think most of them would be found obnoxious to the charge of discriminating in their favor, instead of encouraging the more useful and ornamental varieties. With the single exception of the Asiatic fowls, the largest amount of premiums is generally offered for Games. The premiums for turkeys, the most valuable of all our domestic birds, amount to much less. For geese, still less. Now, if the object of these societies is the promotion of the common weal, the highest premiums should be offered for the birds that are most useful, or for those that promise to be such. The managers should so arrange the list of premiums as to draw out the birds that will be the most profitable on the farm and in the poultry yard. No special inducements are needed for the breeding of Game fowls. That business would take care of itself if the premiums were altogether diverted to the most useful classes.

HAMBURGS.

In writing of Hamburgs, an admirer of this favorite breed says: They have taken their proper place in the list of popular breeds. All varieties of the Hamburg family are beautiful, symmetrical, and stylish in carriage. They have been much improved in the beauty and uniformity of plumage since the era of poultry exhibits, but not in productiveness, as that is hardly possible; for they have long maintained the reputation of being "every-day layers." Birds of the Hamburg family are of only medium size, but their deficiency in size is more than made up for by their fecundity. Both sexes exhibit such glossy and elegantly marked plumage that they are looked upon as special favorites wherever shown or cultivated, and when well-bred are truly ornamental, possessing fancy points that render them pleasing to those who desire to keep pets that will furnish plenty of eggs and also be a gratification to the eye.

Our standard recognizes six varieties of the Hamburg breed,—the Black, Silver-penciled, Golden-penciled, Silver-spangled, Golden-spangled, and White. The

Fig 69.—SILVER-SPANGLED HAMBURGS.

whole family is remarkably attractive in plumage, capital appendages, and the graceful curves which mark the outline of their well-rounded forms. In sprightliness, carriage, and habits they are much alike. The Black is a trifle larger and in appearance stouter than any of the other varieties.

For table use, though small, they are very good; their flesh is tender, with little offal, having a larger proportion than usual of the dressed weight in flesh, from the delicate structure of the skeleton, and is fine in quality.

Fig. 70.—GROUP OF POLISH FOWLS.

(147)

The cocks average about five pounds, and the hens four pounds. They will always be prime favorites with a large class of fanciers and village poultry-raisers.

THE POLISH FOWL.

There are several varieties of these ornamental fowls, differing but little except in their plumage. The main characteristics of each are alike, all being non-sitters, and are by many called everlasting layers. As a class, they are very prolific, and easily raised, feathering out and coming to maturity early. They are small compared with many varieties, but when full-grown weigh from ten to twelve pounds per pair. They are remarkably handsome, and in the yard or lawn have few superiors in beauty. In rearing them tastes differ; some prefer the White-crested Black, others the White and Spangled varieties. They are distinguished by a crest crowning the head, which gives them the appearance of a field-marshal in plumes, though in illustrations this feature is somewhat overdrawn. They are especially adapted to city residences, the lawn, and small inclosures, and extremely domestic in their habits. They seem fond of attention, and become remarkably tame and fond of the society of their keeper; are a hardy breed to raise, but sensitive to cold and wet; require warm, dry quarters, their heavy topknots hanging so far over their eyes as to interfere with their sight. They lay a large white egg of oblong shape, very creamy and rich, and for culinary uses is among the best quality. But the peculiar merit consists in their tame and quiet dispositions and fondness of attention, their extremely ornamental appearance on the lawn, graceful carriage, and the glossy and metallic lustre of their plumage. They are quite liable to pick each other's crests, and while in this condition render the top of the head bare and disfigured. Their coops shou'd be kept clean, and feed supplied them regularly, as they are poor foragers, and little inclined to scratch and wander. Never sitting, they must be raised by other hens; and when first hatched a brood of the White-crested Black look like a line of diminutive grenadiers with white caps. Several gentlemen have turned special attention to improving this family and restoring them to their original purity, and by careful breeding are producing specimens that command the admiration of all. For many reasons we regard the Black and White Polish as the most fascinating and desirable breed of fowls for the young amateur to handle, always observing our standing admonition with this as with all other varieties, to breed but one strain, and that as nearly perfect as possible. If your taste fixes upon the White-crested Black, take that and breed for beauty; or upon the White or Golden, give that your best care. Whichever variety you select, give that your special culture. There is no variety that so quickly develops the error of a cross and disfigurement of a mixture as either variety of Polands, and when carefully and purely bred we know of none giving more pleasure and satisfaction to the breeder, or that can approach them in beauty as ornamental appendages to the yards and lawns of a city or suburban residence, and winning the attention and praise of our most prominent fanciers of pets, while as egg-producers they are not easily excelled.

WHITE-CRESTED WHITE POLISH FOWLS.

The origin of crested fowls is somewhat obscure. Cuvier and Buffon mention them, but are unable to fix upon their original source. It is supposed that they

Fig. 71.—WHITE-CRESTED BLACK POLISH FOWLS.

were first described by an Italian author, about 260 years ago, in whose treatise rough wood-cuts of some crested fowls were given as "Paduan Fowls." Paduan was an Italian city, and these crested fowls were, therefore, Italian. Buffon refers to the Paduan fowls, and supposed them to have been descended from Asiatic stock ; he also described a variety with white body and black crest, which has long been extinct, although breeders have made many efforts to restore it. The vareties of the Polish fowls now known are the White-crested White, the White-crested Black, the Golden, and the Silver-spangled, with some bearded varieties. Of these the most beautiful is, perhaps, the first mentioned. The Polish fowls are profuse layers, non-sitters, delicate table fowls, of handsome appearance ; they possess an oddity in their crests, which makes them attractive to the fancier and the amateur. They are contented in confinement, and bear close quarters very well; are easily kept within bounds and, becoming readily attached to their owners, make pleasing pets. When young, they are unusually elegant with their full crests, gracefully shaped little bodies, and tame disposition. On the whole, there is hardly any other breed which would give more satisfactory results in every way, where but one is kept, than this. For ornament, the pure white breeds have a decided advantage over the colored ones, because they show so conspicuously upon a green lawn or a field. The White Leghorn is very popular on this account, as well as for its prolific egg-producing ; but the White Polish has an advantage over the graceful Leghorn in the possession of a crest, a heavier body, and better flesh, as well as being equally valuable as an egg-producer. For ornament, therefore, as well as for use, the White Polish should be popular fowls.

THE BLACK SPANISH FOWL.

Doubtless there exists no breed of thoroughbred fowls in any country, except the Game, which can lay claim to priority of origin or to such an unbroken line of pure lineage as the Black Spanish. Nearly two thousand years ago Columella wrote about them; they were then indigenous to Spain, and not generally known in the Roman Empire. Faint traces of their origin to the Phœnician colony of Carthage, through the doubtful media of Celtic poetry, are not sufficiently reliable of themselves to substantiate the claim.

The Black Spanish is possibly the fourth in the order of Gallinæ, or, in other words, the fourth distinct variety of the *Gallus bankiva*. Time has effected but little change in them during those years of close breeding. The same vital element, the same stamina, and the same power of reproducing their like in plumage, contour, symmetry, carriage, and facial markings are as characteristic of the breed to-day as they were of them in past centuries. Some writers assert several varieties of the Black Spanish, as the Minorca, Red-faced, Black, the White. the Blue, Andalusian, and the Gray or Mottled Ancona. Although each of these varieties was produced by the amalgamation of the Black Spanish with other provincial breeds, yet, strictly speaking, each is definitely classed by the best-informed Spanish breeders as distinct varieties, inasmuch as they belong to the Mediterranean islands and provinces of Spain. Their resemblance to the Spanish is indeed close. Affinity no doubt exists; but nowadays, when skillful discriminations, careful selections, and thorough breeding produce those nice and fine points not found in the original congenitors, the progeny in time assumes distinctive features, plumage, and peculiar characteristics, so as to be considered a

EUROPEAN BREEDS. 155

distinct variety of breed. The white face on the Spanish is purely Castilian, and it is a mooted question whether this feature is natural or was produced by years of study and skillful cultivation.

Fig. 72.—WHITE-FACED BLACK SPANISH COCK.

The feathering of the Spanish is close and hard. The metallic lustre which tips the hackle, back, and wings contrasts beautifully with the white face, bright-red comb and wattles.

The carriage of the cock should combine stateliness, alertness, and gracefulness; he should be proud and carry his breast full and projecting; his color should be jet-black; white or partially white feathers is a serious fault; the comb, single and extending from the fore part of the nostrils in an arched form. The white face is the most important feature. It should be pure white, rising well over the eye and extending to the back of the head, covering the deep-sided cheeks, and jointing the long and well-rounded white ear-lobes and thin wattles.

The Black Spanish are great layers; none surpass them in beauty, nor excel them in size and quantity of eggs. Our northern winters are too severe for them; yet they seem to do well, if we judge by the grand display of our poultry exhibitions. They require great care during chickenhood; cold rains, damp houses and runs, and close confinement are positive seeds of mortality. They love to roam over the ample grounds of the breeder's homestead, where they can bask in sunshine and display their unique and ornamental facial markings.

WHITE AND BROWN LEGHORNS.

The Leghorns have been widely known in this country for the last twenty years. They have been growing in public favor every year, until they now stand in the first rank of pure-bred poultry. They did not spring up in a few years to their present standing and popularity, but with steady strides have gained hosts of admirers among both veteran and amateur fowl-breeders for their remarkable precocity and productiveness.

Without doubt, we have no variety of domestic fowls among the improved breeds at present cultivated in this country that will during the year produce a larger num-

FIG. 73.—WHITE LEGHORNS.

ber of eggs on the average than the Leghorn. The laying of eggs is their great forte; and if they be properly cared for and fed, they will lay well through cold weather, the hens being powerful machines for converting food into eggs.

The Leghorns, on a good range, can pick up the greater part of their own living. They are the most active and industrious foragers known. But if one is obliged to confine them to a small yard, clip their wing primaries to keep them within bounds, and you will be surprised to see how they will scratch and keep busy day after day.

It is true there is some trouble experienced in wintering Leghorns successfully in our frigid climate; so that they will appear at our annual shows and come out in spring with their combs and pendants unscathed by Jack Frost. But, as it often has been said by our leading fanciers of this and other high-combed varieties, they should be kept in quarters where there is no danger of freezing; and no poultryman who values his fowls should allow them in winter to occupy a place that is not warm and comfortable.

From the time Leghorns leave the shell they grow rapidly, are hardy, active, strong, and healthy, mature early, and are comparatively free from disease. During moulting, when other breeds succumb to the drain on the system by shedding and putting on their coat of feathers, they take on their new plumage quickly, and show little signs of weakness or debility.

They are a proud, sprightly, and handsome variety of fowls. They are singularly precocious, and it is quite common to see the pullets developed and doing their duty as layers before they have attained the age of five months; and the cockerels—such little scamps—making love before they are four months old.

The general objection to the Whites is the difficulty in keeping the plumage unsoiled. Where, however, they receive proper care there is little trouble.

BROWN LEGHORN.

The Leghorns have a high reputation as layers. Of these Italian fowls, the brown variety has recently become very popular. Said to have been introduced by Mr. F. J. Kinney, of Massachusetts, who bought the first trio that was imported, in 1853, from on board a ship in Boston harbor. Since then Mr. Kinney has made several importations from Leghorn, in Italy. The character of these birds is of the very best. They are yellow skinned, and excellent table fowls, are extremely hardy, and enormous layers. Hens have laid on the average 240 eggs in the year in some flocks. Pullets often begin to lay before they are five months old, and continue laying during the whole winter. They are gay plumaged birds, and have become popular amongst fanciers. The Brown Leghorns are described as having the comb of the Black Spanish fowl, with its head and body, and the plumage or color of the Black-red Game. The Brown Leghorn cock is black-breasted, with hackles of orange-red, striped with black ; the ear-lobes are white. The hen is salmon-color on the breast, with the rest of the plumage brown, finely penciled with dark markings. They thrive fairly well in confinement. A prominent English poultry fancier is of the decided opinion that this breed is the best of all our "American" breeds, when size and product of eggs are taken into consideration. The Leghorns are all called in England American breeds, because American fanciers first developed them as pure breeds, and, so to speak, "brought them out."

They are non-sitters, which is a great advantage when eggs are the product mainly desired. There is scarcely any stock of the farm which is so poorly managed as the poultry, yet there is none that may be more productive.

Fig. 74.—BROWN LEGHORNS.

A yield of two or three dozen eggs and a brood of half a dozen chickens is generally considered a fair season's production for a hen. This is the consequence of keeping poor stock, or neglecting that which is better, and capable of doing better with proper treatment. Poultry may be improved by careful breeding as well as a pig or a cow. An infusion of new blood should be procured every year or two, and a bird of undoubted excellence should be bought.

THE FRENCH BREEDS—HOUDANS AND CREVECŒURS.

If profit is the chief end of poultry-keeping, and this is certainly the purpose for which farmers and those who raise poultry for the market, as well as those who compete for prizes at the poultry shows, are all in pursuit of, then the French breeds of fowls are worthy of high consideration. There is no other country in the world where poultry is so popular a product in the market, or so frequent a dish upon the tables, as in France, and a breed that is in favor there must possess positive merit. In addition to the vast number of eggs which are consumed in every possible shape in cookery, and in various arts, millions of dollars' worth are exported from France every year; and the *poulet,* variously presented, is not only a very conspicuous item on the bills of fare, but its delicacy and succulence entitle it to the prominence it enjoys. That it is acceptable in France should be to a breed a passport to popular favor everywhere. Yet the French fowls are not nearly so popular in America as they deserve to be. The Houdans and the Crevecœurs are both prolific egg-producers, grow rapidly, and possess white and juicy flesh. Yet we have admired these fowls in the yards of other people, and have listened favorably to frequent praise of their profit and their beauty. The Houdan is doubtless a very handsome and attractive bird, and a flock of them, well bred and well cared for, is very showy in the yard or the field They are square and massive about the body, with short legs, a spirited or even a fierce carriage, on account of their

Fig. 75.—GROUP OF FRENCH FOWLS.

(163)

peculiar crest, beard, and muffling, and the lively markings of their plumage, which, when perfect, is of a mixed "pebbly" black-and-white. They have the fifth toe,—a useless, objectionable member, which they inherit from the Dorking strain in their ancestry, although along with it they have the fine-flavored flesh and plump breast of that race. Their legs are gray and their bones remarkably light. They are egg-producers rather than breeders; and if properly fed, the hens will lay on without stopping to "sit." They will thrive in confinement, when properly kept, as well as when roaming at large; and when allowed to range, exercise the liberty now and then with greater freedom than is convenient upon the farm. The standard of excellence of the poultry-fanciers for the Houdan is subject to some variation as to minor points, such as the shape of the comb; the fifth toe, however, is insisted upon; the feathering should be of black and white, evenly mixed, and not patchy; the saddle of the cock is tipped with straw yellow; the crest is of black and white feathers, evenly mixed, and thrown back so as to show the comb, which is double, evenly toothed upon each side, and with both sides alike in shape; the hackle is black and white, the beard and muffle almost hide the face, and the wattles are long and evenly rounded at the ends. The hen is square-bodied, and low-framed, with plumage like that of the cock; the crest is full and round and not loose and straggling or shaggy. The fifth claw is large and turned upwards, as with the cock. If good birds are procured to start with, they should breed very true to the marks; but if long closely bred, they will in time become mixed in appearance.

The Crevecœur, like the Houdan, is named from the village in France in the neighborhood of which it has long been largely bred for market. These birds are remarkably stately and handsome, although somber in color, except in the sunlight, when the golden-green reflections from the plumage make them very brilliant; but this peculiarity is only brought out in a favorable light. They are much more rarely seen than the Houdans, although as producers of eggs, and for non-sitting as well as for early maturity, and whiteness and sweetness of flesh, they surpass these. They are not winter layers, which is an objection; but when the cock is crossed upon Brahma hens, the eggs produce table birds of heavy weight, excellent quality, and in time for early marketing. They suffer nothing from confinement, and a dozen can be easily kept in a yard twenty feet square. They are very tame and friendly when petted. They excel as table birds, notwithstanding their black legs, which may be objected to by the marketmen or the cooks; this feature has no ill effect upon the color, flavor, or tenderness of the flesh, which is very white and of delicious flavor. Young birds will fatten when three months old, and have been made to weigh four pounds at that age, and at six months, with two weeks' fattening, have weighed seven pounds. The Crevecœur cock should be a heavy, compact bird, mounted upon short, thick legs; the thighs, being well feathered, tend to give the birds a heavier and more solid build. The back is broad and flat, giving a robustness to the figure, and slopes but slightly towards the tail, which is carried high. The general carriage is dignified, their sedateness being somewhat heightened by their somber coloring. The comb is two-horned or "antlered," and the crest is formed of lancet-shaped feathers, which fall backwards and do not straggle wildly in all directions, as in the Houdan The chicks are hardy when properly cared for, but early chicks of this breed are rare, on account of the late habits of the hen. The breast is full; the hackle is long and sweeps gracefully down the neck; the beard and muffle are full and low on the throat, and the plumage, as previously described, when perfect, is of a solid black, with greenish and sometimes brilliant reflections. The hen is similar in color and special points to the cock; her body is massive, and her legs strong to match her stout body. Her plumage is perfectly black, the crest is large, and the beard full, and the comb, which is horned, is much hidden in the crest.

As these birds become aged a few stray white feathers will appear in the crest, which, however, should be an objection in young birds. When but one breed is kept, the Houdan would be preferable to the Crevecœur, on account of its more lively color; but when cross-bred birds are not objected to, a few of the latter, with their remarkably beautiful color when in a bright light, their large size and handsome carriage, their desirable table qualities, and the habit of the hen to lay when others are broody, would make a very desirable addition to a flock of Brahmas or Cochins.

CHAPTER XVI.

AMERICAN BREEDS

PLYMOUTH ROCKS.

The breed known as the Plymouth Rock is generally acknowledged the best for useful purposes that has ever been bred in this country, and as especially adapted to our American climate, markets, and uses. As fowls for the farmer and raiser of market poultry, they are superior to other birds in many respects. They fill the requirements of the farm, while maintaining their purity as a breed. They are good layers, sitters, and mothers. They are excellent foragers, and, being at the same time under easy control, will bear close confinement without injury. They have the desirable characteristic of being self-reliant when roaming at will and dependent upon their own exertions, and contented and happy when restrained in close quarters.

For general purposes we know of no better fowl. They are hardy, and easily raised, and for a breed that is so large they are wonderfully active and industrious, quick and sprightly in their movements. With a good yard of Plymouth Rocks, the farmer or market-poultry raiser has a breed that fills all requirements; the farmer's object being not so much to gratify taste or a love of the beautiful and ornamental, as to keep fowls that will give a good supply of eggs through a great part of the year, and furnish in the fall and winter large-sized, compact birds, possessing a presentable color for the table.

The Plymouth Rocks were first brought to notice when the Brahmas and Cochins were leading the fashion, and did not attract particular attention; but on the score

Fig. 76 (a).—WHITE PLYMOUTH ROCKS.

Fig. 76 (b).—BARRED PLYMOUTH ROCKS.

of their merits alone they have worked their way up, and earned for themselves a lasting reputation for general utility.

This breed is deservedly becoming very popular among those persons who keep fowls for profit. First among the good qualities of a fowl, is size. This the Plymouth Rocks have in an unusual degree. There are many excellent breeds of poultry which are all that can be desired except as to size, and the lack of this is fatal to their popularity; for, after all, profit is the chief object with most people in choosing a kind of fowl to keep. Hardiness of constitution and vigor, pleasing form, handsome and attractive plumage, and prolific production of eggs are all very desirable qualities in fowls, and these all belong to the breed. The future of the Plymouth Rocks will depend greatly upon the care or fortunate success with which they are bred. Difference of taste leads breeders to favor different styles, and thus "strains" are originated. If these styles are made to depart too much from a rigid standard, there is danger that an important and essential point may be sacrificed for some minor fancy. To prevent this, and to induce or enforce care and consistency in breeding, it would be well that a very close adherence to the standard be insisted upon in all exhibitions, and that a very rigid one be adopted. In the case of the birds here represented, they come fully up to the accepted standard of excellence of American breeders, and meet it in every respect. The points required are: The breast to be "broad, deep, and full," and the body to be "large, square, and compact." The form of these birds is therefore nearly perfect, and if breeders of the Plymouth Rocks vie with each other in taking advantage of favorable accidents in breeding, and in fixing them upon their strains, or in using care in selecting birds for breeding, as any skillful breeder may readily do, the future history of this breed will be a very gratifying one. Among some of seventy breeds recognized in the American standard of excellence, there are only three of American origin, viz., the old fashioned Dominique, the Plymouth Rocks, and the Wyandottes. After some years of careful breeding the Plymouth Rock has been brought to such a condition of merit, that it is now one of the most popular breeds, and promises to be one of the most suitable for farmers and attractive to amateurs.

AMERICAN DOMINIQUES.

This old-fashioned breed is said to have been brought over by the early Puritans, and wherever bred in purity is acknowledged to be one of the best, hardiest, and most beautiful of all domestic fowls; and as there has certainly been no importation of any fowls of this breed into this country for a century, they have come to be regarded as strictly an American variety.

They are without doubt the *oldest* of the distinctive American breeds, being mentioned in the earliest poultry books as an indigenous and valued variety. In the *furore* for fancy breeds of fowls, the older sorts are sometimes wellnigh forgotten; yet it is highly probable that the American Dominiques possess as many good qualities as any of the newer breeds. If they do not reach the heavy weight of some of the latter breeds, they have great merit, and none give better satifaction to the farmer than this old American breed of Dominiques.

They should weigh from six to eight pounds when matured.

The Dominiques are excellent layers, very hardy, unexceptionable as mothers, yet are not given to excessive incubation, and are good for the table. They grow both fat and feathers quickly, while their plain "home-spun" suits make them very suitable for countless localities where larger and more valuable-looking fowls would be liable to be stolen. The merits of this breed will recommend it to persons residing in the country as well worthy of promotion in the poultry-yard, whether as producers of eggs or of meat, or as sitters or nurses.

The color of their plumage may be described as a light steel-gray ground, with each feather distinctly striped or barred across with a darker or bluish-gray, the bars shading off gradually from dark into light. The cock is a very showy bird, with full saddle and hackle, and abundant well-curved sickle feathers. The comb should be a neat "rose" form; face, wattles, and ear-lobes should be red; wattles neat, well-rounded, and of medium size; legs bright yellow.

WYANDOTTES.

A breed which for some time was known as the "American Seabrights" has many admirers, who were instrumental in having the variety admitted to the Standard at the meeting of the American Poultry Association held at Worcester in 1883. At the same time the birds were given the name of Wyandottes.

Breeders differ in their statements of the origin of this variety, but it is generally considered to be a cross of the Brahma and Hamburg breeds. It matters little, however, what the history of the fowl is, so long as it possesses the desired characteristics. When well-bred, the Wyandottes are good layers, sitters, and mothers, and their flesh is of the finest flavor. Their plumage is white and black, each feather having a white ground and being heavily laced with black, the tail alone being solid black. They have a small rose comb, face and ear-lobes bright-red, legs free from feathers and of a rich yellow color. Hens will weigh eight to nine pounds, and cocks nine to ten pounds, when matured.

In this breed we have the rose comb like the Hamburgs, but not so large. The plumage is black-and-white-speckled, like the Hamburgs, but darker, with the black tail of the Brahma. The legs are yellow, like the Brahma, but bare like the Hamburg. Fine specimens are nearly as large as the Brahma. The effort has been

Fig. 77.—WYANDOTTE FOWLS.

in this combination to preserve the good qualities and eliminate the undesirable ones of both parent breeds. The Plymouth Rock has been a favorite with those who have wanted a plump, fat chicken of a pound and a half weight as broilers. The Wyandotte is fully its equal in this respect. It feathers with its growth, and is plump at any age, thrifty and hardy in raising, yellow-skinned, and in all respects an excellent variety for forcing early. When grown, they are plump in body and of an attractive appearance in the market. They lay a medium-sized

Fig. 78.—WYANDOTTES.

(175)

egg of dark-buff color. Their laying qualities depend much on the selections and matings of the parent stock. In markings the fowls are very handsome, the hen more so than the cock. In the main, the feathers are white with a black border, which makes them evenly and brightly speckled. The hackle is penciled white and black, and the tail black.

AMERICAN JAVAS.

In writing of our American Javas Mr. Bicknell says: They have characteristics different from any other variety; they present large size, long bodies, deep full breast, and their general make-up is just what is required for a genuine, useful superior table fowl—hardiness and beauty.

Of the two varieties, Black and Mottled, there is little difference except in plumage. They have single combs, feet are yellow, shanks free from feathers, skin yellow; when served on the table the flesh does not present that objectionable dark color common to some other breeds, but is equal to the Plymouth Rock in every particular.

CHAPTER XVII.

DISEASES OF POULTRY.

Poultry generally suffer from preventible ills. It is almost useless, and rarely ever worth while, to treat sick poultry. A chicken is hardly worth the trouble required to physic it, and nine out of ten die in spite of all the treatment that can be given them. Poultry are naturally subject to very few diseases. If kept clean, not overfed, not cooped up close, kept from foul, putrid food, supplied with clean water regularly, and have abundant pure air in their roosting-places, they live and thrive without any trouble, except in rare cases. The fatal disorders which result from ill-treatment cannot be cured by medicine. It is too late. The mischief has been done when the first symptoms appear, and the best procedure is generally to kill the diseased fowls and sav the rest by sanitary measures.

DISTEMPER, ROUP, AND CHICKEN-POX.

An article which recently appeared in a poultry journal is the most practical we have ever seen on these subjects, and is well worth reprinting. Fowls never perspire; the waste of the system is in a large measure carried off in the vapor of the breath, which is far more rapid than is by many supposed. The heart of the fowl beats 150 times per minute, which causes a rapid respiration, and demands twice the amount of air in proportion to weight. Even the bones of the wing are charged with air, and so much so that the windpipe severed and tied, and the wing sawn off, it will admit air enough to sustain life for some time.

Distemper, which seems to be an acclimated disease, yet if neglected often results in roup, is easily detected by a puffed face, deep scarlet in color, and in two or three days discharges from the nostrils appear. In this disease the membrane of the air-passages, tear-tube and throat is inflamed; and when so much so as to close the tear-tube, the discharges become acrid, and roup is the result. To prevent this, it becomes necessary to check these mucus-discharges. The use of kerosene is a handy and sure cure. By holding the fowl so it cannot swallow, and filling the throat with the oil, holding long enough to have the oil thoroughly saturate the throat, then allowing the same to run out of the mouth, and by washing the nostrils out, and injecting a few drops into each nasal passage, the effect is magical; and if attended to during the first two days of the distemper, one application generally proves sufficient. So safe and sure is this remedy that I have not used any other for the past two years. It checks at once the unnatural discharges. The breathing of kerosene for the twenty-four hours seems to have a most marvelous effect, and restoration to health is the result. By neglect we often have an attack of "roup," which is apparent in a fetid breath, swollen head, and inflamed face, a throat and mouth filled with canker. No matter what the cause that has brought this state of things to your flock,—be it bad ventilation, filthy quarters, unclean water-vessels, or neglect to remove roupy specimens till by the taint of the water by drinking in the same vessel the whole flock is effected,—it is safe, when a part of the fowls are so affected, to reason that the entire flock is in a measure poisoned in blood, and means should be taken to prevent its spreading. If we in such a case put in the water-vessel bromide of potassium to the extent of two grains to each fowl, for three or four days, the evils of the ravage may be stayed.

But in treating those bad cases described above, if the patient is so full of canker as to be unable to eat, we must administer the doses.

At the time of the Portland exhibition, I had sent to me a patient in the shape of a fine Light Brahma. The bird did not arrive until I had left for the exhibition; consequently, it was three days before I could attend to him. When I returned I found him in the following deplorable condition: His mouth was as full as it could possibly be of canker; his head was swollen till both eyes were closed, and face and comb were broken out with dry canker, or, as some poultrymen call it, chicken-pox. By the use of a large syringe, I injected the bird's crop full of milk in which four grains of bromide had been dissolved; I then gargled the mouth and throat with kerosene in the way described above.

We see many recommendations to remove the canker by forcible means; this is the very worst thing that can be done (inhuman and retards the cure). In the case of the Light Brahma, by gargling the throat three mornings, the fourth morning nearly all the canker slipped off, leaving the mouth smooth. I administered the milk and bromide for the four days also.

The head, as I have described, was a swollen, shapeless mass. I felt that the case was a hopeless one, and, already knowing the curative properties of the oil for canker in the throat, I bathed the head, face, and throat with the oil, repeating the operation the second morning, when I noticed here and there small blisters on the throat, and a decided improvement in the looks of my patient. I then on the fourth morning applied the oil again, when the swelling subsided, and he opened his eyes and commenced to eat a little, and from that time improved rapidly; the blisters of course dried down.

About a week afterward I was brushing the dry scale from face and comb, and in the process I lifted entire the cuticle and feathers from head and neck for three inches down, which demonstrated the power of the oil as a counter-irritant, and the necessity of care in its use. These two medicines are all I have used since for distemper or roup, and so successful have I been that I think it safe to say I have not lost five birds by roup in the past two years.

Chicken-pox—warty blotches of comb and throat—can be treated with bromide, by giving three grains a day, and isolating the bird till the spots dry and cleave off, which will be in a week or ten days. The plan to remove those caps is a very bad one, and only spreads the disease. Patience, giving time for the bromide to do its work, and the shedding of the dry scales, is all that is needed for a cure.

CHICKEN OR FOWL CHOLERA.

There is nothing more unsatisfactory than a sick chicken, or more difficult to treat, and we find that the best writers upon poultry diseases insist much more upon prevention than upon cures. The term "cholera" is applied to a disease which, though it varies in different parts of the country, is everywhere accompanied by a violent diarrhœa, and is rapidly fatal. In every such outbreak of disease among fowls, the first thing to be done is to separate the sick from the well, and at once give a change of food, which should be of the most nourishing character, and combined with some stimulant, such as Cayenne pepper, or a tonic, like iron. Modern writers upon poultry diseases are greatly in favor of iron in some form as a tonic. The old method of putting rusty nails in the drinking-water had good sense at the bottom of it, but a more active form of iron is desirable. The English poultrymen are much in favor of "Douglas's Mixture." This is made by putting eight ounces of sulphate of iron (also called copperas, or green vitriol) into a jug (never use a metallic vessel) with two gallons of water, and adding one ounce of sulphuric acid (oil of vitriol). This is to be put into the drinking-water in the proportion of a tea-spoonful to a pint, and is found to be a most useful tonic whenever such is needed. So soon as the disease breaks out among the poultry, this should be given to the well to enable them to resist it, together with more nutritious and easily digestible food.

One writer on the subject states that he made a saturated solution of alum, and whenever a bird was attacked, gave it two or three tea-spoonfuls, repeating the dose the next day. He mixed their feed, Indian meal, with alum-water for a week. Since adopting this he has lost no fowls. Another writes that in each day's feed of cooked Indian meal, for a dozen fowls, he added a table-spoonful of Cayenne pepper, gunpowder, and turpentine, feeding this every other day for a week. From what we have heard of chicken-cholera, it appears to be a protest against improper feeding and housing rather than any well-defined disease. Fowls are often in poor condition on account of the vermin they are obliged to support, or they may be in impaired health from continuous feeding on corn alone. When in this weakened state, a sudden change in the weather may induce diarrhea, or a cold, which attacks the flock so generally that the disease appears to be epidemic. And being generally and rapidly fatal, it is called "cholera," and the owner of such a flock at once writes us for a remedy for "chicken-cholera." A recent letter, from a friend in Massachusetts, is the type of many others received of late. This informed us that some of the fowls would leave the rest of the flock, go off and mope by themselves, refuse to eat, and, as a general thing, those so affected soon died. The writer assumed this to be cholera. Our reply was essentially as follows: Separate at once the sick birds from the well. If the poultry-house has not recently been put in order, remove all the fowls until it can be fumigated, by burning sulphur, and then whitewashed in every part of the interior with lime-wash, to each pailful of which half a pound of crude carbolic acid has been added. Mix some lard and kerosene, and, with a rag, or swab, rub all the roosts. Throw out all the old straw from the nest-boxes, and grease with the lard and kerosene the insides of these. Renew the dust-boxes, using fine road-dust, and mixing some sulphur with the dust.

SCABBY LEGS IN POULTRY.

The unsightly disease which affects the legs of fowls, causing them to swell and become distorted, is due to a mite, a small insect which is similar in appearance to that which causes scab in sheep. It is roundish-oval, and semi-transparent, about one eight-hundredth of an inch in length, appearing, when magnified 400 diameters, about half an inch long. If the scales from the leg of a diseased fowl are beneath the microscope, a number of these mites may be found between them. Beneath the scales there are spongy, scabby growths, in which the eggs and pupæ of the mites are to be seen in great numbers. The pupæ are very similar in shape to the mature mites, but are very much smaller, appearing, when viewed with the above-mentioned power, about one tenth of an inch in length. The disease, being of a similar character to the scab in sheep, or the mange in dogs and cattle, may be cured by the same treatment.

We have cured fowls of the disease, before accurately knowing the cause, by applying to the legs a mixture of lard with one-twentieth part of carbolic acid. This should be applied with a stiff brush, such as one of those sold with bottles of mucilage. A very small painter's sash-brush would answer the purpose; but something must be used by which the medicated grease can be applied thoroughly to the crevices between the scales. A mixture of equal parts of lard or sweet-oil and kerosene will be equally as effective as the carbolic-acid mixture. It is probable that lard, or oil alone, would be effective, but the kerosene more easily penetrates between the scales, and the carbolic acid is sure death to the parasites. The remedy being so simple, it will be inexcusable if this disagreeable affection is suffered to remain in a flock; while, however, one fowl is troubled with it, it will certainly spread, as the mites will burrow beneath the scales of the other fowls. If precautions were generally used, the parasite could soon be exterminated. It should be made a disqualification at poultry-shows for fowls to be affected with scabby legs or feet, in any degree whatever, for we know that several poultry-yards are not free from this disease; and whenever affected fowls are sent out, the disease goes with them.

EGG-EATING FOWLS.

When fowls are confined they will eat their eggs, and no persuasion but that of the ax will prevent them. They must be freed from confinement and given their natural employment of scratching, or they will get into this mischief.

If the bird is worth the trouble, a nest may be so arranged that the egg, when laid, will at once roll out of sight and reach.

FEATHER-EATING FOWLS.

The habit of pulling and eating feathers is also common among fowls confined. It is impossible to cure the fault when once acquired, and it is best to kill the fowls for table use at first sight, as they quickly teach others to do the same. The cause is doubtless a need or appetite for something contained in the feathers. A mixture of dried flesh and bone, specially prepared for poultry, with a small quantity of sulphur, will act as a preventive. Bits of fresh lean meat, or scraps, or fine-powdered fresh bones, will answer.

Another remedy is to give them a sheep's pluck, or liver, to pick at, hanging it up within reach, and to give them wheat scattered in the earth or litter of their houses. This will give them food and work to occupy their time.

THE PIP.

Poultry are sometimes troubled with a disease known as "pip." This is inflammation of the tongue and mouth, with the growth of a horny scale on the point of the tongue, which prevents the fowls from feeding. Give each fowl a pinch of powdered chlorate of potash, dropping it into the throat and upon the tongue, and remove the scale with the point of a penknife.

GAPES.

Gapes is the result of parasitic worms in the windpipe. The only cure is to dislodge them. This is sometimes successfully done by putting the chicks in a box, covering the top with a piece of muslin, and dusting fine lime through the cloth. The chicks breathe the lime, and as it comes in contact with the worms, these let go of the membranes, and are dislodged by the coughing and sneezing of the chicks. To prevent gapes, the chicks should not be kept on ground where fowls have previously been. This may be done either by spading old ground deeply each year, or providing a different locality for the poultry-yard.

EGG-BOUND FOWLS.

It is not at all uncommon for hens, especially old and infirm ones, to become egg-bound. The eggs without shells collect in the egg-passage, and form a mass of hard, cheesy matter, which in time causes the abdomen to swell, and finally kills the fowl. In the early stages of this trouble the remedy is to inject some linseed-oil into the passage, and, by dilating it with the fingers, remove the collected matter. The trouble is generally from over-feeding with stimulating food.

LOSS OF FEATHERS.

Poultry will frequently drop their feathers when over-fed upon corn, buckwheat, or other heating food. The remedy is to feed only chopped cabbage or turnips, or turn them into a grass-field for a few days. A few pills of castile-soap, or half a tea-spoonful of castor-oil, will be of benefit.

BUMBLE FOOT.

This is usually caused by a bruise or sliver; inflammation sets in, and pus forms under the skin and be comes condensed into hard, cheesy matter. When discovered, while the pus is in liquid form, if the skin be opened with a knife, the pus-cavity well syringed out with carbolic acid and water, the place kept open by poulticing for a day or two, it heals up. The same trouble sometimes attacks the shank; in such a case open the sack at the bottom and top, and syringe the cavity from the top to the bottom a couple of times; then use strong liniment on the shank, and it will all heal up. When the case is of so long standing that the pus becomes hard and cheesy, the only way is to lay the whole thing open, making an opening large enough to press the core out; then poultice and use the carbolic acid and water baths, finally winding up with a strong liniment.

DEFENSE AGAINST DISEASE.

If cared for, and they have clean, wholesome quarters and not crowded, poultry will always be healthy. If a fowl merely acts a little "cranky," do not imagine that it is sick, and commence stuffing it with drugs; simply remove it to a pen some distance from the flock, and let it alone a few days. If it proves to be very sick, chop off its head and burn it. For cholera, a strong solution of hyposulphite of soda, given three times a day, in teaspoonful doses, is probably the best remedy we have. For gapes, dip a feather in turpentine, and insert it into the windpipe. One application will generally cure; two are sometimes necessary. Dip scaly legs in kerosene two or three times. A little sulphur mixed with the food once a week in winter prevents packing of the crop and irregularities of the bowels, caused by overeating and the constant production of eggs. Gravel and coarse sand are necessary for the digestion of food. Crushed bones, old plaster, lime, etc., are necessary for the formation of egg-shells. Cayenne pepper in small quantities, mixed with the food occasionally during the winter, promotes egg-laying.

CHAPTER XVIII.

PARASITES UPON POULTRY.

It is very common to speak of "Hen-lice" as if there were but one kind of insect parasite upon our fowls. The fact is that there are at least five species of lice which, with several mites, ticks, and kindred creatures, bring up the number of poultry pests to a dozen or more. From the day the chick leaves the egg, to that on which it is prepared for market, it is subject to the attacks of one or more of these parasites. That they interfere with the comfort, and consequently the thrift of the birds, is evident, and to be a successful poultry-raiser one should know thoroughly the habits of these poultry enemies and the methods of getting rid of them. That some are wonderfully prolific is shown by feathers sent us by a friend in New Hampshire, who writes: "They have something on the base, and about every feather in the 'fluff' is like these." (See Fig. 79.)

Fig. 79.—EGGS AT BASE OF FEATHER.

The engraving, of the natural size, gives the appearance of the feathers. A magnifier showed the "something on the base" to be a dense mass of the eggs of a parasite, and it is safe to say that there were several hundreds in each cluster. A portion of the eggs had hatched, and we do not wonder that our friend wrote that the "cockerel is very lousy." Some of the creatures live only upon the feathers of the bird, while others are provided with suckers by which to draw the blood. Where the fowls are in good health, and have free use of the dust bath, they keep the parasites from excessive increase. In winter there should always be a box of fine earth for dusting kept where no water can reach it. Old nest-boxes should be treated to a bath of scalding lye before they are again used.

To get rid of fleas, the chicken-house should be thoroughly whitewashed—not half done—with hot limewash. The floor should be well sprinkled with a solution of carbolic acid, and the roosts thoroughly greased with a mixture of one pound of lard, one pint of raw linseed oil, a quarter of a pint of kerosene, and a quarter of a pound of sulphur.

When kerosene oil is placed on the fowls themselves, it should be used sparingly; properly applied, it is the best known remedy for lice, but to use it recklessly is dangerous.

"THE" HEN LOUSE.

Unfortunately for the fowls, it is impossible to describe "*the*" Hen Louse, for there are so many of them. Here is a portrait, Fig. 80, of one of the easiest to find, as it is one of the largest, being nearly $\frac{1}{12}$ inch long. Unless special care is taken, little chicks, when they are first hatched, are sadly afflicted; and the feathers on the head are all alive with them. Not only common fowls, but all other domestic birds, including the delicate pets, such as the canary, and the wild birds from the largest to the smallest, are infested by *parasites* —as animals and plants that live upon other animals and plants are called. Vermin is the pest of poultry, and when chicken-houses get thoroughly infested, it is not an easy matter to cleanse them. If the house is washed with a hot-lime wash, and the roosts are rubbed with a mixture of kerosene oil and lard, the lice will be made uncomfortable, and if this treatment is repeated a few times, the house and also the fowls will be quite free from vermin. If the house is, as all poultry houses should be, detached from barns and other buildings, it may be fumigated. Shut it up tight and close every opening; then place a pan of live coals on the ground (or if it must be on a wooden floor, put down a few shovelfuls of earth, or cold ashes to hold the pan). Throw on a handful of lumps of brimstone, and get out quickly, closing the door tightly. If the work has been done thoroughly, no lice can be found at the end of a few hours. The white-washing, etc., may then be done.

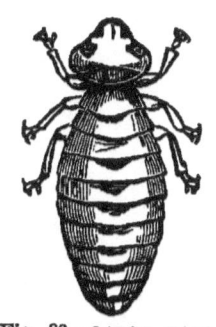

Fig. 80.—LARGE PALE HEN-LOUSE.

In regard to the use of kerosene, it is not more effective perhaps than some other remedies, but is applied more easily than lard, tobacco, sulphur, or whitewash. We apply it to the perches in the hennery from the common lamp-filler. Turn a very small stream from the spout, and move the can rapidly from end to end of the perch. The oil gets upon the feet and feathers, and is soon distributed all over the fowl. The lice leave on very short notice, and the fowls are entirely relieved. It is a greater safeguard against lice on chickens, when first hatched, to use the oil in the boxes, before the nest is made for the sitting hen. It takes but a small quantity, applied to the corners of the box, to keep away insects. Take care that the oil does not touch the eggs. In using a substance like kerosene about the farm buildings, remember that it is inflammable, and must be employed with caution, avoiding every chance of fire.

While the kerosene will destroy vermin by the thousands, its effects are not lasting, as it soon evaporates. To be effectual, it should be applied to the roosts and wood-work frequently, say once a week.

The red color of some of the lice is due to the blood sucked by them from the fowls, as mosquitoes become red after dining on human blood.

CHAPTER XIX.

RAISING TURKEYS.

It is a joyful morning to the farmer when he discovers his first brood of young turkeys following the cautious tread and the low cluck of the mother, as she leaves her nest. The critical season of turkey-raising is now before him. Upon his constant care and watchfulness for the next three or four weeks depend his success and his profits. It is a matter of the first importance that the care of the young broods should be committed to some one individual. There is no substitute for personal responsibility in carrying the young chicks through their first month. They are very tender, and they have many enemies from the start. The mother bird has wise instincts to guard her brood against harm in a state of nature, but in domestication she needs close watching to guard them against birds and beasts of prey, against roaming for food too early in the morning, and especially against storms. If the farmer cannot attend to this himself, he should put the care upon some one else who will look after the broods at short intervals during the day, and see them properly sheltered for the night. Women who have a fondness for the work make the best guardians of the young broods. Each little flock should be counted every night, as they come to their roost, and if any are missing they should be looked after. They can be controlled in their wanderings, at first, by frequent feeding. Like all other birds, they follow the feed very strictly, and will not wander very far from food that is regularly and bountifully supplied.

Why is it that one farmer will raise nearly every turkey-chick that comes out of the shell, and do this nine years out of ten, without much respect to wet or dry seasons, while another loses from a half to three quarters with about the same uniformity? We know of men with whom success is the established rule. They are very systematic in this, as in all their other business. We visited one of these thrifty farmers, who raised one hundred and sixty-five turkeys last year from nine hens, and upon inquiry found that he did about the same thing every year. We wanted to know just how he managed

Fig. 81.—BRONZE TURKEY.

to secure this uniform result, and found him communicative. He insists upon good stock to begin with—the best always selected to breed from. Then he places great reliance upon regular feeding during the fall and winter, so that the flock becomes very gentle, and the hens make their nests immediately about the sheds and barns in places prepared for them. This is a great safeguard against foxes, skunks, crows, hawks, and other creatures that destroy the birds or their eggs. When the young first come off the nest, they are confined in pens for a few days until they are strong enough to fly over a board inclosure one foot high. He feeds frequently with coarse corn-meal and sour milk until four o'clock in the afternoon. He found in his experience that he lost a good many chicks from the food hardening in the crop. There is danger from over-feeding. As the chicks grow the sour-milk diet is increased, and during the summer it is kept constantly in a trough for them. They are exceedingly fond of sour-milk and buttermilk, and they grow very rapidly upon this diet. An incidental advantage, and a very important one, he thinks, is that the young birds are prevented from straying very far from the house. They return many times during the day to the buttermilk trough for their favorite food. This, with Indian meal, constitutes their principal food until midsummer, when insects are more abundant, and they wander farther from the house. This method can easily be tried on dairy farms.

TURKEY ROOSTS.

The turkey instinctively goes to roost at nightfall, and in its native haunts takes to the highest trees, in order to be safe from numerous enemies. The domesticated bird has the same instinct, and prefers the roofs of buildings, or the branches of trees, to any perch under cover. Yet, if taken in hand when the broods are young, turkeys can be trained to roost in almost any place not under cover. For safety the roost should be near the house or barn. If left to roost upon fences or trees at a distance from the house, they are liable to be disturbed, or carried off by foxes, or by poultry-thieves. The roost should be some fifteen or twenty feet from the ground. Poles of red or white cedar, from three to five inches in diameter, are the best material, and these are the most convenient sizes for the scaffolding upon which the birds are to roost. The odor of these woods is a protection against the vermin which sometimes infest the young birds. The size of the poles for the roosts is a matter of importance. It is much easier for these heavy birds to keep their balance upon a large pole than upon a small one. Then, in the freezing weather of winter, the feet of the birds are more completely protected by the feathers. Another advantage of having the turkeys roost together is the saving of manure. If the ground under the roost is kept covered with muck, or loam, and occasionally stirred, several loads of a valuable fertilizer may be made every season. A roost made of durable wood, like cedar, will last for a lifetime. It is but a little trouble to train the young broods to go to their roost every night. And after the habit has once been formed they will go to the same roosting-place regularly every night. One of the secrets of success in turkey-raising is in having a secure roosting-place.

FATTENING TURKEYS.

It is a goodly sight, as the summer days wane, to see the flocks of turkeys coming home from the woods and pastures at nightfall with full crops. If the farm has not been overstocked with these birds, they have very largely made their living upon grasshoppers, crickets, worms, and other small fry. The regular food they have had has been rather to keep them wonted than to supply any lack of forage. As the cool nights come on, and the supply of insects declines, the business of fattening properly commences. It should be remembered that plump, well-dressed turkeys not only bring a higher price in market, but enhance the reputation of the producer, and make his market sure for future years. The turkey is one of the finished products of the farm and one of the greatest luxuries in the market. The farmer should do his best in preparing his flock for the shambles. The main business now is to lay on fat, and the bird should have, every night and morning, a full supply of nutritious and fattening food. Instinctively the turkey follows his feed, and if the supply is abundant at the farm-yard he will not stroll far from home. Boiled potatoes, mashed, and mixed with meal, and fed moderately warm, is a very excellent feed both to promote growth and to fatten. If the pigs can be robbed of a part of their milk, and it be mixed with a part of the hot potatoes and meal, it will very much improve the dish. It is very desirable to supply the place of insects with some kind of animal food, and butchers' scraps is one of the cheapest and most desirable forms of food for poultry. Grain should be given at least once a day with the soft and warm feed. Nothing is better than sound corn. The Northern corn is thought to contain more oil than that of Southern growth. Old corn should always be used for this purpose. The new corn keeps them too loose. In feeding, only so much corn should be thrown out as the birds will eat up clean. Take a little time to feed them, and study æsthetics as you watch the iridescent hues upon the glossy plumage. There is nothing more charming upon the farm in the whole circle of our feathered dependants than a hundred or two of these richly bronzed turkeys feeding near the corn-crib. You can afford to enjoy the disappearance of corn, while the turkeys are increasing in weight. Dreams of a full wallet at Thanksgiving and Christmas will not harm you as you look on this interesting sight.

HABITS OF THE WILD TURKEY.

The males commence wooing as early as February in some of the extreme Southern States; but March is the opening of the season throughout the country, and April the month in which it reaches its highest development. The males may then be heard calling to the females from every direction, until the woods ring with their loud and liquid cries, which are commenced long ere the sun appears above the horizon, and continued for hours with the steadiest persistency. As both sexes roost apart at this period, the hens avoid answering the gobblers for some time, but they finally become less obdurate, and coyly return the call. When the males hear this, all within hearing respond promptly and vehemently, uttering notes similar to those which the domestic gobblers do when they hear an unusual sound. If the female answering the call is on the ground, the males fly to her and parade before her with all the pompous strutting that characterizes the family. They spread and erect their tails, depress their wings with a quivering motion and trail them along the ground, and draw the head back on the shoulders, as if to increase their dignity and importance; then wheel, and march, and swell, and gobble, as if they were trying to outdo each other in airs and graces. The female, however, pays little attention to these ceremonious parades, and demurely looks on while the rivals for her affection try to outdo one another in playing the gallant and dandy. When the strutting and gobbling fail to win her, the candidates for matrimony challenge each other to mortal combat, and whichever is successful in the contest walks away with her in the most nonchalant manner. The easy indifference of the hen as to which she will follow may not be pleasing to persons imbued with romantic feelings, yet she is only obeying a wise

Fig. 82.—WILD TURKEY COCK.

law of nature, which decrees that only the fittest should live, and in the lower animal world these are necessarily chosen for their physical qualities.

The battles between the males are often waged with such desperate valor that more than one combatant is sent to join the great majority, as they deliver very heavy blows at each other's heads, and do not give up a contest until they are dead, or so thoroughly exhausted as to be scarcely able to move.

When one has killed another, he is said sometimes to caress the dead bird in an apparently affectionate manner, as if it were very sorry to have been compelled to do such a deed, but could not help it, owing to the force of circumstances; yet I have seen the winner in a tournament in such a rage that it not only killed its rival, but pecked out its eyes after it was dead. When the victors have won their brides, they keep together until the latter commence laying, and then separate, for the males would destroy the eggs if they could, and the hens, knowing this, carefully screen them. The males are often followed by more than one hen; but they are not so polygamous as their domestic congeners, as I never heard of a gobbler having more than two or three females under his protection. The adult gobblers drive the young males away during the erotic season, and will not even permit them to gobble if they can help it; so that the latter are obliged to keep by themselves, generally in parties of from six to ten, unless some of the veterans are killed, and then they occupy the vacated places, according to the order of their prowess.

Some aged males may also be found wandering through the woods in parties of two, three, four or five, but they seldom mingle with the flocks, owing, apparently, to approaching old age. They are exceedingly shy and vigilant, and so wild that they fly immediately from an imaginary danger created by their own suspicious nature. They strut and gobble occasionally, but not near so much as their younger kindred. Barren hens, which also keep by themselves, are almost as demonstrative in displaying their vocal powers, airs, and feathers as the old males, whereas they are exceedingly coy and unpretentious when fertile. When the season is over, the males keep by themselves in small bachelor parties; but, instead of being exceedingly noisy as they were in the early part of the mating period, they become almost silent. Yet they sometimes strut and gobble on their roosts, though, as a general rule, they do not, and content themselves with elevating and lowering the tail feathers and uttering a puffing sound. They keep at this exercise for hours at a time on moonlight nights without rising from their perch, and sometimes continue it until daylight.

When the hen is ready to lay, she scratches out a slight hollow in a thicket, a cane brake, beside a prostrate tree, in tall grass or weeds, or in a grain field, and lines it rudely with grass or leaves, and then deposits her eggs in it. These, which vary in number from ten to twenty, are smaller and more elongated than those of the domestic turkey, and are of a dull cream or a dirty white color, sprinkled with brownish-red spots. Audubon says that several hens may lay their eggs in one nest, and hatch them and raise the broods together. He found three hens sitting on forty-two eggs in a single nest, and one was always present to protect them.

If the eggs are not destroyed, only one brood is raised in a year; but if they are, the female calls loudly for a male, and when she is rejoined by one, both keep company until she is ready to commence laying again, when she deserts him or drives him away. She builds her nest in the most secluded spot she can find, and covers it carefully with leaves or grass whenever she leaves it.

GENERAL HINTS ABOUT TURKEYS.

The greatly increased attention paid to the turkey crop in the Eastern States, and in the Southern and Western States as well, seems to call for a few more notes. Without a good range it will not pay to raise turkeys; they create trouble between neighbors. I have found that, when confined to a yard, one turkey will require as much food to bring it to maturity as will make forty pounds of pork on a well-bred pig. Where they can have extensive range, they will pick up most of the food they require until autumn. The young are very delicate, and the hen must be cooped until they are well feathered and able to look out for themselves. The same food recommended for chicks is suitable for turkeys. Two weeks before marketing, confine them in a small, clean pen, and feed them all they will eat, not forgetting plenty of fresh water and gravel, and they will fatten up quickly and nicely.

TURKEY-NESTS.

In the wild state the hen seeks the most secluded and inaccessible spot, where there is protection from birds and beasts of prey. Security against attack is the main thing that instinct prompts her to look out for. A tangled thicket of briers, a sheltering ledge, a hollow stump, a clump of brush filled with decaying leaves, suit her fancy. With little preparation she drops her eggs upon the bare ground in these secluded places. Domesticated turkeys usually are left to a good deal of freedom in choosing their nests. Some farmers have prepared nests, made of loose stones and boards, or old barrels, placed by the roadside, or near the barn, and slightly covered with old brush. These are often exposed to the attack of weasles and skunks, and other enemies, besides being unsightly. If there are no prepared nests they will seek the nearest bit of woods, or patch of brush, or fence-corner, where they can find shelter. The whole turkey crop for the year is put in jeopardy by this want of preparation for the laying and breeding season. By having a yard devoted to fruit trees and turkeys, and an open shed with sliding doors, you have complete control of the birds, their eggs and their young, during their tender age. The risk is reduced to a minimum, and the turkey crop is as sure as any other raised on the farm. The nests under the shed should be about three feet square, and arranged with slats in the front so that the birds may be shut in or out at pleasure. The common A-shaped hen-coop on a larger scale, the peak of the gable being about three feet high, is a very good arrangement. If the turkeys are fed under the shed for a few weeks before the laying season, they will take kindly to the nests prepared for them.

EARLY BROODS.

Early broods are very desirable on several accounts, but there is a good deal of risk in having the chicks come out before the grass is well started, and there is settled weather. In the latitude of 40°, and northward, it is quite early enough to have the chicks out by the middle of May. Birds hatched from the middle of May until July 1st will have five or six months in which to grow before Thanksgiving, and that is as soon as they will be wanted for slaughter or to sell as stock. The cold storms of April and early May are likely to prove fatal to the chicks. The laying of the hens is very much within the control of their owner. and can be hastened or retarded by more or less feed at his pleasure. Some of our best breeders feed light after the first of February for the purpose of delaying the laying season. They do not care to have chicks before the first of June. Coming out at that date, they feel reasonably sure of raising the large majority of the hatch. After the birds have begun to lay, and get used to the nests, it is well to feed generously to keep up the strength of the hen while she is laying, and so prepare her for the sitting season. The number of eggs that a hen will lay depends a good deal upon the feed. The average is from fifteen to thirty eggs, while in some cases among the thoroughbreds they keep on laying all summer without manifesting any desire to sit upon the nest. These perpetual layers become very much exhausted in the fall, and it takes them a long time to recover.

SETTING THE HEN-TURKEYS.

As turkeys require a good deal of attention while they are upon their nests, they should be in one yard, or building, or at least not far distant from one another, to take up as little time as possible in the frequent visits. In making the nests, study nature and build upon the bare earth, lined with leaves or hay, or any convenient soft substance; give the eggs room enough, and yet have the nest deep enough to prevent their rolling out of the nest. A hen will lay from fifteen to thirty eggs at a litter, but they cannot always cover the whole litter. Very large old birds will cover twenty eggs. Smaller birds will cover from fifteen to eighteen, and this is about the right average. If you have a dozen turkey-hens in your flock, which is about the right number for a good range, it will not be difficult to set several birds at once, and these may be arranged in nests within a few feet of each other. With artificial or addled eggs you can keep a part of the hens upon their nests a few days, until three or four are ready. Then select eggs of as near equal age as possible and put them under the hens. If the hens, close together, are not set at the same time, there is danger when the first begins to hatch that her neighbors will hear the peep of the first chicks, and become uneasy, and perhaps forsake their nests. If all in the group of three or four nests are hatching at the same time, there is no trouble of this kind. Before putting the eggs into the nest, it is well to sprinkle a little snuff among the hay to guard against insects. If any of the eggs get fouled with the yolk of a broken egg before or after setting, the shells should be carefully cleaned with tepid water, to secure their hatching. Two or three turkeys will sometimes lay in the same nest. This will not do any harm in the early part of the season, but they should be separated before setting, and only one bird allowed to the nest. This may be done by making nests near by and putting a porcelain or addled egg in each new nest. Turkeys are not apt to crowd on to an occupied nest when a vacant one is close by. The group of hens that sit together, and bring off their young at the same time, will naturally feed and ramble together, and this will save a good deal of time in looking after them. The turkey is a close sitter, and will not leave her nest for several days at a time. Grain and water should be kept near the nests.

FEEDING AND RAISING THE CHICKS.

One of the secrets of successful poultry-raising is the art of feeding properly, not merely at regular intervals, but on the most suitable food, and keeping the chicks growing as rapidly as possible from the very start. It is very poor economy to stint turkeys, especially young growing stock; for when once stunted, it takes a long while to recover, if it does occur at all. For the first twenty-four hours after the chicks emerge from the shell, they should remain under the hen unmolested, both to dry and gain strength and hardiness. They do not require any food, as the store nature provides will last over this time. As the chicks hatch sometimes irregularly, the older ones can be cared for in the house until the others are ready to be taken away; when the hen and her brood can be removed to a roomy coop, with a tight-board bottom and a rain-proof roof. They should be fed five times daily, but only just-what they will eat up clean. The first food should consist of stale bread moistened in water or in fresh milk—the milk is decidedly preferable. Do not wet the food, as very moist or sloppy food will cause sickness and a high rate of mortality among young, tender birds. If milk can be spared, give it to them freely in place of water.

The too lavish use of corn-meal has caused more deaths among young chicks than has cholera among grown fowls. Until the chicks are half-grown, corn-meal should be but sparingly fed; but after that time, when judiciously used, is one of the very best and cheapest foods for fowls and chicks. Nine-tenths of the young turkeys and guinea-fowls which die when in the "downy" state get their death-blow from corn-meal, as it is a very common practice (because it is so "handy" and suits lazy people so well) to merely moisten with cold water some raw corn-meal and then feed it in that way.

Young chicks relish occasional feeds of cracked wheat and wheat screenings; while rice, well boiled, is not only greedily eaten by the chicks, but is one of the very best things that can be given. It frequently happens that damaged lots of rice, or low grades of it, can be bought at low figures in the cities. As it increases so much in bulk in cooking, it is not an expensive food for young chicks, even at the regular retail price, though it would not ordinarily pay to feed it to full-grown fowls very liberally or very frequently. In the absence of worms, bugs, etc., during early spring, cheap parts of fresh beef can be well boiled and shredded up for the little chicks;- but care must be taken not to feed more frequently than once in two days, and only then in moderation. This feeding on meat shreds is very beneficial to young turkeys and guinea chicks when they are "shooting" their first quill feathers, as then they require extra nourishment to repair the drain on immature and weakly bodies.

LOSS OF WEIGHT IN DRESSING TURKEYS.

Farmers frequently have occasion to sell turkeys by live weight, and wish to know what is the fair relative price between live and dead weight. In turkeys dressed for the New York market, where the blood and feathers only are removed, the loss is very small. For the Eastern markets the head is cut off and the entrails are taken out. This makes a loss of nearly one tenth in the weight. A large gobbler was recently killed weighing alive $31\frac{1}{2}$ lbs. After bleeding and picking he weighed $29\frac{1}{2}$ lbs., a loss of 2 lbs., or about one-fifteenth. When ready for the spit he weighed $28\frac{1}{4}$ lbs.—a loss of $3\frac{1}{4}$ lbs., which is very nearly one-tenth of the weight. Where the market requires the New York style of dressing, and the price is 15 cents a pound, a farmer could afford to sell at 14 cents live weight, or less, if he counted the labor of dressing anything. In the other style of dressing, if the price were 20 cents, he could sell for 18 cents, or less, live weight, without loss. Farmers who have never tested the loss of weight in dressing sometimes submit to a deduction of three or four cents a pound from the middlemen, who are interested in making this large difference. We have no means of knowing the exact cost of dressing turkeys, but half a cent a pound would probably be a large estimate. The prevailing higher price of dressed turkeys in the Eastern market is not owing simply to the difference in the style of dressing, though this has something to do with it. A large portion of the turkeys that go to the Boston and Providence markets are of extra large size, principally of the Bronze and Narragansett breeds and their crosses, raised in Rhode Island and Eastern Connecticut, where the farmers make it a specialty. Whole flocks of young birds will dress about 12 lbs., on the average, at Thanksgiving, and 14 lbs. or more at Christmas. Young cocks frequently reach 18 to 20 lbs. dressed during the winter, and adult cocks 28 to 30 lbs. These birds are prepared for the market in the nicest style, and are shipped by the ton for the holidays. They always bring extra prices.

14

CHAPTER XX.

RAISING GEESE.

With suitable facilities, breeding geese is profitable, and many a farmer's wife has secured home comforts from this source. It is useless to breed geese with too little room; they must have their liberty to do well, and be furnished with large grass runs, as they are great graziers. Their weakness for fruit, and their ability to trample down small fruits and vegetables, make them undesirable where there are fruit and vegetable plantations. They must be kept away from young chicks, or they will soon destroy them, especially during the hatching season, when they are unusually cross and combative.

Choose only those free from all defects, either individual or hereditary. It is the rule with good breeders to keep the same birds for years successively for breeding, as the progeny is usually stronger and healthier from such stock than from younger ones. The ganders, however, rapidly depreciate with age, and also early pair off with single females. In these cases, a young and vigorous gander is substituted. It is best to make the selection for breeding in autumn, just before culling out for fattening, or selling stock to others. No amount of persuasion, or tempting high price, should induce the breeder to part with his best birds; for if he desires to steadily improve his flock, no matter whether it is of so-called common birds or thoroughbreds, he must take his pick first of the very cream of the flock.

If geese can be set early, two broods may be obtained from each female, thus securing large flocks for each season's sales. The later-hatched birds, generally having favorable weather, will make good weights by late fall, especially if given extra care and food. These late birds make excellent eating about Christmas-time. The goose usually makes her own nest, though it is well to help

Fig. 83.—PAIR OF TOULOUSE.

her a little. She is a careful and constant mother, but her love for the water must be restrained until the goslings are a few weeks old, for many dangers, in the form of musk-rats, snakes, turtles, etc., lurk at the water's edge.

Goslings do not require much extra feed, if they can get all the fresh and tender grass they want, and unless this can be supplied, breeding geese is not profitable. For the first few weeks some food must be given; this should never be corn-meal, for nine-tenths of the mortality among fledgelings, of the various kinds of domestic fowls, can readily be traced to feeding corn-meal. Cottage cheese, or dry curds of sour milk in which red pepper (Cayenne) has been sprinkled, is a very good food, and a quantity of fresh onion-tops, chopped up fine, is relished by them. Stale bread soaked in fresh milk makes an excellent food for all young birds, and the way they develop when fed liberally with it will astonish any one who has not before tried it with his fowls. The greater part of the management of geese consists in keeping them (the goslings) free from dampness while they are still "downy," guarding them from the attacks of rats, cats, weasels, and other of their enemies, in housing them well at night, and in giving them a fresh grass run as often as possible. When they become fully feathered, they are abundantly able to take care of themselves; many breeders then let the geese find their own food, which they can readily do on a large farm, until fattening time, or when the grass begins to get short, when they are brought up, and liberally and regularly fed with corn, still being permitted to have their liberty, until a week or two before they are to be killed, when they are penned up and fed with all they can eat.

VARIETIES.

In breeding for mere fancy, no doubt the odd or handsome kinds, like the white or the brown China, etc., would be satisfactory; but where heavy weights, hardi-

Fig. 84. BROWN CHINESE GEESE.

The color of head of the Brown Chinese is brown; knob dark brown or black; neck light brown or grayish brown, with a dark stripe from the head down to the body. The body is dark brown, breast grayish brown, and the under parts are a shade lighter in color. The China is one of the best layers of all breeds, and the quality of flesh is extra good. Size rather small.

ness, and prolificness are concerned, the Toulouse and Embden are superior to all other sorts, and mature early.

The common gray goose possesses the markings of its parent, the wild goose of Europe and Asia, known in England as the "Gray Lag." The fine variety known as the Toulouse has the same colors, except that the dark plumage is of much richer hues, and, by contrast at least, the light feathers whiter, while the bill and legs are of a deep orange color. The Toulouse geese early develop a deep-hanging fold of skin, pendent, like the keel of a boat, beneath the body. The evidence that the breed originated in the vicinity of Toulouse, in France, is meagre. Nevertheless, we cannot countenance the suggestion that they received their name because their skin was *too loose* for them. The first of the variety which were seen in England came, it is said, from Marseilles, in the south of France. Those purchased probably came 'rom Toulouse to Marseilles, for this name is applied to no distinct variety in France.

Toulouse geese, when not inordinately forced for exhibition, are hardy, early layers, and reasonably prolific, often raising two broods of goslings a year. The young early take care of themselves on good pasture, and grow with astonishing rapidity. It is not well to let them depend wholly upon grass, but at first to give a little wet-up oatmeal daily, and afterwards a few oats or handfuls of barley, thrown into a trough or shallow pool to which they have access. These fine fowls attain, on a good grass range, nearly double the weight of common geese, and, forced by high feeding, a pair have been known to reach the weight of sixty pounds. Twenty-pound geese are not rare. Early goslings, if well fed, will attain that weight at Christmas. The fact is, that common geese make a poor show upon the table unless they are very fat. This is distasteful to many persons, and they can hardly be very fat before the late autumn, because we need grain to fatten them. With this variety, however, and the Embden, which matures early and attains a great weight also, it is different; the goslings are heavy before they are fat, carry a good deal of flesh, and are tender and delicious early in the season, when simply grass-fed, or having had but little grain.

Fig. 85.—EMBDEN GEESE.

In breeding geese, the surplus stock of goslings is killed off every year. None need be saved for wintering and breeding, except it may be well to keep one or two fine geese to take the places of old birds killed or hurt by some accident. Geese lay regularly, brood and rear their goslings well for fifty to eighty years, and it is said grow tougher every year. So if one has a good breeding goose, one which does her own duty well, and is reasonably peaceable towards other inhabitants of the farm-yard, it is best to keep her for years. Sometimes a goose will be very cross, killing ducklings and chickens, attacking children, etc. Such a one is a fit candidate for the spit.

Ganders are generally much worse, and usually one more than five or six years old becomes absolutely unbearable. So provision is naturally made to replace the old ganders every three or four years. It is, besides necessary to do so, for, though a young gander will attend four geese very well, an old one confines his attentions to one only, and often proves infertile at six or eight years old, getting crosser all the time.

PLUCKING.

A part of the profit of keeping geese depends upon their yield of feathers. When geese are bred carefully for exhibition and sale at high prices, only old ones should be plucked, and they only once or twice in the season. But when raised for market, the old ones may be plucked three times, and the young ones once before killing time, and the flock ought to yield, on an average, 18 to 20 ounces of dry feathers, besides considerable down at the summer pickings.

Common geese will yield about a pound of feathers a year, if close picked, and they are often picked cruelly close. This is unnecessary, for at the right time the feathers have a very slight hold, and the operation of plucking them is painless.

CHAPTER XXI.

RAISING DUCKS.

PROFITS IN DUCK RAISING.

Most farmers have a prejudice against water-fowl, especially ducks. They tolerate geese better than ducks, because they will forage for themselves, and live wholly on grass through the summer, after the goslings are started. Ducks will not bear neglect so well; they are more prone to wander and get lost or devoured in swamps or brooks. They have a foolish way of dropping their eggs in water, and of following a brook, or river, into neighboring farms; unless they have suitable quarters, and receive regular attention, it is a good deal of trouble to look after them. The half-starved duck disposes of a good deal of corn at a single feed, remembering the past and anticipating the future. The slipshod farmer is prejudiced against the bird, and will have none of him. But the duck has so many good qualities, matures so early, and furnishes so rare a repast, that the owner of a country home with cultivated tastes can hardly afford to do without a duck-yard. The flesh, in our esteem, is the greatest delicacy raised upon the farm; and if they were much more troublesome than we have ever found them, we should not hesitate to keep them. The fact is, a large part of the trouble is owing to sheer neglect, and the reputation of the bird as a gross feeder is owing to irregular supplies of food. If grain or other food is kept within reach, they devour no more than other fowls that mature as rapidly. If in suitable quarters and well fed, they get most of their growth in four months, and can be marketed in August at the watering-places when prices are highest. The impression that a pond or brook is necessary to raise the ducklings is erroneous. They need no more water than chickens until they are three months old, and are better off without any pond to swim in. We have raised fifty in a season in a quarter-acre yard, and found them no more troublesome than chickens. The best mothers are hens, and we prefer the Asiatic fowls, either Cochins or Brahmas. A hen of these breeds will cover nine or ten eggs. We have found an old barrel with a board at the end to fasten the bird upon her nest, as good as a more expensive coop. They are let off regularly at noon every day, when they have a half hour's range, green food, grain and water. The young ducks are fed with some fresh animal food and coarse Indian meal scalded; this, varied with chopped cabbage, turnips, worms, and liver, is the staple food until they are three months old. They do much better on soft food than on grain.

The paradise of ducks is a location on a tide-water stream or cove, where there is a constant succession of sea-food with every tide. If furnished with a little house or pen upon the shore, and a variety of grain, they will come home regularly every night and lead an orderly life. The eggs are usually laid at night, or early in the morning, and very few of them need be lost. Of the four varieties, Rouen, Aylesbury, Cayuga, and Pekin, we give the preference to the last for size, early maturity, abundance of eggs, hardiness, and domestic habits.

A plan of a convenient house is shown by the accompanying engraving. For fifty to one hundred ducks it should be thirty feet long, twelve feet wide, and from four feet high at the front to six or eight feet in the rear. Entrance doors are made in the front, which should have a few small windows. At the rear are the nests; these are boxes open at the front. Behind each nest is a small door through which the eggs may be taken. It is necessary to keep the ducks shut up in the morning until they have laid their eggs, and a strip of wire netting will be required to inclose a narrow yard in front of the house. Twine netting should not be used, as the ducks put their heads through the meshes and twist the twine about their necks, often so effectively

Fig. 86.—DUCK HOUSE.

as to strangle themselves. To avoid all danger, the wire fence should have a three or four-inch mesh.

Among the most profitable varieties as layers are the Pekins. A fair yearly product for a duck in its second year is a hundred and twenty eggs, and sixty to eighty for a yearling. Their feathers are of the best quality, white, with a creamy shade; and five ducks weighing five pounds each have yielded, killed in the winter-time when fully feathered, more than one pound in all. It will be right to pick the ducks when moulting is begin-

Fig. 87.—IMPROVED PEKIN DUCKS.

(221)

ning; the feathers are then loose and are picked easily and without injury. This will considerably increase the yield of feathers, and will prevent a useless loss; otherwise the loose feathers from twenty ducks will be found spread over their whole range.

It by no means follows because ducks are a water-fowl that much water is required to raise them. Yet this is a very common impression, and multitudes of farmers and villagers deny themselves the enjoyment and profit of a flock of ducks because they have no pond or stream near the house. It is true that adult ducks will get a good deal of their living out of a water privilege, if they have one. It is not true that water to swim in is essential to their profitable keeping. They want some range and grass and good fresh water to drink every day. Ordinarily, ducks can be profitably raised wherever hens can be. They make a pleasing variety in the poultry-yard, and all who have room for them can enjoy them. The first thing in raising ducks is to get them out of the shell, and for incubation we decidedly prefer hens to ducks. They sit more steadily, and take much better care of the young. The wetting of the ducks' eggs daily in the last two weeks of incubation is even more necessary than for hens' eggs. This is sometimes done by sprinkling water upon them, but we think it better to take them from the nest and put them in a basin of tepid water about blood-warm. This moistens the whole shell without chilling the embryo life within. The ducklings out of the shell may be allowed to remain upon the nest with the hen for a day. The hen may then be put upon a grass-plat, under a coop, where the ducklings can go in and out at pleasure. Or if the hen is allowed liberty, the ducklings should be confined in a small pen from which they cannot escape. A dozen in a pen ten feet square is enough for the first two weeks. For water they only want a shallow pan—so shallow that they cannot swim, and in which they can wade at pleasure. The water should be changed often and kept in good drinking condition. For the first food nothing is better than the yolk of hard-boiled eggs or boiled liver, chopped very fine. The food had better all be cooked for the first week. It may then gradually be changed to coarse scalded Indian meal, oatmeal, wheaten grits, or rice, as suits the convenience of the feeder. Bread-crumbs and sour milk are excellent food, as are angle-worms and snails. Ducklings are quite as good as chickens at devouring insects, and nothing seems to harm them but rose-bugs, against which they should be jealously guarded. For this reason they should be kep' away from grape-vines and other plants specially attractive to these insects. As the ducklings grow older they may have more liberty and a greater variety of food. If they have not plenty of grass, its place should be supplied by lettuce, onions, cabbage, or other green succulent food. If you desire exhibition birds of the largest size, it is particularly important that the ducklings should be fed regularly, and at frequent intervals, having all the food they can digest. Five times a day is none too frequent feeding. We have usually succeeded quite as well with ducks as with chickens in a village yard. When grown, we give them a larger range.

AN ARTIFICIAL DUCK-POND.

Ducks and geese may be raised successfully without any pond or stream; yet some prefer to give them an abundance of water, and such can make an artificial pond on the plan shown next page. This is a wooden box ten inches deep and four feet square, or it may be two feet wide and six or eight feet long. This is set in the ground, except the down-hill side, which is partly exposed, and provided with a short spout placed within half an inch of the top, to carry off superfluous water. A peg is inserted at the bottom for drawing off the water when desired. Water may be conducted to the box by a pipe from a spring, underdrain, small brook, or from the well, by sinking a half-barrel between the pump and pond, and filling it with water every day or two, and so graduating the flow that it will merely drop from the barrel through the pipe into the wooden box.

AN ARTIFICIAL DUCK POND.

THE CARE OF DUCKS.

Ducks are a very pleasant feature of farm-yard surroundings. In the last of winter and early spring they are sociable and busy enough, especially on warm days, and begin to lay very early. The duck almost always lays her egg between six and nine o'clock. So the flock must be kept shut up until all have laid. We have found ducks to do better if they can be confined at night, in winter, in a shed where the horse manure is thrown out, than anywhere else. The heaps of manure heat somewhat, and the ducks enjoy the warmth. It makes them lay early, and the eggs are not likely to freeze if we get severe "snaps." Barley and oats are excellent feed for ducks. If these or any grains are thrown into a shallow tub, or trough, they will soak and be all the better relished. Pekin Ducks are among the best layers, by far the best in our experience, laying not unfrequently sixty to eighty eggs each, in the spring, and often again in the autumn, if the weather is warm. If ducks are not confined at night, they will make nests in some hedge-row or secluded spot difficult to find, and one will become broody after laying sixteen to twenty eggs, or as soon as she has a good clutch. When confined as we suggested, they rarely make nests, but drop their eggs about anywhere. Ducks are very fond of water-cress, and if they have access to the water-cress bed at the spring, there will soon be none left for the salad-bowl. Wire netting, a foot in height, will form an effectual barrier.

PEKIN DUCKS.

The Pekin Duck was unknown in this country or Europe previous to the spring of 1873. The following is a brief account of their importation. Mr. McGrath, of the firm of Fogg & Co., engaged in the Japan and China trade, in one of his excursions in China first saw these ducks at the city of Pekin, and from their large size, thought them a small breed of geese. He succeeded in purchasing a number of the eggs, and carried them to Shanghai, where, placing them under hens, he in due time obtained fifteen ducklings sufficiently mature to ship in charge of Mr. James E. Palmer, who was about returning to America. He offered Mr. P. one half the birds that he should bring to port alive, and the latter, accepting the offer, took charge of them. Six ducks and three drakes survived the voyage of 124 days, and were landed in New York on the 13th of March, 1873. Leaving three ducks and two drakes, consigned to parties in New York, to be sent to Mr. McGrath's family (who never received them, as they were killed and eaten in the city), Mr. P. took the three remaining ducks and drake to his home at Wequetequoc, in Stonington, Conn. They soon recovered from the effects of their long voyage, and commenced laying the latter part of March, and continued to lay until the last of July. They are very prolific, the three ducks laying about 325 eggs.

The ducks are white, with a yellowish tinge to the under part of the feathers; their wings are a little less than medium length, as compared with other varieties; they make as little effort to fly as the large Asiatic fowls, and they can be as easily kept in enclosures. Their beaks are yellow; necks long; legs short and red. When the eggs are hatched under hens, the ducklings come out of the shell much stronger if the eggs are dampened every day (after the first fifteen days) in water a little above blood heat and replaced under the hen.

The ducks are very large, and uniform in size, weighing at four months old about twelve pounds to the pair. They appear to be very hardy, not minding severe weather. Water to drink seems to be all they require to bring them to perfect development.

I was more successful in rearing them with only a dish filled to the depth of one inch with water, than were those who had the advantages of a pond and running stream.

AYLESBURY DUCKS.

White occurring without intermixture of other color in the hair or feathers of animals and fowls is evidence of change effected by domestication. This color, or lack of color, becomes a very persistent characteristic. The Aylesbury ducks are pure white, with orange legs, and are one of the most beautiful of the white breeds of poultry. All white fowls are beautiful and attractive. We have white breeds of every kind of domestic fowl, and they all have such notable excellencies that their admirers claim for each that it is the best of its kind. This is noticeable in white geese, which have the best plumage; white turkeys are most domestic, and white barn-door fowls are most prolific. Aylesbury Ducks are claimed to be more prolific and to fatten more rapidly for market than other large breeds. This variety undoubtedly originated in the vicinity of Aylesbury, England, where large numbers are still raised annually for the London market. Its characteristics are distinctly marked, namely: Abundant but close-fitting plumage of the purest white; a beak of peculiar form, being long, straight, and broad, and set on a line with the forehead; most noticeable, however, from its being of a distinct flesh-color; it sometimes inclines to buff, but this is objectionable. The most delicate pink (as an English breeder enthusiastically said to the writer, "pink as a lady's nail") is the color preferred; the legs are of a light orange color. Ducks and drakes are almost precisely alike, the latter distinguished only by the curling feathers of the tail and by the voice, or lack of voice.

This is an old and well-established breed, and in favorable locations breeds very true. Breeders so located find it is not difficult to obtain the pink bills without stain of yellow or blemish of dark streaks or specks. This is supposed to depend upon the purity of the water, and on the gravelly bottom of the brooks with which their bills are constantly brought in contact. Exposure to the sun tans them, and, from some not well-known cause, it is almost impossible to obtain perfect bills in many places, though the birds grow large and fine.

It is customary in and near Aylesbury to confine the ducks in warm houses early in the season, and to induce the earliest possible laying, that the young ducks may be marketed very early in the season, and high prices secured. They come to the market just at a season when game and other poultry are scarce and high. Now, when the Aylesburys are removed from their home surroundings, and, as in this country, are treated like other kinds of ducks, they retain this tendency to lay, and hatch a brood early in mid-winter, only for the first generation from importation, even then to a less degree than the imported birds show it. The tendency to lay very early would no doubt be maintained if it were encouraged as it is at home. In regard to the care of ducks, it is well to observe that the more a variety is changed by domestication, the more attention they need, and usually the more profit they yield. Many common ducks lay a clutch of perhaps 20 small eggs; in sitting, cover half or more, and hatch them out, while the Aylesbury Duck will lay 60 eggs or more, but until she begins to show a tendency to sit, usually a week or ten days before she sits, she makes a sort of nest, and there she deposits her eggs. The only way to secure all the eggs is to shut up the ducks at night. They will usually lay an egg apiece between dawn and eight o'clock; and as soon as each has laid, all may be let out. They all march straight for the water; and if let out too soon, some eggs will be almost surely found in the bottom of the pond. Ducks are voracious and almost omnivorous feeders; they are fond of grass and water plants, water-cress especially, and are diligent foragers for snails and the little shell-fish of fresh-water streams, ponds, and swamps; and, besides, on dry land they are indefatigable insect-hunters, young ducks being often very useful in a vegetable garden, where they gather and destroy many plant-pests.

A pair of Aylesbury Ducks fit for exhibition ought

to weigh at least 12 pounds; in England they often reach 16 pounds to the pair; and are occasionally heavier by one or two pounds, thus almost equaling the weight of the heaviest specimens of Rouen Ducks.

ROUEN DUCKS.

There is a prevalent belief among farmers that ducks are not profitable poultry. This arises naturally from several causes. The habits of indolence which some possess—the tendency not to hunt their food, but to depend upon being fed and the scraps which they pick up about the house—lead farmers to contrast them unfavorably with the wandering turkeys, which find their living and rear their young often in the woods, depending only in winter upon the farmer for their food; and scarcely more favorably with dunghill fowls, which during the summer months require but little food except what they hunt for about the farm. The ducks, besides, though some kinds are excellent layers, are heedless birds, exposing themselves, their eggs, and young to crows, rats, turtles, and other vermin, dropping their eggs about, shifting their place of laying if disturbed, inconstant as sitters, and chilling their young by taking them too soon and too often to the water. Still, all these objections may be obviated, in a measure, and ducks really pay very well both in flesh and eggs for the amount of food they consume.

The duck is an omnivorous animal—eating almost everything vegetable and animal that comes in its way. Insects of all kinds, worms, polliwigs, fish, shellfish (dead or alive), meat, even that which is partly decomposed, and many green vegetables, grass, seeds, grain, etc. Withal, its appetite is voracious; hence it grows

Fig. 88(a).—ROUEN DUCKS.

Fig. 88(b).—AYLESBURY DUCKS.

rapidly and fattens easily. The common tame duck is supposed to have descended from the wild Mallard duck, *Anas boshas*, common to this country and Europe. It breeds freely with this species, and also with several other species of wild duck; in some cases the progeny is capable of reproduction of its kind, in others mule-birds or "mongrels" result. The fact that a very different class of birds is produced where the Mallards are crossed with other species and where the common duck is so crossed, with other points of difference, throws some doubt on the assertion that the Mallard is the parent of our common ducks. Besides, efforts to domesticate the Mallard have not been successful as a general thing. We have, however, many wild ducks capable of domestication, and the experiment ought to be well tried with all, for thus our stock of domestic poultry may be essentially increased and improved.

The Rouen breed is the most highly esteemed of all domestic ducks by many duck breeders. Its habits are quiet, and so it does not wander about and get lost, as ducks do. It attains a great weight, and is unsurpassed as a layer. An English writer reports that he has frequently known a pair of young drakes 9 or 10 weeks old to weigh 12 lbs. Sundry writers report very remarkable laying performances of the Rouen ducks. One laid an egg a day for 85 days; three ducks from February to July laid 334 eggs, besides a few soft ones and five double eggs. One of these laid every morning for 92 days. The young ducks often lay in autumn a good clutch of eggs, and it not unfrequently occurs that a duck which is a first-rate layer will manifest no tendency to sit. This variety of ducks has, in common with many other kinds, great beauty of plumage, which varies somewhat in different individuals. The drakes are heavier than the ducks, but the difference is slight in comparison with the disparity between the sexes in most varieties.

The beautiful green heads and necks of the drakes, iridescent with purple and copper hues, set off with a clean white collar and claret-colored vest, give them a distinguished air which the various colors and distinct markings of the back and wings does not detract from. The females are brown, each feather being marked with black, which gives them a speckled look.

. The only variety which really rivals the Rouen as a useful and economical birds is the Aylesbury. These, a purely white English variety, are beautiful birds and ighly esteemed in the markets of Great Britain, as also .n the United States, where they are known. They are good layers and nurses, not noisy; good feeders, and by some decidedly preferred to the Rouen. The eggs are white, sometimes inclining to blue, while those of the Rouen duck are blue, with thick, strong shells; of the two the Rouen has the reputation of being most hardy. Where ducks are raised for breeders, it is a practice (founded perhaps on prejudice) to set ducks upon their own eggs; but if the young are wanted for market simply, the eggs are put under hens. Hens will hatch a clutch of duck's some two days quicker than ducks will, but it is thought that the young have not so good constitutions. Young ducks raised for market often get injured by being allowed to go freely to the water. They grow faster and stronger if they only have enough to drink, at least for several weeks.

CHAPTER XXII.

ORNAMENTAL POULTRY.

THE PEA-FOWL.

Although the pea-fowl is well known as a bird of fine feathers, few persons are acquainted with its natural history and real merits. It is a good table fowl, and as easily reared as the turkey; still it is rarely seen on a farm or country place, and then only as an ornament. This bird is a native of Asia, from whence have come nearly all our gallinaceous fowls, the turkey excepted. In the time of Solomon, it was an article of merchandise, and was brought with ivory and apes from Tarshish to Judea. One species of pea-fowl was found by an English traveler, Colonel Sykes, abounding in a part of India, where large flocks were kept about the native temples. Another Eastern traveler relates that from 1,200 to 1,500 were seen by him in the passes of the mountain, within sight at one time; and he speaks in extravagant terms of the brilliancy of their plumage. There are three distinct genera, which include several species and varieties, such as the Crested, the Black-shouldered, the Javan, the Japan, the Iris, the Thibet, the Malay, etc. All the domesticated sorts are surpassed by the wild ones in beauty. Culver says of the pea-fowl: "We find in its incomparable robe, united, all the brilliant colors which we admire separately in other birds; we find all that glistens in the rainbow, that sparkles in the mine, the azure and golden tints of the heavens, and the emerald of the field." White, the naturalist, found that the feathers of the train do not belong to the tail, but that they grow upon the back, the real tail feathers being short, stiff, and brown, about six inches long, and serve as a prop to support the immense train. By a peculiar muscular action, the long train feathers can be erected and spread, and their shafts made to strike together and produce a chattering noise. The Pied peacock is white upon the wings, belly, and breast; the rest of the plumage is as showy as in the other species. Pure white birds are very rare, and highly valued; but from the absence of the gorgeous coloring of the common kinds, they suffer greatly in contrast with the latter. It is not until the second year that the difference between the sexes becomes apparent. The bird lives from 20 to 25 years, and reaches maturity slowly. The third year the train of the cock becomes developed, and it is only when it exhibits its full coloring that he is ready to be mated with three or four hens.

The pea-hen lays her eggs on alternate days, and when she has produced five or six she will incubate, unless the eggs have been removed. She makes her nest upon the ground, in a secluded place, beneath the shelter of low bushes, long grass, or weeds. The maternal instinct is well developed in some hens; in other hens it is so lacking that they even destroy their own young, or leave them to perish from neglect. The period of incubation is from 24 to 29 days. The pea-fowls have strong local attachments, and they rarely leave the place where they have been reared and fed. They are sensible of kind treatment, and will become very tame when gently used and petted. They have a habit of roosting high, and will choose an elevated place on the top of the highest tree or buildings to which they can gain access. When but three days old, the chicks are able to reach a roost two or three feet high; and if they can mount from one step to another, they will follow the old birds to their highest roosting places. The birds are naturally shy, and their treatment must be regulated accordingly. The proper feed for the young pea-chicks consists of hard boiled eggs, cracked wheat, coarse oatmeal, and bread-crumbs; and they will soon hunt after and consume insects and worms of all kinds. It is necessary to protect the young birds from wet and cold, and they require the same care which is needed for young turkeys.

TRAINING PEA-FOWLS TO STAY AT HOME.

At "Rose Lawn," Paterson, N. J., there is a flock of pea-fowls—half a dozen or more. They are confined, or rather kept, in a lot of perhaps two acres in extent, which has a high fence of wire net, and where they are associated with a small herd of deer and farm-yard poultry of all sorts. They fly into the tops of the apple-trees to roost, but never fly out of the enclosure. Seeing them so apparetly contented, day after day, and knowing well the restless habits of the bird, especially the male, which generally makes himself a nuisance to the whole neighborhood within half a mile, this domestic trait of these birds interested us, and we learned that if one flies out, he is condemned to wear a ball and chain, or rather a cord and block, for several days. It is thus applied: Strong list of woolen goods, or other soft, strong band, is passed about the leg of the peacock, so that it cannot tighten, and to this is attached a block of hickory or other heavy wood, weighing three or four pounds. The block should be round or conical, and should have a hole through it lengthways, and the cord should pass through this, and be well knotted at the end. It must turn in the block so as to prevent kinking. These gorgeous fowls would be much more frequently kept if it were known that they might be so easily trained.

JAPANESE BANTAMS.

These quaint little creatures weigh about a pound and a quarter each. The plumage is white, excepting some

Fig. 89.—BLACK TAILED JAPANESE BANTAM.

of the wing feathers, the tail, and sometimes the tips of the neck feathers, which are black. The legs are bright yellow. The tail is the most curious part of this breed,

Fig. 30.—SEBASTOPOL GOOSE.

being large, and carried so erect as to nearly touch the head. The legs are so short as to be almost invisible, and this gives the birds a curious creeping sort of gait The little hens are exemplary mothers, and one of them, with a brood of tiny chicks, would be the delight of a boy or girl, as well as attractive pets for old folks. This breed has the virtue, rare amongst bantams, of being exceedingly peaceable and quiet.

ORNAMENTAL WATER-FOWLS.

In this country we have much to learn in the way of utilizing natural waters, whether streams, springs, or ponds. Any place, anywhere, be it a farm, large or small, or merely a country-seat, has its value greatly enhanced by the possession of water, whether running or still. Of the money value of such water, whether for stock, irrigation, or as motive power, we do not propose to speak just now. The value of water in these respects is as far from being appreciated as it is in its ornamental aspects. We know of one body of water—a small pond, which is so treated by its owner as to be both profitable and ornamental. It is a conspicuous object from the road, and being not far from the house, its surroundings are planted with a view to ornamental effect. The water is at the same time made useful as the pasture-ground for a fine collection of water-fowl. The flock contains some birds raised for the table, but is largely of the kinds known as ornamental, and these are made profitable; the place being in a populous vicinity, the birds do their own advertising, and there is a sufficient demand for all the increase. The practical part of the establishment, including the breeding-houses, coops, etc., is at some distance from the pond and hidden from view by a screen of evergreens planted for the purpose. Among the birds regarded as both ornamental and useful are the

SEBASTOPOL GEESE.

This is a most peculiar variety of the goose, one of its peculiarities being that no one knows why it is called "Sebastopol." It is said to come from the Black Sea country, but even this is doubtful. The characteristic of the breed consists in having a large share of its pure white feathers, especially of the back, wings, and tail, very long, lax, curled, waved, and frizzled. These feathers give the birds a somewhat bedraggled look, when on land, but impart a most elegant appearance when they are on the water. For the rest, though rarely weighing ten pounds, they are useful table birds, are hardy, prolific, and good sitters and mothers.

THE WHISTLING DUCKS

are among the ornamental ducks, in which beauty of plumage is regarded rather than weight. They are from South America, and there appear to be several sub-varieties, distinguished mainly by the color of the bill, but all agree in having a peculiar whistling note. All are very domestic, and remarkably quaint and amusing in their habits and movements. The birds shown in the engraving are known as the "Widow Whistler" and the "White-faced Whistler." Their general color is a light shade of chocolate, with black below; the head, neck, and bill are also black, making the white face all the more conspicuous and very attractive.

Fig. 91.—WHISTLING DUCKS

THE AMERICAN WOOD DUCK—OR SUMMER DUCK.

We have in this country many beautiful varieties of wild ducks, some of which we know are capable of domestication, and more which have not been experimented with. One of the former is the "Summer duck" of Southern and the "Wood duck" of the Northern States. Either name is appropriate, for it is the only duck which

Fig. 92.—AMERICAN WOOD DUCK.

remains with us during breeding season, except now and then a stray pair of Mallards, and perhaps a pair of one or two other kinds are very rarely seen ; and its natural haunts are the deep quiet woods far from the dwellings of men. The bird is rather rare in New England, especially so in the Eastern part, more plenty in New York, and abundant in Pennsylvania, and to the westward and south, wherever a wooded country offers pools and secluded river and lake margins, close to which it delights to make its nest and rear its young. The engraving represents a beautiful bird, but one not familiar with these ducks would hardly credit the correctness of an accurate description of its colors. The bill and legs are red, the dark feathers of the head exhibit gorgeous steel-blue, coppery and green iridescence, and in some lights are jetty, velvety black, or purple. The white feathers on the head and neck, in the queue-like tuft of the back of head, and on the shoulders, wing covers and sides are all clear, vivid dashes in every case contrasted with black bands or bordering of dark, nearly black feathers. The back shows the brilliant rainbow hues and metallic colors of the head, while the breast is of a delicate wine color, spotted with white, and the belly white, shading into ash-color on the sides. These colors belong to the drakes; the ducks are similar, but much less showy. In Pennsylvania and northward they pair in April or May, and the female brings off her brood of eight to fifteen in June. They migrate just before winter sets in and are very likely to return to the same locality. The flesh of the young birds are highly esteemed. During the winter they go into the Southern States, and are there seen in large flocks.

This duck has been repeatedly domesticated, so as to be as familiar as any denizens of the farm yard. The best way to get them is to find the nests, which are usually in a hollow tree not far from the water (they use an old woodpecker's or gray squirrel's hole if they can find one big enough), and transfer the fresh eggs to a sitting hen, or else take the very young ducks as soon as they are hatched.

CHAPTER XXIII.

BREEDING AND CROSS-BREEDING.

The foundation of the breeding of fowls is the same as that of the other domestic animals; the rule that like produces like, or the likeness of an ancestor. That is, if the parents and grandparents are what is wanted, the chick will almost always be what is wanted. Find two parents that represent the idea that you are breeding for, and the chick will repeat that idea.

When show birds are to be bred the sire must be of strong constitution, and perfect in color and symmetry. The vigorous red color of his head should denote strong vitality. Not only should the individual be perfect, but his pedigree should be such as to show that his qualities are a family trait. It is thought the male influences the color of the chicks more than does the female, while the female has fully as much influence in deciding the practical qualities of eggs and flesh-making.

The tendency of the mixed color breeds is to run lighter, if left to breed for themselves. Hence, males with faded or light plumage should not be used for breeders. Males that are darker colored than wanted can often be used to good advantage by mating with light-colored hens, thus striking the balance; but matings of light males with dark females are not usually successful.

Do not select overgrown specimens. Those which come up to about the average of the breed, and are not too fat, will give best results. This rule applies especially to the larger breeds, but may often be disregarded with the smaller ones.

RULES OF I. K. FELCH.

The following matings are among those recommended for some of the leading breeds, by Mr. I. K. Felch, the well-known authority:

BLACK OR WHITE BREEDS.—A metallic-black male mated to females of same hard smooth surface color is the best for both males and females, but such a cock

1. Comb.
2. Face.
3. Wattle.
4. Deaf-ears, or Ear-lobe.
5. Hackle.
6. Breast.
7. Back.
8. Saddle.
9. Saddle-hackles.
10. Sickles.
11. Tail-coverts.
12. True Tail-feathers.
13. Wing-bow.
14. Wing-coverts forming the "bar."
15. Secondaries, lower-end, forming the wing or lower butts.
16. Primaries, or Flights, not seen when wing is clipped up.
17. Point of breast-bone.
18. Thighs.
19. Hocks.
20. Legs, or Shanks.
21. Spur.
22. Toes, or Claws.

FIG. 93. CHART OF POULTRY TERMS.

mated to females dead black, lacking in brightness and metallic surface, will breed fine pullets, but the male progeny is generally much poorer than the female. In black there is little to do beyond these two distinctions of color. The metallic-hard-finished surface and the dull black, if crossed, restore to the progeny the metallic-black desired. Birds of this cross should be mated to those of the metallic-black mating. In solid white specimens, the points to consider are purity of plumage color, that is, white in web and shaft. Males from yellow females are not satisfactory. Females with yellowish tinge and quills must be mated to pure white males.

PLYMOUTH ROCKS.—Males with breast of the color desired in the females, with yellow back and legs, with

FIG. 94. BLACK JAVAS.

neck, back and tail evenly barred, the light shade predominating, yet free from any white feathers in flights or tail, mated to females in plumage slightly darker than, yet accurately described by, the standard. This should be the mating to preserve the male line. Again, mate cocks like the one described above with females a little too light in color. This mating produces good females.

WYANDOTTES, COLORED.—A male like that in standard, except that the breast be black with small white centers, thighs stone color, with fluff dark stone color, approaching black. Mate pullets weighing fully five and three-quarters to six pounds, full breasts, plumage of same fully laced, yet the white center of good size, and to grow smaller in the plumage and the black lacing wider as it approaches the tail, when it merges into a full black tail and dark, stone-colored fluff, with thighs nearly black, beak and shanks yellow, comb as described in the ancestors. This mating to produce one line of sires, and no sire should be used from any other mating if we hope to see this breed reach that accuracy and uniformity of breeding we see in Light Brahmas.

LIGHT BRAHMAS.—Mate males with hackles that have a good, fair, black stripe, but edge of feathers free from any smoky tinge, nearly white undercolor and cape, wing flights about one-half black, coverlets of tail black laced with white, lesser coverlets white. Females of standard form, intense black stripe in hackle, very dark cape, undercolor of back so dark as to show black spots in the web but not on the surface, tail black, flights black; standard in other respects.

FIG. 95. FEATHER OF BARRED PLYMOUTH ROCK.

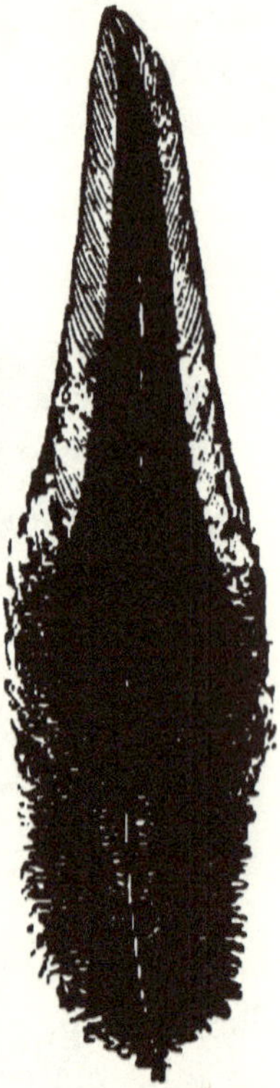

FIG. 96. FEATHER OF SILVER LACED WYANDOTTE.

DARK BRAHMAS.—*Mating No. 1.* Hens that are

standard, which were nearly perfect, steel-gray pullets in their first year mated to a cockerel, metallic-black in breast and thighs, medium dark beak, hackle and saddle, broad in the black stripe and decided in shade. This mating should be made in producing the male line.

Mating No. 2. Hens that were fine as pullets but have become bronze-hued as fowls mated to a cockerel with a black breast, evenly dotted with minute white spots, black thighs, hackle and saddle well striped, and medium dark beak.

PARTRIDGE COCHINS. — *Mating No. 1.* Cockerel weighing ten to eleven pounds, hackle and saddle rich bay, the black in the same being metallic greenish-black, and broad in the stripe, metallic-black breast and thighs, fluff showing a bronze tinge, indicative of rich, brown blood. Hens are described in the standard. This mating is the best that can be made for the male progeny.

Mating No. 2. Cock weighing eleven to twelve pounds, and of the same color as described for cockerel in Mating No. 1. Pullets large in size, and in color reddish-brown ground penciled with a deep brown, with standard neck and tail. This mating will produce finer females than males.

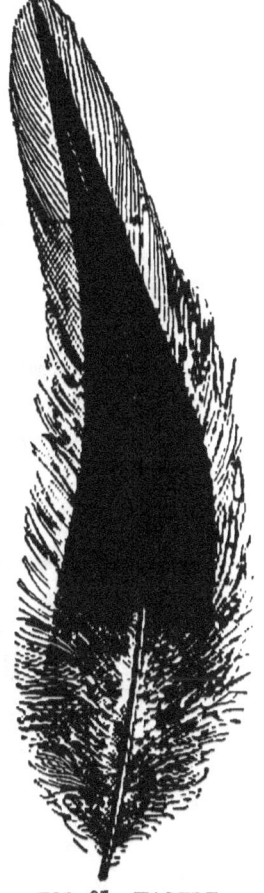

FIG. 97. HACKLE FEATHER OF LIGHT BRAHMA COCK.

BUFF COCHINS.—The mating most to be coveted would be a cock of one even reddish-buff color from head to tail, with no white undercolor in him; his tail black, tipped out with chestnut; the coverts chestnut, streaked with dark color; lesser coverts reddish-buff, and in form standard. To such a sire mate pullets of the same rich buff color, free from white in flights and undercolor, tail chestnut or buff, dark color showing in flights. Pullets fully up to standard weight. With such a mating males and females would appear in the progeny of a high order.

SELECTION FOR EGGS.

The best time of the year to pick out breeding stock is when the hens are not laying very well, say in July or August. Any hen will lay in the spring and the best ones cannot be selected. As soon as the best ones have been taken out, they are placed by themselves and a record kept, in order to find the average yield. The best laying type is usually rather large framed and long in leg, neck and back, legs well apart, breast well developed, flesh firm, not inclined to fatness, eyes bright, never sunken, disposition active, appetite good, and great foragers. These characteristics will help in selecting layers. Patent contrivances have been invented for registering the number of eggs laid by each hen, but these have not come into general use.

FIG. 98. TYPICAL LAYER (Leghorn).

The best layers can generally be selected by careful observance of the general characteristics above noted. Good layers have always strong vitality, and should be mated with strong males bred from a noted egg-laying line. It is best, if possible, to have the pick of a large flock, and to choose the males, not for fancy points, but for the degree in which they possess the typical qualities of the breed. Select from the best egg-laying strain, not necessarily from the flock which has taken the most prizes in the poultry shows. Care of the breeding stock is very important; good feeding will improve the qualities of any strain. The older breeds will impress their characteristics more strongly than those which have been more lately originated. The oldest breeds, like the Black Spanish and Games, are likely to be weakened by excessive inbreeding, in some strains, and should be selected with special attention to health and vigor.

SYSTEMATIC CROSS-BREEDING.

The continual advocacy of fancy poultry for common farm use is an error. The poultry papers, and most agricultural papers, advise the breeding of certain pure breeds, as if they possessed merits far superior to the barn-door fowls and common poultry. This is a mistake. No one advocates the use of thoroughbred horses, well-bred trotters, pure Percherons or Clydes, pure-bred pigs, or sheep, or cattle, to the exclusion of common ones, but farmers are urged to improve their common stock by breeding up, by gradually introducing better blood, and breeding with some definite aim. Thus, our common mixed sheep, which are regular breeders, good mothers, and have plenty of milk, are crossed with pure rams of one of the established breeds. If size is wanted, with long wool, the Cotswold is perhaps employed; if the wool is to be improved in fineness without so much reference to the mutton, one of the Merino breeds will be selected; while if early lambs of fine quality are desired, one of the Down breeds is chosen by the raiser. This is precisely the course which should be followed by farmers in poultry raising. The advantage of grading up common poultry is, however, not so profitable in most cases as cross-breeding. This is, properly, the interbreeding of two pure varieties. We have, however, usually no pure breed of fowls upon the farm, and of course wish to utilize those which we have. Therefore, the first thing to do is to grade up the flock. After two or three years, when they have the looks and qualities of pure-breds, the hens may be crossed with cocks of

FIG. 99. CROSS-BRED GEESE (Wild Gray and African).

another breed, and then most of the advantages of cross-breeding will be realized. In this use of pure-bred cocks which we recommend, no male bird should run with the same flock more than two years. If he is healthy and vigorous, and his progeny of the first year take strongly after him, in form as well as feather, he may well be kept the second year to run with pullets of his own get. After three years the blood of the original flock will be reduced to one-eighth; after four years to one-sixteenth. One may have a flock of hens which have been carelessly bred, and into which no fresh blood has been introduced for years. They are small, hardy, active, fair layers, good sitters and mothers, and get their own living all summer—but the garden suffers. How can the flock be improved? This, we conceive, is the question which may be put by ninety-nine in a hundred of the keepers of hens in the country. The answer suggests itself, but first we should know whether eggs, or broilers, or full-grown fowls for market (chickens in autumn or winter) pay best. The farmer must treat his flock of hens exactly as he would his flock of sheep or his herd of cows, or other stock; that is, secure the use of full-blood males having the desired characteristics. Thus, if he wishes eggs, he will buy cocks of some *one* of those breeds famous for the number of eggs the hens lay. Size and beauty of eggs may be an object, or simply a large number may be most desirable. The French breeds and the Spanish usually have large eggs; Leghorns, eggs of medium size; Hamburgs lay many but small eggs; while all are persistent layers of beautiful white eggs. The half-bloods, as a whole, will take after the pure breed in a good measure, and in so far may be said to be an improvement upon the old stock. The second year the three-quarter bloods will closely resemble pure-bred ones; some will only be distinguished from pure-bloods by an expert, while others will show their dunghill origin very clearly, and yet, as layers, these may be the very best. So improvement goes on. The flock will in two or three years assume the appearance of "fancy" poultry of the breed selected with which to produce the improvement. The question naturally arises, Will they be improved?—be better and more profitable than they were before? Perhaps not for all uses, but as layers, yes. **The hens will lay more eggs; they will be less** inclined to sit; if they sit at all, they will probably be broody only for a few days, and as producers of eggs no doubt the flock will be more satisfactory.

GUIDE TO CROSS-BREEDING.

By careful selection of the breeds, desirable qualities of both may be combined in the cross. Defects in one side may be counterbalanced by strong points in the other, and the chicks excel either parent in practical qualities. The best results are usually obtained upon the first cross, and the cross-bred male should not be used for breeding. Breed the cross-bred pullets to pure-bred males. Experiments after the first cross often show defects of remote ancestors.

The most profitable use of cross-breeding on the farm is grading up the flock of common hens with pure-bred males of general purpose breeds, or if eggs are specially desired, males of the laying breeds. The best plan is to use the pure breed each season, raising the cross-bred stock. This is the only kind of pure-bred poultry that the ordinary farmer will find it worth while to buy, namely, the pure-bred males for grading up the flock. A selection of the best individuals is of more importance than the breed, even. It is best to visit a large flock noted for egg production and choose for oneself. Hardiness and vigor are of more importance than other points.

The effect of a cross between pure breeds can only be determined by experience. While some breeds combine well, others, apparently as well adapted for crossing, do not give good results; hence the results of actual tests must be studied. The objects to be obtained by crosses for table use are yellow legs and skin, hardiness, quick growth, early maturity, compact shape, abundance of breast meat. Some of the most common crosses among producers of market poultry are the Leghorn and **Light Brahma,** the White Wyandotte and **Brahma,** and **Plym-**

outh Rock and Brahma. With the idea of discovering other crosses which might equal or surpass those ordinarily made, extensive experiments were conducted at the Rhode Island station in 1892, and these remain the most accurate and detailed account of crossing breeds which can be obtained. Of all the crosses, the chickens from the Indian Game and Light Brahma, and Indian Game and Buff Cochin, seemed to do the best. Those from the White Wyandotte and Indian Game came next, remarkable for quick growth. The Indian Game and Golden Wyandotte cross was next in thrift. The Plymouth Rock and Buff Cochin cross was unsatisfactory, likewise the Dark Brahma and Silver Wyandotte.

FIG. 100. CORNISH INDIAN GAME HEN.

Indian Game and Light Brahma.— Cockerel, plumage similar to Light Brahma but darker, with some yellow. Larger than Brahma and between the two in shape; comb and wattles the same as Brahma. Body wide, legs long. Pullet, plumage brown with penciled feathers, dark hackles. . Resemble Brown Malay hen except in the slight leg feathering. Lay well, eggs as large as Brahmas. Each sex is as uniform in size and in color as a pure breed. They are hardy, quiet, good feeders, and are closely feathered. There was hardly any loss among the chickens. A very desirable cross.

Indian Game and Houdan. — Plumage black, or slightly mixed with white, small crests. Cockerels have flesh colored legs, and pullets dark legs. Are active, grow quick, and fairly hardy. There is not much difference in size between cockerels and pullets. Are uniform in appearance.

Indian Game and Golden Wyandotte.—In plumage and appearance most like Golden Wyandotte. Markings uniform. Fairly hardy, quick, active, and plump at any age. Disposition rather excitable. Cockerels much larger than pullets. But slight loss among chickens.

Indian Game and Buff Cochin.—None but pullets reared. Similar in plumage and appearance to Light Brahma cross. Not so closely feathered, legs shorter and more feathers on them. Larger and brighter comb.

White Wyandotte and Light Brahma.—In appearance between the two. Both rose and single combs appear. Body more stocky than Brahma, legs shorter, plumage faded and muddy. Show more red in comb and face than Brahmas. Disposition quiet; good feeders and hardy. Cockerels grow very large.

White Wyandotte and Indian Game.—Plumage similar to Silver Wyandotte, dark with gray neck; breast feathers in pullets slightly spangled with white; legs and neck short; rose comb. Grow quickly, and are always plump and hardy. Pullets are excellent layers. Cockerels not much larger than the pullets. A desirable cross.

Houdan and Partridge Cochin.—Plumage a mixture of the two. Small crests; legs both light and dark, and feathered; active, quick growers.

Judging from these experiments, the raiser of market poultry will not make a mistake if he crosses Indian Game cockerels or cocks on Light Brahma hens, or on any variety of Wyandotte hens; or Wyandotte males on Indian Game hens or Light Brahma hens. It was found that Indian Games and their crosses were harder to pluck and more difficult to caponize than any other of the crosses.

Various crosses were tried the following year at the Rhode Island station, but none were found equal to those already mentioned. Aseels were crossed with White Wyandottes and Pea Comb Plymouth Rocks; Indian Game with Langshans; Houdan with Langshans and Indian Games; White Game with White Brahmas and White Plymouth Rocks, and White Indian Game with Pea Comb Plymouth Rocks. Neither the White Indian Game, White Game nor Aseel was found to be satisfactory for the production of table poultry as the dark Indian Game. Aseels were found to be unsuited for use in the practical production of table poultry.

FIG. 101. ROSE COMB WHITE LEGHORN COCKEREL.

In crosses made for eggs mainly, suitable combinations of the smaller breeds will give the best results. White Leghorn on White Wyandotte are excellent layers, and pullets can be selected which lay a fairly dark colored egg. Crosses of such similar breeds, as White and Brown Leghorn, give splendid vigor. White Leghorn on Light Brahma, and the progeny bred back to the Leghorns, has been a popular cross for eggs.

The objection to crosses repeated every year is that no progress is made beyond the first year, the cross-bred males not being desirable for breeding. By grading up the flock, however, this difficulty is avoided. Males of the same breed are used each successive year, and the flock each year becomes more like the pure breed, until at last it is practically identical with that breed. But being a cross and containing some outside blood, and no inbreeding having been practiced, the hens have fine vigor and are an improvement on the pure breed.

CHAPTER XXIV.

FEEDING FOR GROWTH.

Chickens intended for layers and breeding stock must be kept growing rapidly, but will not bear forcing so hard as chickens meant for broilers. When they are to be killed and sent to market at eight or ten weeks of age, they will endure high feeding and restriction of exercise the last two weeks, while the breeding stock must be fed for framework and stamina.

A farmer in one of the shore towns of Massachusetts, Mr. L. S. Richards, who keeps several hundred fowls as a branch of his farming operations, who believes in the incubator for farm use, and who is very successful in the management of both chicks and hens, gives his experience as follows:

The chicks are left in the incubator two days after they are hatched, then they are removed to the brooder, which is heated by a kerosene lamp in the rear, outside. The brooder is warmed by top heat, through tin pipes running on either side within, one in the middle and another across the front, all connected, of course, with two outlets in the rear portion. I have six brooders, each large enough for seventy-five chicks. The first week I keep the temperature between 80° and 90°. When two weeks old 75° will answer, and at four or five weeks, 70°. In the bottom of the brooder there is a platform slide resting on the lower one and covering it, on which the chicks rest. After a few days I pull out the slides and remove the droppings, then re-cover with hay seed and replace them. They should afterward be cleaned every day. Have a sand floor or ground for them to run on and pick to grind their food. The first week, if cold, I use outside of the brooder a small 75 cent oil stove or heater to warm the house for them, especially while they are out feeding.

For the first two weeks they require a great deal of warmth, and I am convinced that the cause of death among so many small chicks is due to lack of warmth. I speak from experience. The same is true with chicks brooded by the hen. We have often found an apparently dead chicken, chilled outside, and brought it to life by warming it; in nine cases out of ten it will revive and thrive. When the small chicks are out feeding in the brooder house during the first week, watch them more, or less and see that none get chilled. After the first week they will generally go in and under the brooder at their own option, and when the sun is out and shining through the glass they will crowd together in the sunshine, and during a very cold day they will get chilled, even in the sun's rays (unless the house is very warm), rather than go under the brooder where it is warmer. They like the sun. During the first week I have a fine wire shutter with which to close them in the brooder when they have been out long enough, and always at night for a week, and perhaps two, if cold. If not so restrained, they would get out too early in the morning, become chilled, and die. After the first week or two I do not use it, but let them go out and in at will. This, I think, will answer for the incubator and brooder. One other point should be mentioned, and that is, I should advise one not to touch an incubator

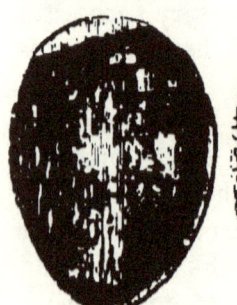
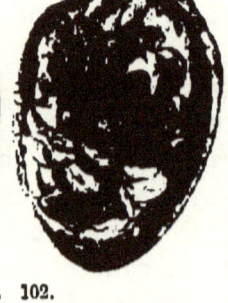

FIG. 102.
UNFERTILE EGG.   FERTILE EGG.

until he has raised chicks successfully by the hen. It is one thing to hatch chicks, and quite another to raise them successfully.

In regard to feed for chicks, which, of course, applies to chicks with the hen as well as those in the brooder, we give them the first day or two, when they are old enough to eat, cooked eggs chopped fine. Get the hen well filled with corn, or some soft feed, before feeding the egg to the chicks, otherwise the hungry hen will gobble it up. After this give them some baked Indian meal and flour bread mixed, chopped fine, and milk to drink. After the first week give them ground oats, cracked oats, cracked wheat and sifted cracked corn, boiled broken rice and white flour bread or graham bread. Milk, if you have it, if not, water, for the brooder chicks. Give them meat scrap which contains ground bone, and also cut fresh bone. You can, perhaps, keep a small chick alive on cracked corn alone, the same as half the farmers do; but that is not what the man or woman wants who is raising chicks for profit, and who desires to get three-pound-per-pair chicks in ten, or at the farthest, twelve, weeks; and to do this you must work them for all they are worth. But do not feed on cracked corn alone. I assure you, they get tired of it, the same as we would

FIG. 103. BARRED PLYMOUTH ROCK.

upon a diet of bread alone. Let them have free access to coarse sand or any kind of grit. Don't leave any holes open at night in your houses for rats to crawl through.

Mr. I. K. Felch, the well-known breeder, feeds his chicks by a fixed schedule. The first meal is boiled eggs chopped fine, shells and all, also corn cake and his excelsior meal crumbled into scalded milk. After the first 24 hours, the early morning feed is excelsior meal, bread and scalded milk. At 10 o'clock, a feed of very fine cracked corn; at 2 o'clock, excelsior, bread and milk; at 6 o'clock, canary seed, millet seed and the fine cracked corn. If the season be winter, meat and green food, steamed clover, fine grit, etc., are added. After the chicks are two weeks old, and until they are eight weeks of age, the bill of fare is as follows:

Monday—Breakfast, excelsior meal, bread and milk; ten o'clock meal, boiled meat, chopped fine, with steamed clover; two o'clock dinner, excelsior meal, bread and milk; supper, granulated corn, oats and barley.

Tuesday—Breakfast, the broth in which meat was boiled, thickened while it was boiling (and when the meat was taken out) with excelsior meal; ten o'clock, chopped mangel-wurzel beets, and after eating what they would, allow to finish filling their crops with granulated corn; two o'clock dinner, the balance of the broth, mush, and a pan of sour milk, if to be had, to pick at till five or six o'clock; supper, all the granulated corn, oats and wheat they would eat should be given.

Wednesday—Breakfast, fish chowder made palatable with salt and pepper, boiled potatoes, and thickened with corn meal and shorts; ten o'clock, oats and wheat, and all the steamed clover or green chopped oats they would eat; dinner, cracked corn, and balance of chowder if not wholly disposed of at the morning meal; supper, cracked corn and barley.

Thursday—Breakfast, chopped sheep's haslets, and warm mush of wheat, bran and corn meal; ten o'clock, cracked corn and wheat; dinner, all the steamed clover they would eat, and as dessert what excelsior meal cake they would dispose of; supper, cracked corn and oats. Give sour milk in a pan to go to at will.

Friday—Breakfast, the meat soup thickened with excelsior meal; ten o'clock, green oats, chopped onions

FIG. 104. WHITE WYANDOTTES.

and light feed of granulated corn; dinner, balance of the broth, mush and barley to finish up; supper, cracked corn and wheat.

Saturday—Breakfast, raw chopped meat and excelsior meal mush, scalded and fed warm; ten o'clock, chopped cabbage, lettuce and turnips, or mangel-wurzels, throwing them a little granulated corn; dinner, excelsior mush with barley; supper, granulated corn and oats.

Sunday—Breakfast, fish chowder, warm (made as above); ten o'clock, steamed rowen clover and barley; dinner, excelsior meal cake and scalded milk; supper, cracked corn and wheat, with sour milk ad libitum.

For the benefit of those who wish to make it, Mr. I. K. Felch's rule is given for his excelsior meal bread. "Grind into a fine meal in the following proportions: Twenty pounds of corn, fifteen pounds oats, ten pounds barley, ten pounds wheat bran. We make the cakes by taking one quart of sour milk or buttermilk, adding a little salt and molasses, one quart of water, in which a large heaping teaspoonful of saleratus has been dissolved, then thicken all with the excelsior meal to a little thicker batter than your wife does for corn cakes. Bake in shallow pans till thoroughly cooked. We believe a well-appointed kitchen and brick oven pays, and in the baking of this food enough for a week can be cooked at a time." Some growers obtain stale bread very cheaply and use it in place of a cooked bread like the above.

A correspondent furnishes this excellent bill of fare: First week—at 6 a. m., cracker mixture; 9 a. m., clabbered milk; 12 m., cracker mixture; 3 p. m., chopped cabbage; 6 p. m., cooked oat meal. Second week—6 a. m., cracker mixture; 9 a. m., clabbered milk; 12 m., oat meal, dry; 3 p. m., chopped cabbage; 6 p. m., cracker mixture. Third week—6 a. m., cracker mixture, omitting the egg; 9 a. m., chopped cabbage; 12 m., cracked wheat; 3 p. m., clabbered milk; 6 p. m., oat meal, cooked. Fourth week—6 a. m., cracker mixture; 9 a. m., clabbered milk and oat meal, dry; 12 m., chopped cabbage and cracked wheat; 3 p. m., cracked corn; 6 p. m., cracker mixture. Skimmed milk is allowed freely, but no water. The cracker mixture consists of cracker dust soaked in milk and mixed with boiled yolk of eggs, fine ground bone and ground beef scraps; the first week it should be nearly half egg.

R. G. Buffinton writes: I feed the young chickens the first three days on hard-boiled eggs, and then stale bread or broken crackers for a few days longer, or until they get smart enough to run out. I then give them the same as I do the old fowls in the morning—corn meal, fine feed, boiled potatoes and beef scraps, always using a little of the egg food. After they are two weeks old, I keep cracked corn and wheat by them all the time.

Pigs' liver is one of the best forms of animal food for chicks. It is extensively used by Plymouth county poulterers who hatch artificially. Codfish has killed chicks.

The coops should be often moved to fresh locations, on dry, green grass plots if possible, and plenty of fresh

FIG. 105. WHITE WONDERS.

water given daily; put old nails, or other iron, in the water, as iron is good for their health. When the chicks get strong they may be allowed to roam at will with the hen. If there is danger of hawks, a run or yard covered with a wire screen may be necessary. It is also a good idea to make a box out of slats wide enough apart to admit chicks of various sizes, and yet exclude hens, and throw the feed for the chicks in this, so that they can eat without being robbed by the larger fowls. The chicks of different ages should be kept at quite a distance from each other for this reason, allowing only flocks of same age to feed together. When the chicks are six weeks old they may be removed to some other part of the farm, where they will have a fresh hunting-ground for insects, which will form an important part of their food. They should be placed in small, portable houses, eight feet long, four feet wide, three feet high in front and two feet high in rear, with tight floor and roof. The sides of this building should be boarded perpendicularly, leaving one-inch space between each board to secure perfect ventilation without a draught.

When the chickens are removed to these houses they should be placed at quite a distance from, and out of sight of, their former habitation; if this is not done, they are liable to go back to their former coop. They should be moved at night, and shut in the house for a day or two, when they may be let out just at dusk, always feeding them near their new quarters. After a day or two they will be contented, and will always be found at night in their new home. If they are placed near some cornfield they will do no injury to the growing crop, and it will serve as a shelter for them from the burning sun. As the season grows later and the hay crop is gathered, the colonies may be scattered all over the mowing fields to a great advantage to the next season's crop. The chickens will destroy all the insects, and the fertilizer that they will deposit will make the fields look green.

FATTENING AND MARKETING.

Old hens are unprofitable, and should be weeded out, and autumn is the time to do it if they were not sold in the spring or used for potpie during the summer. They will never be heavier and fatter than they are then, and the feed they will consume will be all loss. For fattening fowls, the following arrangement will be found effective: A long, low box (a shoe box, laid upon its side, answers very well) is lathed up and down in the front, leaving an opening all along the front, a bar being fitted across the box, three inches above the bottom. This bottom opening is to clean out the box with a scraper, once every day; after which dry earth is thrown in. This box will hold six fowls, and a feeding trough and a water can should be fitted in front. A number of boxes may be tiered one over the other, and when the fowls have fed, the front should be covered and darkened, by hanging bagging over it. This will keep the fowls quiet. Two weeks of this treatment will fatten them. The finest flesh is made by feeding cornmeal and boiled potatoes, mixed with skimmed milk, quite thick, and four feeds a day should be given. Fowls are best slaughtered and dressed as follows: A barrel is provided, with a number of nails driven in around the open edge. A number of loops of twine, about six inches long, are also provided. The bird is fastened by noosing the loop around the legs, and is hung in the barrel, head downward. The head is then taken in the left hand, and a sharp pointed knife is pushed through the throat, close to the vertebra, and drawn forward so as to cut the throat clear through, by which sensation is at once arrested, and the fowl bleeds to death rapidly and painlessly. Being confined in the barrel, the splashing from the fluttering is avoided, and everything is done in a cleanly and easy manner. Dry picking is preferred by the marketmen, but the extra price will hardly pay for the trouble over the scalding of the fowls, and the easier picking in that way. To scald a fowl, take a pail three-quarters full of boiling water, and plunge the bird into it, drawing it up and down a few times. Keep the water up to the scalding heat by adding a quart of boiling water occasionally.

Ducks are fed nearly the same as chickens, except that they need rather more animal food as they increase in size. They should be carefully guarded from rain for the first fortnight. They should also be yarded while young, for if allowed free range, they greedily devour all manner of insects, which they do not stop to kill, and too often pay the penalty with their lives. Boiled potatoes and vegetables should be fed freely, at least once a day, to young ducks, which should have four meals each day until five weeks old. Cracked corn and refuse wheat may be kept by them, but while fattening they should have all the soft food they can eat at least three times a day. Ducks should be marketed at nine or ten weeks old, as soon after that the pin feathers begin to grow and they are off condition and soon become poor, while it is an immense job to pick them. If not marketed at the time above mentioned, they will not be in condition again till after they are four months old. Pekin ducks at nine weeks old, if well fed, will dress from eight to eleven pounds per pair.

PACKING AND SHIPPING.

In packing poultry, assort them carefully, putting the large ones, also the small ones and any old bulls or cocks, each by themselves, and mark the number in the package. During Thanksgiving week, large fancy turkeys, weighing from twelve to fifteen pounds each, generally command the best prices of the year. The market is then usually filled with "fair to poor" stock, which goes at low figures; but even ten-pound turkeys, fat and well dressed, bring good prices, unless, as is sometimes the case, warm, rainy weather demoralizes the market. Make your packages as uniform as possible. Nice boxes of regular dimensions are much better than irregular ones. We subjoin a cut giving best sizes used for turkeys and chickens, and showing style of packing generally preferred. Western shippers who send large quantities had better adopt these packages and style of packing, even if at considerable trouble and expense, as it will give them a decided advantage over other shippers who use old boxes of all sizes, ready to fall apart on arrival—because, when shipped as above suggested, it insures quick sales, prompt returns and highest market prices for quality of stock.

During cold weather, poultry can be shipped any day in the week, either by express or freight. It should be

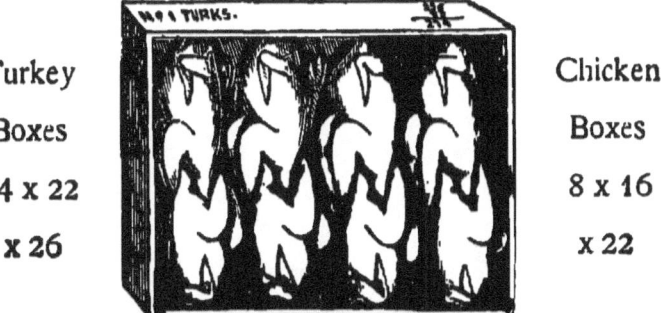

Turkey Boxes 14 x 22 x 26

Chicken Boxes 8 x 16 x 22

FIG. 106. TURKEYS PACKED FOR MARKET.

entirely cold, but not frozen, before being packed. Boxes are the best packages. Line them with paper and pack so closely that the contents cannot move, but never use straw, and never wrap dressed poultry in paper. On the cover, distinctly mark the kind and quality of contents —the gross weight and correct tare in plain figures, thus:

20 No. 1 Turks.	250 40
	210
ADDRESS OF COMMISSION MERCHANT.	

Choice Chicks.	125 20
	105
ADDRESS OF COMMISSION MERCHANT.	

Also the merchant's name and that of the shipper, unless he is known by the number of his stencil. Stencils are furnished free for this purpose, when desired. When the correct tare of a package is omitted, the entire contents have to be removed to ascertain the weight of the poultry, and if frozen, it is often impossible to do this without tearing the package to pieces, and if not frozen it causes much extra work and delay, which will sometimes prevent the sale, especially if the customer is in a hurry, as is usually the case in the busy poultry season.

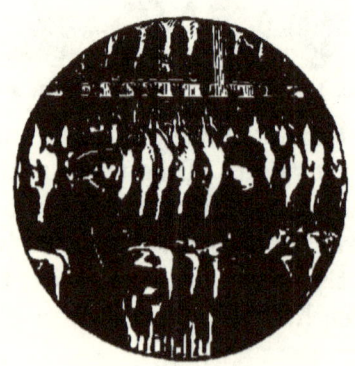

CHAPTER XXV.

FEEDING FOR EGGS.

Anybody can get eggs in spring and early summer, but there is little money in them at the prices which then prevail. The poultry keepers who make hens pay are those who know how to get eggs in autumn and winter.

A right start is very important. Pullets, not old hens, must be kept for fall and winter laying, and pullets which are mature enough to begin laying before cold weather begins. To get such pullets, the chicks must be hatched in April, for the large and medium breeds. For the small breeds, like Leghorns, May hatching will answer. The pullets must be kept growing right through the summer, for if they cannot be induced to lay by November, good-by to any great profits for the year. Cross breeds and grades will lay better than pure breeds, unless the pure breeds have been bred and selected more for eggs and vigor than for fancy points.

Having secured the early pullets, and having placed them in warm, light, dry houses, they must be properly fed.

HOW TO FEED.

Feed in the morning a warm, cooked meal of various ground grains, including a good proportion of middlings, shorts or bran. Season it slightly with a very little salt. About twice a week mix in a liberal dose of meat scraps of some kind, and occasionally season it with cayenne pepper. Vary the proportions of the different feeds daily. This will keep them in good appetite and make them anxious to see you as soon as 'tis time to leave their roost. Give them also, occasionally, in the cooked food, a quantity of bone meal or ground bone.

For the other one or two meals a day—some feed only twice, others three times; young stock that are confined should have a light feed at noon, the heavier feed being

FIG. 107. BROWN LEGHORNS.

given at night just before going to roost—give them whole grain, making the variety as great as possible, and vary their meals as much as possible. No two meals alike in a day is a first-rate plan. Only feed Indian corn, whole or ground, once or twice a week, unless to fattening fowls. It is a poor egg food, but will put on fat quicker than any other.

There should have been stored, in the fall, all the culls from the cabbage crop, for the use of the fowls. When no green stuff can be had from their runs, and when confined to the house, hang a head up in the open yard where it can just be reached by jumping a little, and see how eagerly they will go for it, and how much fun and enjoyment they will get from it. Good clover, rowen, and in fact almost any good, clean, sweet hay cut in short pieces, is good for them and will be thankfully received and appreciated and good interest paid on its cost. Vegetables, either cooked or raw, are much relished also, and serve in some measure to supply the place of a green diet. Onions chopped fine and mixed with their food are exceedingly wholesome, and, if not a cure, are certainly a preventive of disease. Growing chickens are even more anxious for green food than laying hens. But if the poulterer feeds too many onions the eggs will taste of them; feed moderately, and if chopped up raw, nothing is better for laying fowls. Raw apples or other cheap fruit, chopped up fine, is relished in winter. Below is the ration of R. G. Buffinton, a well-known and extremely successful producer of eggs for market. He says:

"Much depends upon the feed, especially for hens that are yarded all the time. It will not do to keep feed by them. If we did, they would be liable to get sick or get too fat. Then they would not lay any eggs, and instead of a profit there would be a loss. We cannot afford to keep hens around half of the time doing nothing. My morning feed consists of corn meal and fine feed in equal parts, ground beef scraps, and in the winter boiled potatoes. This is all mixed together with hot water, adding a little salt and egg food. This is fed as soon as the fowls can see to eat, except in the longest days in summer. This feed is put in troughs eight feet long, eight inches wide and three inches high. The ends are put in so the bottom of the trough will be three inches above the ground. This same trough is used for the dry grain on stormy days, and in all winter weather. At other times the grain is fed in the yards. For dry grain feed, I use equal parts of whole corn, oats and wheat. This grain is mixed together in a basket that holds three pecks, and I always use a two-quart flour scoop to deal out both wet and dry feed. This mixture is fed twice a day, in the morning after breakfast, and at night. I never feed in the middle of the day or disturb the hens in the least. I want them to spend all the time they want in laying eggs. I used to feed at noon, but found if all the hens were called off the nest to eat dinner the same number would not go back again that day."

FIG. 108. HAMBURGS.

Four quarts of feed per day for twenty-six hens would be about right. If they were large Brahmas, they might require more; if Leghorns, less. The proper way would be to give them what they will eat up readily. Wheat screenings contain a large quantity of foul seed; some of them the hens will not eat, and of course they will take root and grow. We have known hens to die from eating the seed in screenings. The better way would be to feed good wheat. A good winter feed for laying hens is equal parts of corn meal and fine feed; add to this one-twentieth as much ground beef scraps and some boiled potatoes, mix with hot water and feed every morning. Give whole corn, oats and wheat in equal parts at noon and night, giving a very light feed at noon and all they will eat at night.

MAKE THEM WORK.

In no one point do so many fail as in that of giving the hens exercise. Unless they are kept scratching a great part of the time, they will not lay as they should. Upon this point all are agreed. The usual plan is to keep the floor covered with leaves, straw, cornstalks or hay several inches deep, and to make the hens scratch it over by scattering grain, and by stirring up the litter with a fork. The more time spent making the hens scratch, the more eggs they will lay, other things being equal, and the less time they will have for mischief and learning bad habits. One man does in this way: "My new poultry house opens into the barnyard, where I unload the manure that is drawn from the city in the winter. Every morning I scatter four quarts of wheat on the manure heaps, and the fowls spend most of the time scratching for it. When not so occupied they are on the nests laying, or are clucking contentedly in the hen-house. Every evening before the fowls go to roost a feed of corn is given them. I get plenty of eggs and the fowls are contented and healthy."

Whenever the ground is bare of snow, during the winter, give the birds a chance to run. After their first meal in the morning, give their feed on some grass plot, or where the dead leaves are accumulated, and make them scratch for it. They need just such exercise, and will be all the healthier and hardier for it. When snow covers the ground, keep them confined in the house and the open shed connected with it. Eating snow and drinking snow water will keep them poor, no matter how well you may feed them. Feed the whole grain in the open shed, in which you can put leaves or cut hay or straw, so that they will have to scratch for the grain or go hungry, which latter they won't do.

Another successful egg raiser says: "Into the pens (which are 11x12 feet) is put about four bushels of fine earth, and then dry forest leaves to the depth of one foot or more, over which scatter whole corn, at the afternoon feeding time, and I can assure you there will be no lack of exercise. During the winter I keep fifteen fowls in each pen of the above size, and occasionally add plaster and fresh leaves as they are reduced to powder, which serve to keep the fowls warm and dry. All droppings will be worked down through the leaves. I have never had a diseased fowl, feather-puller or egg-eater since I began using leaves in this way. Don't let any fear of filling your houses with woodmites deter you from using leaves, when kerosene oil and Dalmatian powder are both cheap and effective."

HEALTHY FOWLS.

Thorough ventilation, a comfortable house, plenty of exercise and varied food, are the safeguards against disease. Colds must be looked for, and treated as soon as noticed. If this is done promptly and thoroughly, there need be little fear of roup. A warm place for the ailing ones, soft feed, cooked, of wheat middlings and bran mixed, ground oats, with small allowances of Indian meal, in which a dose of prepared roup pills has been dissolved, and made smart with cayenne pepper, is a good treatment. If they have a cough with the cold, burn flowers of sulphur in their house after they have gone to roost, until they are affected by the gas so they sneeze well. This has a wonderfully good effect. Put a small bunch of shavings in an old tin pan, or on a shovel, with a handful of the sulphur, light the shavings, and let it burn; shut the house up tight till they begin to sneeze, and then take it out. The quantity named is sufficient to "sneeze" two or three houses of fifty fowls each.

The dust bath should be provided at all seasons of the year. In winter a generous box of dry dust by a sunny window will be sufficient for forty or fifty hens if its supply of dust is renewed once or twice. Add half a pound each of lime and sulphur to each bushel of dust used; these greatly assist in killing lice. Fine sifted coal ashes are excellent. If wood ashes are used, they should make up but one-fourth of the dust, as their potash is too strong when used alone. In summer, wallowing in the dry earth is best.

SPRING AND SUMMER.

At these seasons, hens should be fed twice a day. Give a warm mash in the morning, composed of all the odds and ends from the table, anything but bones, cut and jammed up and mixed with Indian meal and shorts or fine feed, about half and half; then scald and give as warm as they will eat it. About nine o'clock give them a pan of milk which has been soured and thickened, and a pail of apples partly decayed, which they will devour voraciously. About four or a little after give them a generous feed of Indian corn and wheat, half and half. Keep ground oyster shells by them, and mix scraps or meat cut up, or grease, with their breakfast, every two or three days. If the chicks are all right, the hens will lay all winter with this slight care.

FIG. 109. SEVERE CASE OF ROUP, SHOWING THE WHITISH DISCHARGE IN PASSAGES (see P. 318).

USEFUL HINTS.

To use pans for feeding, take a common milk pan and two wires—one two feet long and the other one foot long. Bend the long one in the middle into a loop.

Fasten the short one to it so as to make three ends about ten inches long. Fasten these at equal distances around the edge of the pan. Hang it by a string in the henhouse, so as to have the top edge six inches from the ground. The biddies can then reach and eat from it without being able to get into and soil the food.

The old practice of feeding fowls on the ground should be abandoned. It was formerly supposed that the more sand, grit and dirt that was taken into the crop with the feed the better, but the ground plan conduces to disease, for there is a constant accumulation of filth, to say nothing of disease germs, on such places. Either feed on a long broad board or from a trough, for fowls prefer cleanliness to filth at all times. It is also wasteful to throw food upon the ground, to be trampled into the mud on wet days, there to ferment and cause annoyance from time to time, to say nothing of the struggles and combats that are more liable from the system.

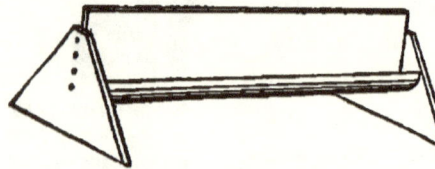

FIG. 110. FEED TROUGH.

Economy in feeding is a very important chapter in the hen diary. When fowls are fed all they will eat, and food is left standing by them, it must be protected against waste. Arrange a box, opening at the top by a lid, and slats on two sides, running up and down. Put feed inside, so the fowls can get their heads in, but not their feet; or make a box-shaped coop, with slats running up and down, open at the bottom, tight at the top. Place this over the feed dish.

A simple and efficient feeding trough may be made by tacking a piece of tin about three and one-half inches wide along the edge of a half-inch board, so that the tin projects about an inch and a half on either side of the board, bending the tin so as to form a shallow trough, and fastening the board to blocks which raise it from one to two inches from the floor (see Fig. 110). The trough may be from one to three feet long. It is within easy reach of the chickens, and so narrow that they cannot stand upon the edges. Food placed in such feeding troughs can be kept clean until wholly consumed.

Drinking vessels protect in the same way. We consider galvanized iron dishes the best. You can get them made, of any size or shape. They are not to be broken, will not rust, and can be cleansed with hot water, and will last for years. They should be kept in a shady, dry place, rinsed out every day, and scalded out every week. A common water pail can also be utilized.

Saw out two staves even with the top hoop on opposite sides of the pail, leaving a stave between those cut out; cut a notch one inch deep and one or two inches wide on opposite staves.

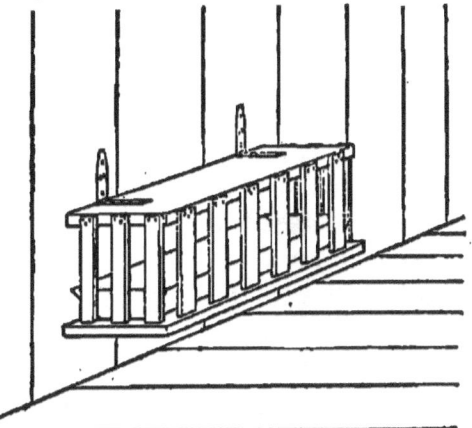

FIG. 111. DRINKING FOUNTAIN.

Make a cover and nail on a cleat long enough to project by at each end about one inch; then fasten another cleat to the first, just long enough to fit into the top of the pail, and fasten a strap to the other side of the cover for a handle. When the cover is on and the cleats are in place, the hens cannot knock it off.

The drinking dish should, in any case, be arranged to promote cleanliness. A good plan is to raise it and enclose it in a frame of laths. Take a long, narrow dish, something like a tin bread tray, on a low shelf a few inches from the floor, and hinge the cover to one side of the poultry house, so that it can be tipped up in front for the removal of the dish or for filling it with water (see Fig. 111). Whatever device is used, it must be easily cleaned and of free access to the fowls at all times.

Cleanliness in all pertaining to the food and feeding is essential. Punctuality in feeding is a matter the French esteem of great importance, and it is being more and more regarded in the same light in this country. Hens are early risers, also, and do not like standing around on one foot waiting for their breakfast. The morning meal, with them, is the most important one of the day.

In feeding grain to laying fowls, if the flock is a large one, great care must be taken that the grain is scattered, so that the weaker fowls are not jostled aside by the stronger ones. Our rule, in feeding all stock, is to see that the weakest ones have abundant room. While we soon can detect the unthrift of large animals when thus crowded away from their just share, we cannot so easily individualize the egg record of each hen in a large flock, yet we must charge the minor members of the household, when entrusted with feeding, to see that the least aggressive hens have room enough to get their due share.

COMMON MISTAKES.

In looking over the average poultry house in winter, the most common defects are as follows: Bare, damp floor, upon which the fowls stand and mope, and some times get rheumatism; broken windows, letting cold air blow upon the roosts or upon the fowls in daytime. Both the above will check laying, and are common causes of roup. Damp droppings left for weeks to heap up under the roosts; lack of a supply of water, obliging the hens to eat snow, thus stopping the eggs; lack of plenty of good, sharp grit, which alone is a sufficient cause of failure; lack of fresh meat and cut bone fed twice a week; overfeeding, overcrowding, and no inducement to scratch for a living. These are the most common and important mistakes, and those who wonder why their hens do not lay, will do well to go over the list.

See that your house is tight, so that on cold windy nights the fowls will not suffer any more than can be helped. A good plan is to keep a barrel in the building, and the coldest nights put in the birds that are liable to have their combs freeze, and cover the barrel. Above all, do not crowd the fowls. During the long winter months, when they cannot exercise out of doors, they will need at least seven or eight feet square per fowl. Scatter some hay around and throw the grain into it. This will make them exercise and will be what they need, and the eggs will hatch better in the spring. Avoid feeding stimulants to

FIG. 112. RHODE ISLAND REDS.

fowls you are going to breed from, and do not give them any more food than they will eat up clean. The rest is very apt to be left and become filthy. Another thing is, pure, fresh water; do not fail in this. You may think snow will answer, but it is not good for poultry and will make them poor. Warm the water on cold days, and put a spoonful of red pepper in it. Fowls are always thirsty, and a great deal of roup is brought on by allowing them to drink impure water. Kindness is never thrown away in poultry. Show us a person who studies their wants and loves to care for them, and we warrant he will be successful.

Some growers keep, for laying, hens without a male. Under such conditions, the hens will lay an equal or greater number of eggs, and the eggs are claimed to keep better than those which have been fertilized. According to experiments at the New York station, eggs were produced at about thirty per cent less cost where no cockerel was kept. The only objection to the plan is the annoyance occasioned by the uneasy and peculiar behavior of the hens. When eggs are wanted for hatching, the cockerel may be added about four weeks before beginning to save the eggs.

ABOUT CERTAIN FOODS.

Old cheese can sometimes be had for a very low price, and such has been found to be a very good egg producer.

Ground oyster shells, fine sea shells, refuse plaster from houses, a little slaked lime, etc., should be supplied to provide the lime necessary to form egg shells. Good, clean gravel, to aid the digestion, should be provided.

Pork is not good to feed to poultry, and if used must first be thoroughly cooked. It is sometimes recommended in disease.

Sunflower seed, especially the large Russian variety, is fine for poultry.

Clear rye bran will swell and cake in the crop, so don't feed it whole. Rye should not be fed too freely to fowls, as it is very loosening to the bowels; it is the least desirable of any of the various grains for the production of eggs, and if fed at all, it should be used sparingly.

Cabbage for poultry feed may be hung up in the poultry house, head down, and high enough from the floor so that the birds can pick at it and yet not soil it.

Animals which die on the farm, if the disease is not infectious, may be fed to poultry.

Fish food is liable to cause bowel trouble, and should be fed only in small quantities.

Bone meal is excellent for layers. One pound of bone meal per day is about right for fifty hens.

Lawn clippings are good green food for poultry confined in summer, and good also as dry fodder in winter.

Scraps of all kinds should be fed daily about the middle of the day, when least liable to freeze. Bits of meat, soup bones, apple parings, cabbage leaves, celery tops and small onions, or almost any refuse from the cook, should be fed in a roomy box, where the fowls can kick it over with pleasure. Pulverized clam shells, raw or burned bones, with gravel, should always be accessible. The cracked bone can be purchased by the pound from many of the fertilizer companies, also the oyster shells, but nothing seems to suit the fastidious taste of some hens so well as the clam shells. A shallow box is a convenient receptacle for this food. The lights (lungs) of beef make excellent meat if boiled till very tender and chopped moderately fine. They are too tough if fed raw, and would only be wasted; they may be obtained from the butcher for very little cost, and will help much to fill the egg basket. Tallow scraps or lard scraps are good, and can sometimes be purchased from a distant market, but there is some danger that the tallow was allowed to become tainted before trying, in which case the scrap might induce disease.

Dried blood is fed by some poultry men, but is mentioned with hesitation, because cases have been known of disease apparently caused by the hens eating the blood, which may have come from diseased animals.

AMOUNT NEEDED.

Experiments at the New York station resulted in the following statement of the amount of food consumed per day in winter for each fowl:

	Corn.	Raw apples.	Ground oats.	Total grain.	Total food
	oz.	oz.	oz.	oz.	oz.
Larger breeds...	3.06	2.32	1.27	4.33	6.65
Smaller breeds..	1.48	1.57	.47	1.95	3.52

Those who wish to go below the surface, in the science of poultry feeding, should study the composition of foods. Following is the Lawes and Gilbert table, which shows the make-up of the common foods:

There is in every 100 lbs. of	Flesh-forming material, gluten, etc.	Warmth-giving and fattening material.		Bone-making material or mineral substance.	Husk or fiber.	Water.
		Fat or oil.	Starch			
	lbs.	lbs.	lbs.	lbs.	lbs.	lbs.
Beans and peas...........	25	2	48	2	8	15
Oatmeal...................	18	6	63	2	2	9
Middling thirds or fine shorts...............	18	6	53	5	4	14
Oats.......................	15	6	47	2	20	10
Wheat	12	3	70	2	1	12
Buckwheat...............	12	6	58	1½	11	11½
Barley....................	11	2	60	2	14	11
Indian corn...............	11	8	65	1	5	10
Hempseed	10	21	45	2	14	8
Rice......................	7		80			13
Potatoes	6½		51	2		50½
Milk......................	4½	3	5	¾		86¾

OTHER POULTRY FOODS.—(Hatch Station.)
[Lbs. in 100.]

	Water.	Bone-making matter or ash.	Husk, etc.	Fat.	Flesh-forming matter.	Starch, etc.
Ground clover...........	9.53	7.43	27.80	1.93	13.65	39.66
Wheat bran	9.56	5.27	6.85	5.37	17.69	53.26
Animal meal	5.08	28.63		16.18	40.03	10.08
Cut bone..................	29.67	24.06		26.13	20.19	
New process linseed meal	9.35	4.48	6.58	6.39	38.06	35.14
Buffalo gluten meal......	7.14	.84	7.07	12.67	23.31	48.97
Chicago gluten meal.....	8.10	.83	3.34	5.57	36.51	45.65
Wheat middlings	10.93	4.03	6.95	5.30	17.28	55.51
Whole wheat.............	10.60	1.69	2.17	1.93	13.19	70.42
Whole oats	10.06	2.77	8.71	4.87	14.53	59.06
Soja bean meal..........	9.24	5.02	3.87	16.25	34.75	30.87

In general, whatever concentrated food is good for making milk will also produce eggs. The following analysis shows the general similarity of the analysis of milk and of eggs, casein being equivalent to albumen:

ANALYSIS OF MILK.			ANALYSIS OF HENS' EGGS.			
	Cow's milk.	Skim milk.		White.	Yolk.	Mixed.
Water	86.3	89.0	Water	64.8	51.5	71.7
Casein	4.1	4.3	Albumen	12.0	15.0	14.0
Milk fat	3.7	0.4	Fat	2.0	30.0	11.0
Milk sugar	5.1	5.5	Membranes, etc.		2.1	2.0
Ash	0.8	0.8	Mineral	1.2	1.4	1.3
Total	100.0	100.0	Total	100.0	100.0	100.0

Albumen and albuminoids are the actual flesh and egg-formers; starch and fat are heat-producers and force-givers; husk is chiefly waste matter; ash, or mineral matter, contains phosphate, etc., necessary for bone-making, feather-forming, etc.; in milk the albumen is usually known as casein, this casein being the chief ingredient in milk for cheese-forming.

THREE MONTHS' RECORD OF EGGS LAID BY DIFFERENT BREEDS.

BREEDS.	No. hens on trial.	No. eggs laid.	Average per hen.	REMARKS.
Brown Leghorn	1	72	72	European origin.
Minorca	3	127	43	" "
Houdan	1	24	24	" "
Silver Spangled Hamburg	1	37	37	
Langshan	3	147	49	Asiatic origin.
Light Brahma	2	116	58	" "
Partridge Cochin	1	27	27	" "
Buff Cochin	2	92	46	" "
Barred Plymouth Rock	1	46	46	American origin.
*Houdan-Minorca	1	45	45	" "
Bronze Turkey	1	27	27	" "

*A cross of Houdan and Minorca, by the station.

The trial was made at Louisiana station, and the experimenter's comment is as follows: The Brown Leghorns gave the best record for three successive trials. They are followed by Light Brahma and Langshan and Plymouth Rock, Buff Cochin and Minorca. The Europeans are the best spring and summer layers, but nonsitters. The Asiatics are winter and early spring layers, good mothers and brooders, and excellent for table purposes. Indeed, the Langshan is one of the best all-round fowls known, and close to them are the Plymouth Rocks, Wyandottes and Light Brahmas. However, it is hard to decide the merits of a fowl confined to close pens, and fed only vegetable foods raised upon the farm.

CHAPTER XXVI.

TURKEYS ON THE FARM.

Not every one can engage in the turkey business as an occupation or means of livelihood, because so much is dependent upon surroundings. All farmers are not so situated that they can raise turkeys without incommoding their neighbors. The laws of trespass are rigid in most States, and any neighbor who objects to your birds roaming over his fields can make you trouble, if he be so disposed. Turkeys must have range, and if your own fields are not wide enough to allow them that necessary element of success, either be sure of your neighbors' good nature, or do not embark in the business at all. Many turkey-growers believe that turkeys have a perversity of disposition, which impels them to leave their own premises, where there is plenty of room, grain and grasshoppers, and trespass on some neighbor's land, to get less food.

A few turkeys can be grown on a small farm; but there are plenty of abandoned farms in New England, which can be bought for the price of the buildings alone, large enough to grow large flocks. The convenience to large markets enhances the profits. In the Western and Southern States still greater numbers may be kept, owing to wider ranges and cheapness of grain. Common fowls, with proper care, can be kept with profit in any city or village lot, but centuries of domestication have not changed the turkeys' natural love for a necessity of free range. They can be made tame by gentleness; they learn to be familiar with those who care for them, and can be taught to come home every night; but, as soon

TURKEYS ON THE FARM.

FIG. 113. NARRAGANSETT TURKEYS.

as they have left the stage of "infancy," as shown by "shooting the red," their propensity to wander in search of their food asserts itself, and they must have that privilege or they will sicken and die. This is a fortunate trait, for two reasons. First, it makes the birds' flesh better food for man; second, it limits the business to fewer persons, who get paying prices for their labor. If turkeys could be raised at a profit in confinement, their flesh would not be so wholesome, and so many people would go into the business that the price would come down to a non-paying point. Turkey nature itself effectually prevents all danger of overdoing the business.

Turkeys are not hard to raise after you know how. For the first few weeks of their lives they require more care than any other domesticated bird, but after they are fully feathered and have "thrown the red," they require less care than any other fowl. It requires but little capital. Houses, except in the extreme North, and turkey sheds in other sections, are not needed. Turkeys must be raised on farms, and farmers raise much of the grain they need. One tom and three to five hen turkeys are enough to begin with. When you can raise all, or nearly all, of their progeny, then it will be time to think of enlarging your business. From a flock of six you ought to raise seventy-five to one hundred turkeys.

Turkey raising is an excellent business for women. Many a farmer's wife, whose husband does not care to "bother with poultry," can earn from fifty to three hundred dollars a year, according to the size of the flock, the range and the market, without seriously impeding the other necessary work which falls to the lot of farmers' wives.

Rhode Island Experiment Station: "To the foregoing it should be said, that we have found the largest and most thrifty looking turkeys on rather light land,

and where new blood is frequently introduced. If a flock becomes diseased, the land which they wander over may become contaminated, and affect other flocks which occupy the same ground, hence it is sometimes necessary to change the land on which they run, from one year to another. If turkeys are kept where they may drink from stagnant pools in barnyards, pigpens or privy vaults, sudden and fatal attacks of bowel trouble must be expected. A running stream is of great value on a turkey farm."

BREED AND CARE.

In reserving or selecting parent stock from which to raise turkeys for the market, do not overlook a most important matter, the age of the parents. Ten- or twelve-months-old turkeys are not sufficiently mature to produce the strongest progeny. Old turkeys lay larger eggs, and the young are larger and stronger when hatched. If necessity forces you to breed from stock of your own raising, keep the hens three, four, five or six years, if necessary. No judicious farmer will kill off his good heifers after they have dropped their first calves. He knows the progeny will become better and better, until age enfeebles the parent. So with turkeys. The same breeding stock may be kept, after they have proved their value, for some time. When you wish to replenish or renew the parent stock, select the best of your young hens and get a first-class tom not related to them; then you have your new stock to take the place of the others, whenever it may be deemed proper to dispose of the old ones.

The Bronze turkeys are at present the favorites with the majority of those who grow turkeys for the market. Size and hardiness are the important factors which cause this favoritism. Sometimes private customers prefer white- or yellow-skinned ones, just as they prefer yellow-legged chickens. Boston has made the present taste in New England, which decidedly prefers yellow-legged chickens, and though the preference is not emphatic for the skin of White Hollands, yet, doubtless, it is because it is difficult to obtain them. The compiler of this book has sold yellow-legged and yellow-skinned poultry at fifty per cent advance on the price of dark-legged chickens. It may be a fancy, but if you get your money, what matters it? By persisting in raising white turkeys for the New England market for a series of years, a demand may be made for them. Outside of New England, unless we may except the Philadelphia market, the color of the skin and legs of a fowl or turkey receives but little consideration.

By "common" turkeys is meant mongrels,—all sorts of breeds mixed. Too many farmers have such flocks. Get a first-rate male of the variety you want and mate him with your hens. From their progeny select the best females, and mate them with a fine male of the same breed, but not related to their sire. Pursue this course, "grading up," for two or three years, and you will have as good a flock as you need for market purposes.

GETTING READY.

Much depends upon the care of breeding stock, turkeys being quite liable to disease when kept in confinement. The floor should be covered with litter, which should be renewed when badly soiled. Make them scratch for their grain in the litter. Dryness, cleanliness and a variety of food are important. Feed some meat. Furnish plenty of grit. Overfed turkeys will get too fat. Feed the old turkey hens clover and less starchy food in the latter part of winter, and they will give better satisfaction. Throw them some grain at noon. Then just before sundown, give them all the hot whole grain they can eat. Let them out as early as possible in the spring.

When the laying season approaches, the turkeys must be watched. One man, who has great success with turkeys, encloses a large space by a high fence of wire netting, to prevent the turkeys laying and sitting in the woods and fields. Nests are provided within the enclosure. During the laying season, the hen turkeys are driven within the enclosure to roost, and confined during the forenoon each day, until all have selected nests. When hatching, they and their young are more readily cared for and controlled. Humor the turkey's love for secrecy, if you prefer to have her lay out of doors, by setting laying coops for her in secluded places not far from your house and barn. Barrels, or "A" coops, with dried leaves or litter in them, will do. If she steals her nest in some bushes not far from the house, leave her alone, but remove the eggs daily, leaving a nest egg in the nest. When she has layed her litter she will rest awhile, and then lay another litter, when she should be allowed to sit. The eggs should be taken into the house and kept in a cool (not cold) place, packed in wheat bran, small end downward.

Turkey eggs require twenty-eight days for incubation. Coincide with the hen turkey's desire for secrecy, and let her sit in places hidden from the sight of men and dogs. Bottomless boxes that will shed rain, old barrels with two or three staves knocked out, "A" coops, measuring not less than three feet square at the base, placed in retired situations not far from the house, are all that are necessary for hatching purposes. If the turkeys were taught to lay in them, all the better. The nest should be upon the ground, and made of forest leaves or chopped hay. The turkey's first litter may be taken away and set under common hens.

Mr. Samuel Cushman says, from his own experience, that turkeys can be made to sit whenever required. A young turkey hen that never laid an egg was shut on a nest of china eggs, and there was no trouble in getting her to settle down. The first two times she was put off to feed, she was caught and placed on the nest and shut in, but after that the nest was left uncovered and she came off whenever she chose. We never found her off

FIG. 114. BUFF TURKEY COCK.

the nest. The shed in which she was set had a slat front, so she was confined and could not go out of sight of the nest or get away. This turkey was not a tame one, by any means. We can control our turkeys better if set within a large building or enclosure. Turkeys can be used to hatch the eggs of hens, ducks and geese, and the raiser who does not have an artificial hatcher will not have to delay operations until hens get ready to sit, or until he can secure the desired number.

REARING THE TURKEY CHICKS.

The turkey chicks having been hatched, they will require the breeder's utmost and constant attention for the first eight or ten weeks, for on the management of the chicks depends the success or failure of turkey rearing. Turkeys, when chicks, being exceeding delicate (the most delicate of any domesticated poultry), and liable to be not only decimated, but entire broods exterminated by a sudden cold wind or a slight shower, and requiring, as they do, feeding every two hours, or six times a day, it is advisable for those who are unable to spare the time to give the necessary attention, not to attempt breeding turkeys, for they will only meet with severe losses and disappointment.

The chicks, having broken the shells by themselves, without any fussy interference by the owner, may be left to themselves for twenty-four hours, though the shells may be removed and something placed in front of the nest, if it be made in a box, to prevent any of the chicks falling out and getting cold. The chicks having, just previously to emerging from the shell, drawn into their body the yolk, they are sufficiently sustained for twenty or twenty-four hours or so, and require no feeding until the following day. If the day be warm and fine, they may be placed outdoors, in a dry situation; if cold and damp, or windy, they are better kept under cover, though not in a close atmosphere, but where there is plenty of ventilation, a large open shed protected from the wind being the best. A warm bed having been provided, made of chaff, dry sawdust or dry horse droppings, all over a bed of dry sand and coal ashes, to prevent damp arising, place the coop, which should be previously lime-washed, over it, facing south, and the mother and chicks inside. The poults hatched under common hens should be given the mother turkey in the night. Some breeders prefer bottoms to the coops, but unless the ground be very damp, that is not necessary. If you dusted the mother with insect powder two days before hatching, there will be no lice to annoy them.

On the second day the chicks may receive their first meal. On one point all turkey growers agree; no "sloppy" food must be given the young birds. In a natural state, turkey chicks feed largely upon flies, spiders, grasshoppers, grubs, snails, slugs, worms, ant eggs, etc., and if watched on a bright day will be seen to be constantly chasing flies, etc., about the meadows and woods. Berries, seeds, etc., make the variation. The first meal should be hard-boiled eggs (boiled twenty minutes), and stale wheat bread dipped in hot milk, the milk squeezed out, and both crumbled fine and seasoned with black pepper. This feed may be continued for two or three weeks, with now and then a variation to thick clabbered milk, or Dutch cheese in place of the egg. Let it be known that the egg is a substitute for insects, which the young turkey has in its wild state; so, as opportunities open for the chicks to get insects, the egg should be omitted. Dry meal must not be given them, nor wet meal insufficiently swelled. If the meal swells in their crops, death is almost certain. The best way to feed Indian meal is in the form of corn bread or "Johnny-cake." After the young birds are three weeks old, omit the eggs and give meat scraps and ground bone. Clean water or milk must be before them all the time. For runs, the best are three fourteen-inch boards set on edge so as to form a triangle, with the coop in one corner, or shorter boards over one corner, for shelter from the sun by day and dews by night. Every day or two, move two of these boards so as to form another triangle, Fig. 115, adjacent to the site of the old one. By the time the chicks are old enough to jump over the boards, they may be allowed to wander about with their mother, after the morning dew is off. After that time, three feedings a day are sufficient, and when they are weaned, feeding at morning and night only is enough. With a good range over wheat stubble, which they can have in the Western States and territories, and plenty of grasshoppers, no other feeding is necessary after they are educated to come home to roost.

Mr. Barber writes: "Our turkeys lay and sit in large, roomy coops, two and one-half feet long by two feet wide, two feet high in front, with a slope of six inches to the rear; we keep the turkey hens, with their broods, in a lot, on short grass."

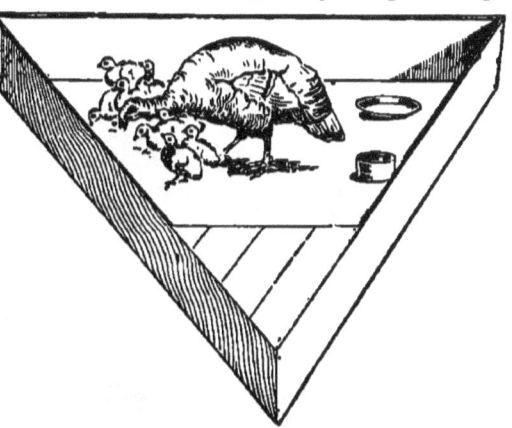

FIG. 115. PEN TO CONFINE LITTLE TURKEYS, UNTIL OLD ENOUGH TO JUMP OVER; MOTHER AT LIBERTY.

Instead of cooping brooding turkeys to prevent them from roaming too much, W. P. Lewis, who raises 90 per cent of his hatch, fastens the hen with a cord to a peg in the ground, after the manner cows are tied out to pasture. After being pegged down for a few days, the hens are "shingled," so they cannot fly over walls and fences, and are then allowed free range. In "shingling," or "boarding," turkeys, a thin board or shingle, in which holes are bored, is fastened across the shoulders of the bird by soft cords, tape or strips of cloth. When of the proper shape and the boards are in the right

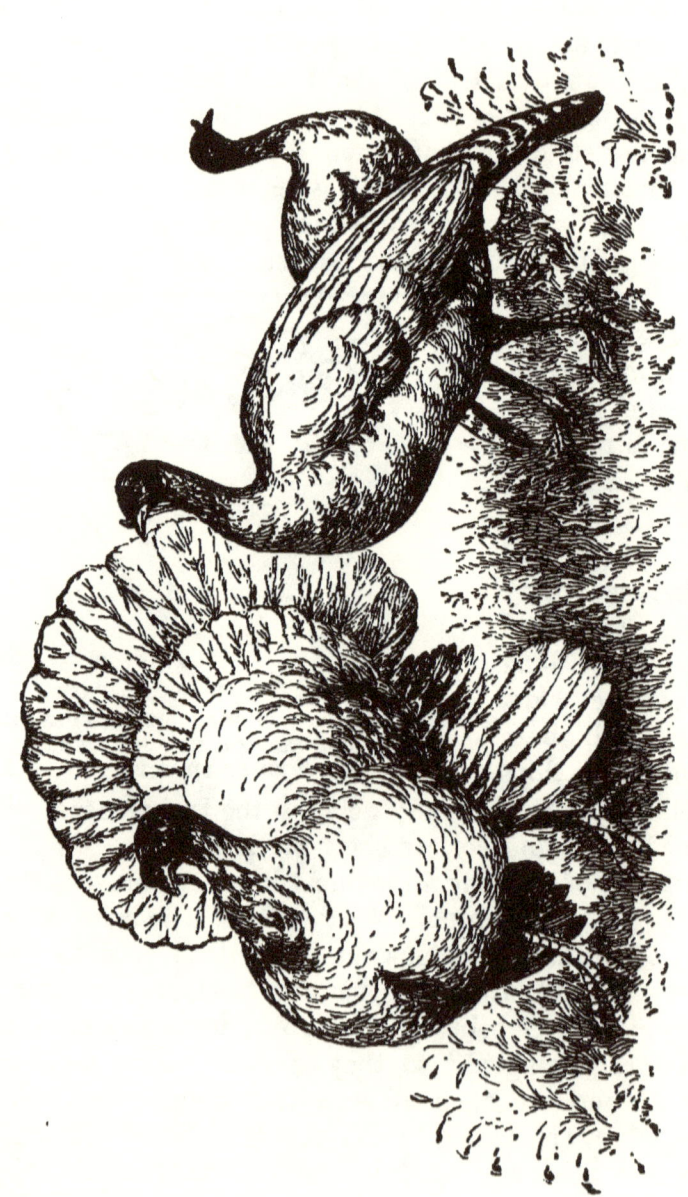

FIG. 116. WHITE HOLLAND TURKEYS.

place, and the cords are not tied too tightly, they may be worn twelve months without injury to the turkey. By this method the birds may be confined to one field as easily as sheep. This is better and surer than clipping one wing. The only objection to it is that turkeys thus hampered are almost at the mercy of dogs. When the board is first adjusted, the turkeys try to free themselves, but they usually accept the situation in less than an hour, and do not seem to mind them afterward. The strings are usually tied on the top of the board. In fastening

FIG. 117. COOP FOR BROODING TURKEY, WHILE THE CHICKS ARE AT LIBERTY.

the common style of board, the string is passed down from one hole in front of the wing, close to the body, and around under the wing and up through the other hole, and is tied on top of the board. An ordinary shingle is strong enough for most hens, but large gobblers require something stronger, and light barrel staves are often used; a three-eighths-inch auger hole is then necessary, but usually a gimlet is sufficient.

The young chicks must have green food. If they cannot obtain plenty of grass, give chopped lettuce, dandelions, onion tops (these last sparingly), turnip tops, etc. Buckwheat, cracked corn and wheat may be given at night, after they get large enough. Do not leave food around. Feed each time only so much as will be eaten up clean. After the first two weeks give sour milk freely. After they can get insects, no other meat than the milk will be necessary. The particular enemies of the young turkeys are lice and diarrhœa, but both may be conquered.

During the feathering period, the chicks must have plenty of bone- and feather-forming material. This is supplied best in the form of finely chopped meat and green bones. A good bone mill or cutter is indispensable when much poultry is kept. See that they have grit, in the form of pounded crockery, oyster shells and clean gravel. The best thing I ever used was small sea shells from the sea coast of Connecticut. They cost about a dollar per barrel.

FIG. 118. SHED FOR SHELTERING LITTLE TURKEYS AT NIGHT.

In addition to the foregoing, the following hints brought out by the most careful inquiry by the Rhode Island Experiment Station, of the methods pursued by the best turkey specialists in that State, are of interest: Little turkeys do best if kept and fed separate from fowls and chickens. They are weak and tender creatures, and as they grow very fast, require an abundance of nutritive and easily digested food, but it must not be too concentrated. Too rich food, too much food that is hard to digest, or a lack of green food, will cause bowel trouble. Little turkeys require food oftener than little chickens. Feed little and often. Give cooked food until they grow enough to develop the red about the head, or green food, like chopped onions and lettuce, if they are confined to a pen. Remember that little chickens thrive under confinement that would cause disease and death among little turkeys. If the little turkeys are cooped, remove them to fresh, dry ground frequently. Dampness, lice and filth make short work of them. Give them their food on clean surfaces.

Young turkeys should not be out in heavy showers until their backs are well covered with feathers. If they get wet, they may die from chill, unless put in a warm room to dry. Black and red pepper and ginger in the food or drinking water aid them to overcome a chill, and are of great value on cold or damp days, and are a preventive of bowel trouble in both old and young turkeys. Some find that young turkeys do best when neither they nor the hen is confined, providing they are put in a pasture lot, high and dry, where the grass is short and there are no trees. No more than three litters are cooped in a five-acre lot.

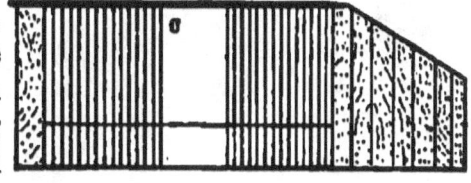

FIG. 119. SHED FOR SHELTERING LITTLE TURKEYS AT NIGHT.

At the Rhode Island Station it was found that confining the little turkeys at night prevents their being entangled and lost in the long, wet grass, but it is detrimental to their welfare and should not be continued too long. If possible, they should have full liberty where the grass is short. Their nature is such that they need cold air and a great deal of exercise. Restriction of liberty, with light feeding, soon puts them out of condition; while full feeding, even with liberty, prevents their taking full exercise, and causes disease of the digestive organs, and they are lost or do not thrive.

FIG. 120. BLACK TURKEYS.

If the young birds have done well at six or eight weeks, they begin to "throw the red," as it is termed, viz.: To develop the red carunculous formation about the head and neck, so characteristic of the turkey. If the turkey chicks be late hatched or weakly, it is retarded sometimes another month. Should the growth, from whatever cause, be checked when young, they will never make large and vigorous birds. After they have "thrown the red," the sexes can be distinguished, and they are then termed poults. They should not be allowed to perch too early, but bedded down upon chaff, leaves, etc., or they will have crooked breasts. Later on, the fleshy appendage over the beak, and the billy or horsehair-like tuft on the breast, make their appearance in the male birds, which, with tail erected and outspread, and with the whole body inflated with pomp, can be easily distinguished from their more somber sisters. At the time of "throwing the red," the young turkeys pass through their chicken molt, another critical period in their life. The birds lose their appetite and languish several days. They require now more stimulating food and a larger meat diet. Being insectivorous, the best range young turkeys can have is among shrubbery, bushes and such like. If the weather be open and fine, and the birds have a little extra care for a short time, they become as hardy, as adults, as they were delicate when young.

MARKING TURKEYS FOR IDENTIFICATION.

SAMUEL CUSHMAN.

As previously stated, turkeys do not thrive unless allowed free range. If enclosed in a large park by woven wire fence, or kept on an island, they can be controlled, but when given full liberty they roam over adjoining farms. In a neighborhood where many keep them, the different flocks are liable to meet, run together and get

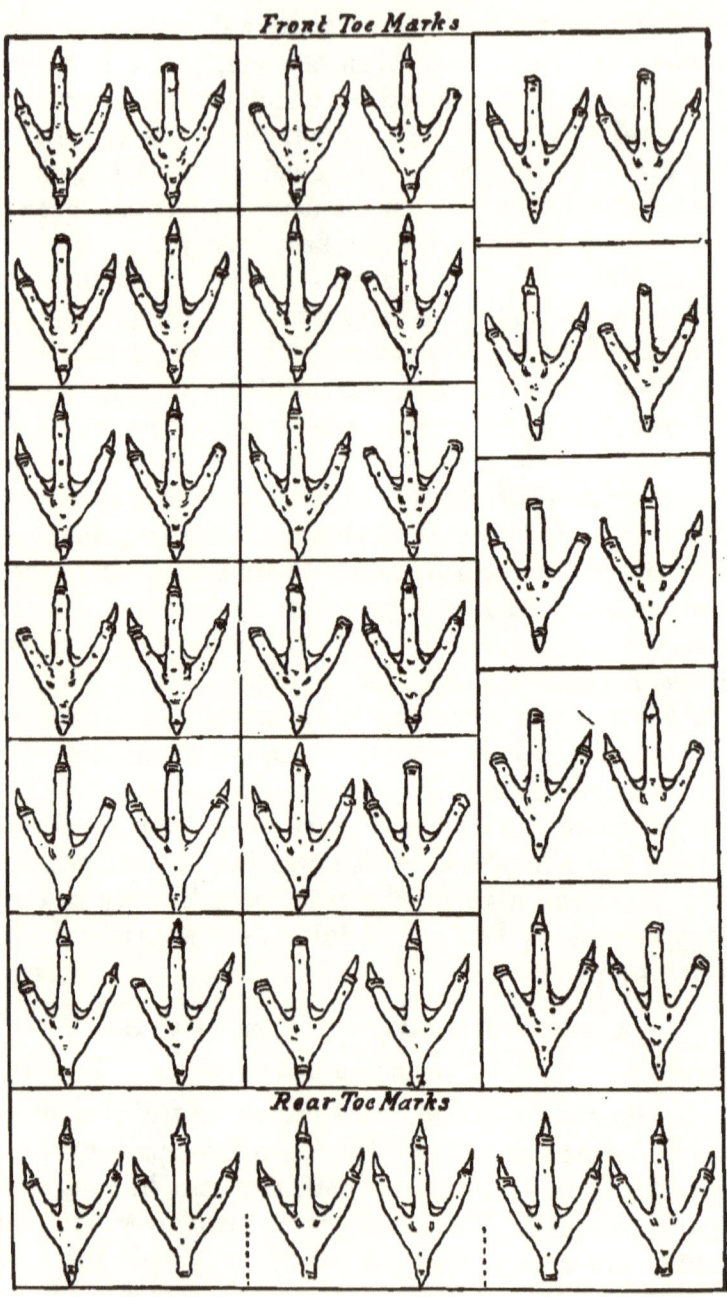

FIG. 121. SUGGESTIONS FOR MARKING TURKEYS BY THEIR FEET.

pretty well mixed. If not separated immediately, they may roost together, and roam as one flock the rest of the season. The first night a flock fails to return to its home roost, it should be looked up, separated from the other flocks and driven home. To do this is comparatively easy if immediately attended to, but each day they run together makes their separation more difficult.

To readily distinguish their own birds, many raisers try to have turkeys of a different color from any of those of their neighbors. By breeding for several seasons from a gobbler of a breed different from those kept near by, the flock takes on characteristics of its own, and each individual is readily distinguished. The White, Buff, Slate and Red or Golden varieties are valued principally for such use by growers. An additional advantage is gained, because first crosses between pure breeds are much more hardy, and some combinations are much larger. The grading up of common stock by the repeated use of males of a pure breed also improves its profitable qualities.

This means of identifying a flock is an excellent one, but is not sufficient for all purposes, for it is often desirable to distinguish the birds of a flock from each other, the stock raised one year from that of another, or that of a favorite hen or gobbler. Your turkeys may be lost among similar colored birds, or they may be captured by thieves, and dressed before you get a clue to them. If you have a private mark you can tell them, dead or alive. A private brand is desirable, for many reasons.

In turkey-raising sections, where there is a flock on nearly every farm, a system of marking their feet is followed. This is done by clipping off one or more of their nails, or tips of their toes, as soon as the little turkeys are hatched. At this age they take very little notice of the operation, and there is little or no bleeding.

Each raiser has a different mark, and in some towns these are registered at the town clerk's office, the same as the brands of sheep or cattle. As a turkey has three front and one back toes on each foot, or eight toes altogether, many different brands may be made by clipping the different toes. Fig. 121 shows some of them.

Six different marks may be made by clipping only one front toe. Nine more by clipping but two front toes. By clipping either the right or left back toe, the number may be doubled or trebled. By clipping more toes, combinations almost without number may be made, but it will be rarely necessary to remove more than one to two nails, even in a turkey-growing section.

Should mature turkeys thus marked be stolen and dressed, they may be identified, as the marks cannot be changed without showing the fresh mutilation. The marks of little turkeys may be changed without detection, provided sufficient time passes to allow them to heal before they are examined. The more toes you clip, the more difficult it is to change your marks.

Other marks, in addition to the foot marks, are sometimes necessary. The beak may be filed, holes punched in the skin or web of the wing, or a loop of colored silk fastened in the flesh where it cannot be seen. Although you may feel that such a precaution is not necessary in your case, probably if you follow this practice, you will at some time be very glad that you have done so.

PRIZE ESSAY ON TURKEY CULTURE.

MRS. A. J. SEXSON, FURNAS COUNTY, NEBRASKA.

The first requisite to successful turkey growing is carefully selected stock for parent birds. Selections of the best, for years, have produced the most improved and profitable breeds of stock. The future stock depends very much upon the parent birds, or their ancestry. Repeated breeding from inferior birds makes inferiority hereditary. After having faithfully tried the White, the Wild Black and the Mammoth Bronze turkeys, I prefer the latter for several reasons. They have proven hardier than the White, are equally strong, more gentle and more easily handled than the Black, less apt to roam far away and with proper care are ready for market at an earlier age than either of the other varieties, and I believe are less liable to disease. After complying with the first condition and having secured large, strong, parent turkeys, at least one year old, see that they are in the right condition for breeding.

Breeding fowls should not be overfat, as the offspring of such fowls are less vigorous. If the hens are young (late hatched) they require more food at breeding time, as they are still growing and immature. If hens are old they should have millet and clover, where it can be grown, and less carbonaceous food in the latter part of the season. Too much corn will produce overfat turkeys, unless they have abundant exercise in insect hunting and plenty of green food. When the laying season begins, usually in March, a watchful lookout for the eggs must be kept. It is natural for all turkeys to hide the nest, but petting will do much toward keeping them near the house. Each egg should be gathered as soon as laid and placed, small end down, on cotton or some soft material and kept in a dry, cool, dark place. If not used at once, they should be turned occasionally, to prevent settling or adhering to the shell. As the eggs are removed daily from the nest, it is better to return a hen's egg, until there are five or six in the nest, as a turkey is suspicious and easily discomfited. My turkeys lay entirely in the grove near the house and arrange their nests with skill themselves, my only task being to protect them from natural wild enemies. The nest should always be dry and large, and on the ground if possible. Fifteen eggs are sufficient for a large hen, and if small, thirteen will give better results. Four weeks, and often thirty days, are required to hatch the eggs. This makes a long period of rest for active Mrs. Turkey, yet she must be compelled to do her work faithfully, consequently should have easy access to an abundance of food and pure water, that she may not be forced to remain too long a time off the nest to procure food, thus allowing the eggs to chill.

CARE OF THE YOUNG.—About the twenty-seventh day I throw a hard-boiled egg, mashed very fine, close to the nest, not into, lest it adhere to an egg, rendering the egg air-tight exactly over the beak of the young turkey, which would prevent his escape from the shell. The mother turkey may eat this egg and the one given the following day or two, if it is not needed for her young, but in case she is hatching, she will use it for the little ones, and this food will often save the first-hatched birds. I have had the mother turkey refuse to leave the nest for three days after the first eggs hatched. If she leaves too soon, the remaining eggs may be placed under hens, or hatched by wrapping in wool and keeping warm near the fire. Should an egg become broken in the nest, the soiled eggs should be carefully washed immediately in warm, but not hot, water, and dried and returned at once to the nest. The trying time in the life of turkeys is the first week, when they require constant watching, then great care until they are eight weeks old, or until the quill feathers are well started. The producing of these feathers seems to weaken the fowl, and exhausts the system, and therefore they need especial treatment to counteract this difficulty.

For the first week, the mother and young must have a warm place, free from draughts of air, free from dampness, and where they will be undisturbed by other fowls.

The first three weeks the food should consist of sweet

milk (fresh from the cow is best), very hard-boiled eggs and fine wheat-bread crumbs for the little ones, wheat, corn and fresh water for the mother. Feed the mother first and she will not take much of the egg and bread, which is more expensive. During this time, if the weather be warm and sunshiny, let the mother out during the middle of the day, keeping her near the coop, taking care to shut her in before sunset, as the dew is harmful to the young turks. During the first week the little ones are apt to get onto their backs, from which position they cannot rise, and will die if allowed to thus lie for any length of time. Care must be taken not to place the pens near the hills of the small red or black ants, as these are enemies to young turkeys. They not only attack the head and kill the turkey, but if eaten, will almost instantly choke them to death.

The fourth week the food may consist of oatmeal, sour milk curd in small quantities, cracked wheat and scraps from the table, taking care that the scraps contain nothing salt. Salt, salt meat, brine or salt fish will kill them. After the eighth week, give mother and brood their freedom. Feed only in the morning, and this is not needful if they have access to grain fields.

If a turkey becomes sick, it should be isolated at once from the others, to prevent spread of the disease. Land over which diseased fowls wander will be contaminated and infect other flocks. Turkeys require plenty of pure water and must not be allowed to drink from stagnant pools, as this may produce bowel troubles. It is useless to doctor a very sick turkey—better to kill and bury deep at once. Prevention is better than cure, and if the following dose is given fortnightly, or even monthly, throughout the year, to either turkeys or chickens, there will be little necessity for cholera cure: Two ounces cayenne pepper, two ounces sulphur, two ounces alum and two ounces copperas. Mix all together and add two tablespoonfuls to eight quarts of corn meal, and wet the mixture with sweet milk or warm water. This will feed forty fowls.

One may profitably practice giving two broods of young turkeys to one mother when hatched at the same time, as one turkey can hover from twenty-five to thirty little ones during the critical period in their lives, after which they do not need much hovering. The other mother, after being closely confined out of sight and hearing of the little ones for one week, will quickly mate and lay again. This is very practicable and desirable when the first broods are hatched in May, or earlier, as the second hatchings are often the best, only a little later ready for market.

THE RHODE ISLAND SYSTEM.

Of late years Prudence Island has been one of the leading turkey-producing sections. Over 800 turkeys were raised there in 1892. George Tucker raises the largest number, and probably produces more turkeys than anyone in Rhode Island. In 1888 he raised 225 turkeys from 22 hens; in 1889, 306 from 28 hens; in 1890, 340 from 30 hens; in 1891, 322 from 36 hens, and in 1892, 425 from 35 hens. Previous to 1888 he had only average success, but since that time, owing to an improvement in his management, he has had but very little loss. He credits his present success to having gained a clearer understanding of the requirements of turkeys, as well as to having procured from Connecticut a very fine gobbler, by means of which he increased the hardiness of his flock. He has since been more careful in selecting new blood.

He found that young turkeys that were kept near the house or under the trees in the orchard, did not thrive; many had swelled heads and soon died. On the other hand, those placed on the highest and dryest pastures,

FIG. 122. PART WILD BLOOD BRONZE TURKEY.

This bird, Eureka, was from a thoroughbred Bronze hen, while his sire had one-fourth wild blood. At sixteen months he weighed thirty-six pounds, and at twenty-eight months tipped the scales at forty-eight and one-half pounds, winning first prize both years at New England and York State poultry shows. The accession of wild blood only three removes back, even if it added nothing to the great weight of this bird, unquestionably contributed to its vitality and the brilliancy of its plumage.

where there were no trees and but a light growth of grass, did the best of all. He usually winters from twenty to thirty-five hen turkeys and two gobblers. One gobbler is sufficient, but the second is kept in case one should die or fail in any way. The gobblers weigh from thirty to thirty-five pounds and usually are kept two seasons, and the hens two or three seasons, old hens being the surest breeders. They roost out in the trees the year through, and but few are lost. In the spring a sufficient number of nests are made for the hens by placing barrels by the walls and fences near the house and barns, or by laying wide boards against the walls. In them is placed leaves or cut straw. The turkeys readily take possession of these nests, although some persist in seeking out one of their own. This is usually allowed, unless a swampy location, or one too far away, is chosen, when the nest is broken up and the hen induced to choose another.

Sometimes several lay in the same nest. To prevent this, a nest in which a turkey has commenced to lay is, after she has deposited her egg, shut up for the remainder of the day, to keep out intruders. When the crows eat eggs laid in the nests that are far from the house, they are frightened away by strings stretched across near the nest. Glass nest eggs are used. Eggs are gathered daily, to prevent their being chilled, and that rats may not get them. They are kept in pans, having a few oats in the bottom to prevent their rolling about. Each panful holds two sittings, and is dated, that their age may be known. When a hen stays on the nest for two nights, seventeen of the oldest eggs are given her; the eggs laid by her during the two days are not left in the nest. The nests are first shaped, so that they will not be so flat as to allow the eggs to roll out, or so deep as to cause them to be piled one upon another. The turkeys seem to do better if not fed while sitting. Those occupying nests

TURKEYS ON THE FARM. 313

FIG. 123. THE PRIZE BRONZE TURKEY.

This bird won the grand prize offered by the New York fanciers' club some years ago. He was two years old, weighed forty-five pounds, and was bred by Sherman Hartwell, of Connecticut. With seven fine hens, he was bought by William Simpson, and exhibited at numerous poultry shows in England, capturing prizes in every case, and proving superior to any English-bred turkeys. The fine picture we present is from an instantaneous photograph by Smalls, taken for the *American Agriculturist*, and drawn by Keeler.

near together are looked after daily, to see that they return to their own nests.

Mr. Tucker at first experienced some trouble in having turkeys come off with a few young, those late in hatching being left to their fate. This was partly overcome by setting eggs of the same age. By feeding hens with dough when the eggs are due to hatch, they are also contented to stay on the nest longer. When the turkeys are a couple of days old and seem quite strong, they are placed in a basket, and, with the hen, removed to a remote part of the farm. Triangular pens, made of three boards, twelve feet long and one foot high, are placed in the fields, where it is intended the flocks shall stay until nearly grown. They are not located near together, lest the different flocks attract each other's attention. But four or five of the pens are put in a twenty-acre field. The little turkeys or poults are put in one of these pens with some dough, and the hen is gently placed beside them. In releasing the hen, Mr. Tucker takes pains to step quickly back toward the wind, that, if frightened, she may go in a direction in which the cries of her young may be heard and bring her to them. The pens are removed to fresh ground frequently. Care is taken that the pens are placed on ground free from hollows that may hold water, for some turkeys, when hovering their brood in such places, will remain in them while they fill with rain and the brood is drowned. After five or six days, when the young are strong enough to follow the hen without being worn-out, and have become so familiar with the attendant that they will come when called, they are let out of the pens and allowed free range.

In feeding and looking after this number of turkeys, the attendant, usually one of Mr. Tucker's daughters, has to walk about three miles to go the rounds. Until four weeks old their food consists of corn meal mixed with sour milk, and they are given sour milk to drink, no water being given them. When four weeks old, cracked corn is mixed with the meal, and the quantity is gradually increased, until at eight or ten weeks old their feed consists of cracked corn moistened with sour milk. Until June 1st they are fed three times each day. From June 1st to July 15th they are fed twice a day. After this Mr. Tucker used to give them no feed until they commenced to come to the house, in the latter part of September, when a little whole corn was given them daily, but of late years, he has thought they did not get enough without it and has continued the feed the whole season.

In November they are given all the corn they will eat. They like northern white flint corn the best, fatten most rapidly on it, and the quality of the flesh is also finer when it is given. If fed new corn, they have bowel trouble. Mr. Tucker usually gives old and new corn mixed, for fattening. When the young turkeys get to be the size of quails, two hens and their flocks usually join forces and roam together until fall. In the fall the sexes separate, the gobblers going together in one flock, and the hens in another. About Thanksgiving, the litters hatched in the latter half of May weigh, gobblers eighteen to twenty pounds, and hens ten to eleven pounds each. Mr. Tucker does not care to raise second litters. When he has them, it is because the hens have stolen their nests. He has considerable loss among late turkeys, and if such birds are kept over winter they get sick more readily, and as disease spreads very quickly among turkeys, he looks upon them as disease breeders.

The turkeys of the early litters that are lost generally die during the first week, or in August, when two or three months old. There are no foxes, weasels or skunks on the island. Mr. Tucker prefers birds with short legs, as they have the plumpest bodies. His turkeys are a mixture. Many are of a light gray color, similar to Narragansett turkeys. There are also buff, brown and dark ones. He prefers the brown and gray to the black, as they look better when dressed. He finds medium weights sell best except at **Thanksgiving, Christmas** or **New Year's.**

CHAPTER XXVII.

DISEASES AND PESTS.

BY JAMES RANKIN, WITH ADDITIONS BY THE EDITOR.

ROUP.—This is a disease very prevalent among fowls, and in its incipient stages sometimes makes its appearance in the form of a cold or slight catarrh. These troubles, if taken in time, are easily removed, but, if neglected, often result in serious loss.

When fowls are confined in damp, filthy quarters, or when cold drafts of air come in contact with the fowls, or when they are kept in poorly ventilated buildings, roup is a frequent visitor (See Fig. 109).

As this disease is very contagious, and often fatal, the affected fowl should be removed at once and placed in dry, warm quarters. The dried mucous should be removed from the nostrils; the passage to the roof of the mouth thoroughly cleaned; the head and throat bathed in kerosene twice each day. The bird should be fed on stimulating and highly nutritious food. In the latter stages of the disease, the discharges from the nostrils become very offensive, the head begins to swell, and sometimes one eye and occasionally both are closed.

All this can usually be prevented if the birds are taken in time, but when in this condition must be fed by hand, with soft food mixed thin with milk and a little red pepper dusted in. Unless a fowl is very valuable the axe is the best remedy.

The severity of roup varies from that of a mere cold in the head, to cases which are like diphtheria in human beings. In fact, there is doubtless more than one disease, but all are commonly known as roup. While some forms are easily cured, others are often fatal. But whether it be called roup, or distemper, or influenza, or fowl diphtheria, the symptoms, in a general way, are similar, likewise the treatment. It is claimed by some that the diphtheritic form of roup can be given to human beings, and it is well to use care in handling the sick fowls, and to keep them away from children.

Dr. V. A. Moore, of the U. S. Department of Agriculture, recommends the following mode of prevention and treatment:

(1) Fowls which have a discharge on any of the mucous membranes of the head, or which have come from flocks in which such a disease exists or has recently existed, should not be introduced among other poultry.

(2) If the disease appears in one or more fowls of a flock, they should be immediately separated from the well ones. If possible, the source of the infection should be determined and removed.

(3) The quite common practice of allowing fowls from different flocks to run together during the day should be discouraged.

(4) Care should be taken to avoid the possibility of bringing the poison of the disease from affected flocks, in the dirt or excrement which naturally adheres to the shoes in walking through an infected chicken yard. The same care is necessary in the interchange of working implements, such as shovels, hoes, etc.

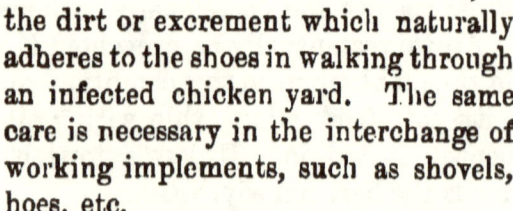

FIG. 124. APPLYING MEDICINE FOR ROUP.

It is evident to any careful observer that the fact is too often overlooked that fowls, owing to their method of living, are more liable to infection than other farm animals. This is especially true when they are allowed to run at random, as they too frequently are, picking their living from the garbage pile and barnyards, or securing even more unwholesome food.

There is little doubt that many so-called outbreaks of contagious disease among fowls are brought about by improper care. The efficiency of these few suggestions in reference to the prevention of this disease, is demonstrated by the success of certain poultry raisers who adhere strictly to the teachings of sanitary methods.

The wide distribution, the large number of fowls affected, and the usual chronic course of this disease render it one of the few poultry affections for which curative measures promise to be of practical value. Although prevention is the safest of cures, when the disease is once introduced as it is in a very large number of flocks, the necessity for remedial treatment is apparent, and where economy is to be considered should be recommended. The practice sometimes followed of destroying all of the affected birds should be discouraged. Although experiments have not been made to test the efficiency of remedies already recommended, or to investigate the practicability of others, the testimony of many practical poultry raisers is, as previously stated, to the effect that the disease is amenable to treatment.

The most certain of the known methods of treatment is the local application of certain disinfectants, among which a weak solution of carbolic acid appears to be the most satisfactory. The fact that the lesions are so much exposed renders the disease especially favorable for local applications. The administration of mild stimulants has also been recommended. In addition to the medicinal treatment, it is of much importance that the affected fowls be provided with proper food and kept in dry, warm, and well-ventilated apartments.

If the disease has reached its third stage, it is frequently necessary to remove the sloughed exudate before the disinfectant is applied.

The following, recommended by another authority, will be found to be excellent treatment for all stages of the disease, combined with nutritious, soft food:

Pills.—Sulphate of copper, half grain; cayenne pepper, one grain; hydrastine, half grain; copaiba, three drops; Venetian turpentine, quarter section. 1n pill night and morning.

Lotion.—Sulphate of copper, quarter ounce, dissolved in a pint of rain water. To wash out the mouth and nostrils, if required.

CRAMP, though usually attributed to damp quarters, is mainly the result of too highly concentrated food, coupled with too little exercise. Who ever saw chicks troubled with cramp when allowed to run out of doors, even in warm rain and dew, so long as they had plenty of grass and insects for dessert, and plenty of exercise to stimulate action in their digestive organs?

On the contrary, I was once called to a case where a man had just lost two hundred fine chicks from this trouble, and three hundred more a little younger were just coming down with it, and this in a building the floor of which was made of dry boards on which had been spread an inch of dry sand. A uniform temperature of 70° had been preserved in the room night and day. These chicks had been carefully shielded from dampness. This was in March.

I told him to clear away the snow from his building, in front, turn his chicks out when pleasant, give them plenty of boiled potatoes, chopped cabbage, feed on bread crumbs and baker's dust mixed with sour milk, with a little animal food, and report the result to me. At the end of a fortnight a letter from him reported two of the cases dead and the rest as lively as crickets, every symptom of the disease having disappeared.

BUMBLE-FOOT usually confines itself to the Asiatics and heavier breeds. When it first appears, the bird should be removed to dry quarters, with clean straw. The skin over the inflamed part should be shaved away a little, and caustic applied, which will nearly reduce the swelling. If that fails and the swelling becomes large, soft, and full of pus, it should be opened the pus removed and the wound thoroughly washed out with warm water, when it will usually heal.

SCALY LEGS.—Scabby leg, leg rot, scaly leg, elephantiasis, and bumble-foot. This well-known disease, under its various names, is also due to a mite, the *Sarcoptes mutans*. This mite affects most birds, and has been known for some considerable time. The creature apparently only affects the legs of birds, the similar disease of the head being due in all cases to a fungoid pest.

The diseased limbs become covered with rough, lumpy crusts, which can be removed with a blunt knife, but unless the limb is moistened with soft soap and warm water, the removal leads to violent bleeding, which should be avoided.

FIG. 125. BAD CASE OF SCALY LEG.

This sarcoptic mite lives and breeds under the scales of the feet and legs, gradually raising them up and forming beneath them a white, powdery mass. The crusts formed are generally hollow, and contain a spongy mass internally, in the lower parts of which are to be found the pests in all stages.

FIG. 126. MITE WHICH CAUSES SCABBY LEG (magnified).

They sometimes produce such violent inflammation and disease that the toe or affected parts drop off. The disease grows very slowly, some birds living over a year, but if neglected, leads to emaciation and death. The disease is contagious, but not severely. If fowls have plenty of run they are less liable to contract these sarcoptic diseases than when kept in confined spaces. Dorkings seem comparatively free from this disease. Houdans and Cochins seem very liable to it. The diseased growth may readily be mistaken for the deformities seen on birds' wattles, but the cause is quite distinct. They both, however, yield to the same treatment. Several cases of so-called "Bumble-Foot" that I have examined, were due to the work of the mite, but others contained no traces of sarcoptes.

Prevention and Remedies.—Isolation of patients and disinfection of runs is most essential. Removal of crusts without causing bleeding, and then the application of either creosote (one part) and lard (twenty parts), or balsam of Peru, will be found sufficient. Oil of turpentine has still more definite results, I find, but the dressed limbs must afterward be treated with sweet oil, to allay subsequent irritation.

GAPES.—This disease is caused by small red worms accumulating in the throat of the chick, and the disease is usually a denizen of damp, filthy quarters. The first thing is to thoroughly clean and disinfect the buildings and yards. Put the affected chicks into barrels and circulate dry air-slaked lime freely among them. Inhaling this will cause them to cough and throw up the worms. Gapes may be prevented by rubbing the neck with one part turpentine thoroughly mixed with three parts lard.

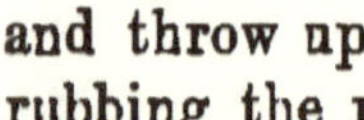

FIG. 127. GAPE WORM (male and female) NATURAL SIZE.

Entomologist McCarthy, of the North Carolina Experiment Station, recommends boiling salt water sprinkled on the ground as a disinfectant, and a teaspoonful of turpentine and one of asafœtida in warm bran mash for each twenty-five birds. A pill of camphor, the size of a wheat grain, pushed down the throat, often gives good results. One-third ounce of salicylic acid should be added to each quart of the fowls' drinking water. By the fumigation treatment, the sick birds are shut in a large dry goods box, in which is burned a mixture of equal parts of turpentine, sulphur and pine tar. After a quarter of an hour, or as soon as the fowls begin to be overcome by the fumes, take them into the open air.

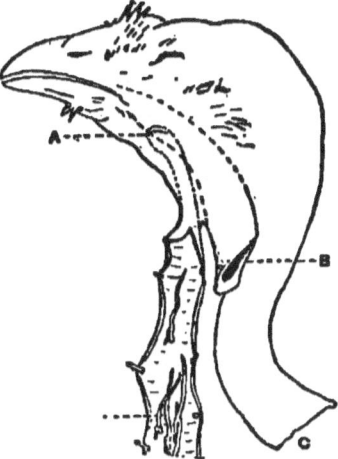

FIG. 128. CHICK WITH GAPES, the trachea pinned open. A, the glottis or opening through which air enters the trachea from the mouth; B, the cut end of the œsophagus; C, the cut neck.

FEATHER-EATING is more an idle, vicious habit than a disease, superinduced by idleness and close confinement, or possibly a craving for animal food. Separate the offending bird, or the feather-eating will become general. Rub the feathers near the picked places with powdered aloes mixed with lard.

DIARRHŒA.—Dust a little powdered chalk and cayenne pepper into boiled milk, feed on soft food, and withhold vegetables for a few days.

Whenever a fowl hangs its wings, and looks drooping, let it be seen to at once, whether it appears purged, and if so, give immediately, in a teaspoonful of warm water, a teaspoonful of strong brandy or whisky saturated with camphor. Repeat this the next morning, and in most cases the disease will be checked; care being, of course, taken to give the invalid warmth and good shelter. The best food is warm barley meal, or rice meal mixed with lime water. If these measures do not promptly check the discharge, give the following powder, mixed up with a little meal: Take powdered chalk, 5 grains;

cayenne pepper, 2 grains; powdered rhubarb 5 grains. This scarcely ever fails when the case is not desperate.

TAPEWORMS.—Tapeworms are very common in poultry, and are sometimes so numerous as to close the passage, or cause diarrhœa, sluggishness and fits. Not only hens, but ducks, geese and turkeys are infected. The worms do come to the fowls directly from the egg, but the young of the tapeworms infest earthworms and other insects which are eaten by poultry. When swallowed by poultry, they develop into full growth. Young birds

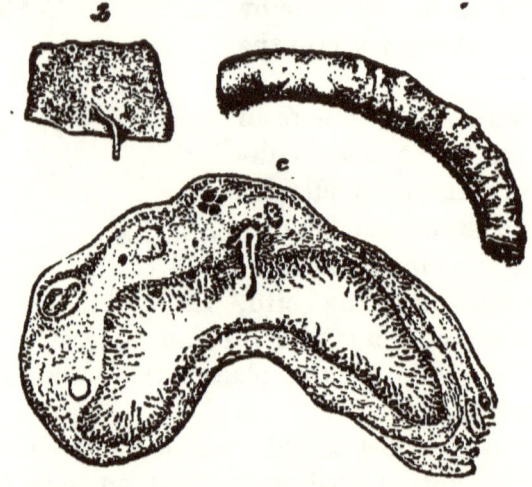

FIG. 129.

a, Piece of intestine of fowl, showing nodules, several small worms, and one large worm. b, Intestine, roughened by tapeworms. c, Interior of intestine, showing wall thickened by action of worms; also part of a worm which has penetrated the lining.

suffer more than old ones, and more in wet seasons than in dry. If numerous tapeworms are present in the intestine of young or old fowls, a more or less extensive intestinal catarrh develops, corresponding to the greater or less number of parasites present.

The intestinal catarrh shows itself, especially in chickens and geese, as follows: The sick animals become emaciated, although the appetite is not especially disturbed. At times the appetite is even increased. The droppings are thin, contain considerable yellow slime, and are passed in small quantities but at short intervals. The poultry raiser must direct his attention to these thin, slimy, and often bloody droppings, for if any treatment against the tapeworms is to be undertaken, this must be done as early as possible. In observing the droppings, it should be noticed whether tapeworm segments or eggs are present. The eggs can be seen, of course, only with the microscope. The birds become

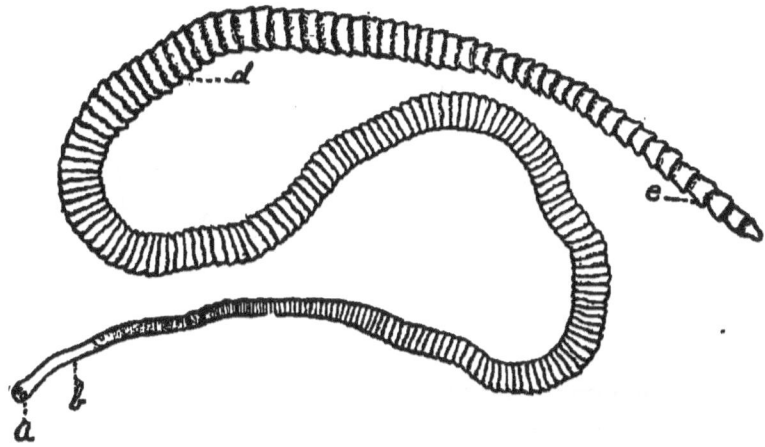

FIG. 130. TAPEWORM FROM A TURKEY.

listless and drooping, with ruffled feathers. An unusual desire for cold water is considered a symptom.

The best method for the farmer to follow is to kill one of the sick chickens, when he suspects tapeworms, and to cut out the intestine; he should then open the intestinal tract from the gizzard to the anus, in a bowl of warm water, and look for the tapeworms.

In the line of prevention, chickens will be less likely to become infected if not allowed to roam until the sun is well up and the ground dry. To prevent spread of the worms, destroy the manure of infected fowls, or use it where it can do no harm. Sulphuric acid and water, or quicklime, will destroy the eggs.

Treatment.—First, separate the fowls; second, destroy infected droppings. The chief drugs used against tapeworms are: Extract of male fern, turpentine, powdered kamala, areca nut, pomegranate root bark, pumpkin seeds and sulphate of copper (bluestone). According to Zürn, powdered areca nut is the best tapeworm remedy for fowls, but he calls attention to the fact that turkeys are unfavorably affected by this medicine. He advises the administration of powdered areca nut in doses of 2 to 3 grams (=30 to 45 grains), mixed with butter and made into pills.

Liquid extract of male fern is very effectual against tapeworms. Hutcheon advises a teaspoonful for young ostriches three to four months old, to a tablespoonful for a full-grown ostrich; it may be made into a pill with flour. The dose recommended by the department of agriculture is from one to three tablespoonfuls of turpentine, according to the size of the chicken.

The illustration, Fig. 129, shows a form of tapeworm disease sometimes mistaken for tuberculosis. The nodules in the intestines look like the tubercles of the other disease, but if the surface of the intestines is carefully washed the small worms can be seen.

CHOLERA is a terrible scourge—the worst with which the poultry grower has to contend. It not only decimates, but often destroys whole flocks. It is far more prevalent in the West and South than in the East and North. There is no doubt but that low, marshy grounds, and damp, filthy quarters, will encourage the disease and predispose fowls to its ravages. In careful experiments by Prof. Pasteur, of the London international medical college, it was found that the blood, body and excrements of the diseased fowl were filled with minute organisms. One drop of this blood introduced into a little chicken soup will speedily affect it in the same manner, and so on even to the hundredth departure, and one drop of the last dilution is equally as deadly as the original drop of blood from the diseased fowl.

The disease first makes its appearance in the urates, giving them a yellowish cast. These discharges, as the disease advances, gradually become more frequent and copious, and the bird becomes weaker, sometimes living several days, and often dying in twenty-four hours. Fowl cholera is not only the most fatal, but the most contagious of all poultry diseases.

Now, as every part of these excrements is filled with the microscopic life of the cholera, it will be seen how necessary it is to thoroughly clean and disinfect the building and confine the affected fowls by themselves.

In an experiment, some time since, a number of diseased fowls were confined by themselves, and fed on soft food into which was mixed a small quantity of medicine composed of equal parts of asafœtida, hypophosphate of soda and saffron, ground together, a little cayenne pepper being sprinkled in the food also. The drinking water was treated with the Douglas mixture. Three-fourths of the fowls thus treated recovered. In another lot, simply confined and fed without any treatment, the disease proved fatal in every case.

The great point is to avoid contagion. Deodorize everything in connection with the buildings, and have all infected matter burned. This alone will destroy the minute organism of fowl cholera.

BLACKHEAD OF TURKEYS.—An infectious disease of the intestines and liver, commonly known as blackhead of turkeys, has prevailed very extensively in Rhode Island, Massachusetts, Connecticut, and probably also in other turkey-raising districts, although the disease has been scientifically investigated in the New England sections only. The disease is caused by a small parasite, which first attacks the cæcum or pronged part of the lower bowel, causing it to become thickened, enlarged, and full of sores. Next, the liver becomes spotted, and covered with round, yellowish patches. Young turkeys are attacked. Many die in July and August and in the fall. The symptoms are, diarrhœa, roughened feathers, and purplish or "black" head. The disease spreads from one bird to another.

Dr. Theobald Smith, of the U. S. Bureau of animal industry, recommends the disinfection of the coops and other structures designed to give shelter to turkeys. The following disinfectants are strong enough to kill spores of bacteria:

(a) Corrosive sublimate (mercuric chloride), one ounce in about eight gallons of water (one-tenth of one per cent). The water should be put into wooden tubs or barrels, and the powdered sublimate added to it. The whole must be allowed to stand for twenty-four hours, so as to give the sublimate an opportunity to become entirely dissolved. Since this solution is poisonous, it should be kept covered up and well guarded. It may be applied with a broom or mop, and used freely on all woodwork. Since it loses its virtue in proportion to the amount of dirt present, all manure and other dirt should be first removed before applying the disinfectant. The manure should be covered with lime.

(b) Chloride of lime, five ounces to a gallon of water (four per cent). This should be applied in the same way.

(c) The following disinfectant is very serviceable. It is not poisonous, but quite corrosive, and care should be taken to protect the eyes and hands from accidental splashing: Crude carbolic acid, one-half gallon; crude sulphuric acid, one-half gallon.

These two substances should be mixed in tubs or glass vessels. The sulphuric acid is very slowly added to the carbolic acid. During the mixing a large amount of heat is developed. The disinfecting power of the mixture is heightened if the amount of heat is kept down

DISEASES AND PESTS.

by placing the tub or glass demijohn containing the carbolic acid in cold water while the sulphuric acid is being added. The resulting mixture is added to water in the ratio of one to twenty. One gallon of mixed acids will thus furnish twenty gallons of a strong disinfecting solution, having a slightly milky appearance.

(*d*) Ordinary slaked lime, though it does not possess the disinfecting power of the substances given above, is nevertheless very useful, and should be used more particularly on infected soil.

LICE AND MITES.—These pests are a great trouble to the poultry grower, and need incessant vigilance on his part. There are two kinds of lice with which he has to contend. The larger, or body, lice find their home among the feathers of the fowl. She will usually rid herself of them when provided with a proper dust bath. The smaller parasite, or the little red mite, is the most troublesome.

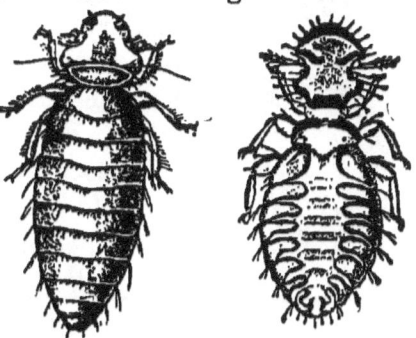

FIG. 131. COMMON KINDS OF HEN LICE.
N. Pallidum.   *G. Abdominalis.*

When once they have obtained possession, the only remedy is to fumigate thoroughly with burning brimstone. No living thing can withstand that. Then whitewash the whole inside of the building.

As in everything else, so here, a little prevention is worth a great deal of cure. These little mites originate on the perches, and are never on the fowl's body except to feed. Judging from sad experience, they have astonishing facilities for the reproduction of their species.

It is easy to avoid the red mites when you know how. Procure for perches planed spruce joists, two by three inches in size, and as long as required. Cover them with hot coal tar, and you will have no lice for at least one year. I have perches that were so painted three years ago; they have been in constant use ever since, and there has been neither tar nor lice on them since. Every one knows that this tar is an odoriferous compound. It is excessively obnoxious to the lice. Kerosene or diluted carbolic acid applied to the roosts and crevices is a good remedy.

An insect which almost makes life a burden to the southern poultry keeper is the nest bug, a near relative of the bed bug. It commonly infests nests, and will often compel sitting hens to leave their eggs. As will be seen by the smaller illustration, it is an insect of considerable size. The treatment is the same as for the small ticks, or mites. Kerosene is a good remedy, also insect powder and tobacco dust. Burn old nests.

FIG. 132. NEST BUG.
An insect very troublesome in the South. Natural size and magnified.

The lice may be found, by careful examination, especially about the head and neck and under the joints of wings and legs. Whenever a fowl appears out of sorts, it is safe to suspect lice. A great deal of apparent sickness is merely lice. Young chickens are most dangerously affected. They mope about, will not eat, bodies are small, thin and stunted, they peep a great deal, sometimes lose their feathers, or waste away and die. Large lice on the head or throat often cause the apparently mysterious death of chicks. They hide at the base of the feathers, and are not easily seen. Most chicks raised by hens are somewhat infested. A single big head louse is enough to make trouble for a chick.

Mr. E. W. Parker, writing in one of the poultry papers, gives a good idea of how indifferent one may be.

He says: "In July and August especially (but at all times of the year) lice abound more than at any other time, and chicks will become infested with them unless great care is taken. Many persons wonder why their young chicks droop and die, mope around for a week or two, all the time getting thinner and weaker, finally become unable to stand, and die—these persons claiming all the time that 'lice is not the cause of it,' because they have searched under the wing for the red or yellow

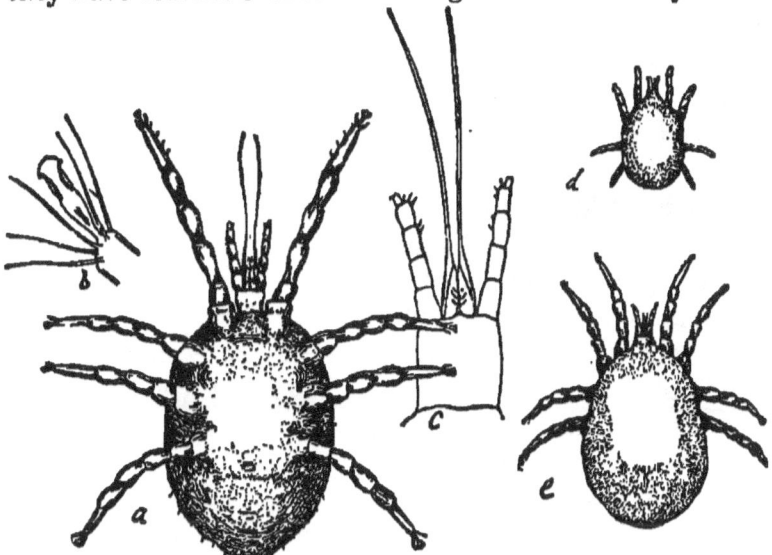

FIG. 133. THE TICK, MITE, OR SPIDER LOUSE.
a, Adult; *b*, tarsus; *c*, mouth parts; *d* and *e*, young—all enlarged.

louse, or the head for the large head louse, and in fact have looked them from top to bottom for parasites and have found none. I wonder if they have ever looked on the throat, or at the side below the ears, for the large head louse. I wonder if it entered into the brain of such breeders that the head louse could destroy the life of chicks from two to six weeks old by sucking the life-blood from the throat and under the head. If it has not, I can tell them that such is the case, and I say without fear of contradiction that when the chick appears weak, growing weaker and thinner, the skin seems to shrink upon the body, and there is a slimy discharge from the body, and when the chick eats it is usually with difficulty, and as the supposed disease advances it seems almost impossible for the chick to swallow, finally refusing to eat. When any or all of these symptoms appear, then examine the under part of the head and the throat and at the sides for the head louse, and nine times out of ten he will be found snugly at home among the down or sprouting feathers; then apply two-thirds glycerine, one-third carbolic acid, and five times as much water as the above mixture."

A few general measures will answer for all kinds of lice. To smoke them out is a very thorough way, if the house is tight enough to hold the fumes. Where the house can be made tight an excellent plan is to fumigate it with pure carbon bisulphide once every two months. This is done by simply pouring the bisulphide into an open saucer, using about one pound for each one thousand cubic feet of space in the house. Close the house tightly, and leave for at least twelve hours. Bisulphide of carbon is very explosive, and must not be brought near a fire or light. It is very sure, and will kill any insect. Besides sulphur, already mentioned, tobacco stems are very commonly used for smoking. The smoke must be very dense, and should remain in the house at least twelve hours. If the first smoking does not kill all, repeat the operation. Another good way is to drench the roosts with kerosene or hot water, followed by whitewashing, and the use of tar on the ends of the poles and wherever they come in contact with supports. The addition of four ounces of crude carbolic acid to the gallon of whitewash increases its efficiency for this purpose. Repeated applications may be necessary, but due attention to reaching all points to which the pests resort will keep the nuisance in check at least. For the red mites much the same treatment is needed as for common lice. Clear the house, then spray well with kerosene or kerosene emulsion, taking pains to reach the cracks; thoroughly drench the roosts with hot water or kerosene, benzine or gasoline, whitewash the house, or dust with carbolated lime, and then daub the ends of the roosts, where they come in contact with supports, with coal tar, so the mites will have to cross it to reach the fowls.

DOUGLAS'S TONIC POULTRY MIXTURE.—Take sulphate of iron, half a pound; sulphuric acid, 1 oz; pure soft water, 2 gallons. Mix, and give to the fowls by adding one teaspoonful to each pint of their drinking water.

PARRISH'S CHEMICAL FOOD (An English tonic).— Protosulphate of iron, 10 dr.; phosphate of soda, 12 dr.; phosphate of lime, 12 dr.; phosphoric acid, glacial, 20 dr.; carbonate of soda, 2 scruples; carbonate of potassa, 1 dr.; muriatic acid and water of ammonia, each a sufficient quantity; powdered cochineal, 2 dr.; water sufficient to make 20 fluid ounces; sugar, 3 lbs. troy; oil of orange, 10 minims.

CHOLERA DISINFECTANT MIXTURE.—Mix sulphuric acid, 8 ounces; pure soft water, 8 gallons. This dilute. Sulphuric acid is a good preparation whenever the houses or grounds need purifying after an infectious disease.

FIG. 134. TYPES OF FEATHERS.
1. Striped. 2. Laced. 3, 4. Spangled. 5. Pencilled. 6, 7, 8. Mottled.

CHAPTER XXVIII.

POULTRY DICTIONARY AND CALENDAR.

Beard—A bunch of feathers under the throat of som breeds, as Houdans.

Breed—Any variety of fowl presenting distinct characteristics.

Brood—Family of chickens cared for by one hen.

Broody—Desiring to sit or incubate.

Carriage—Bearing, attitude, or "style."

Carunculated—Covered with fleshy protuberances, as on the neck of a turkey cock.

Chick—A newly hatched fowl. Used only while but a few weeks old.

Chicken—This word is often applied to any age indefinitely until twelve months old.

Clutch—This term is applied both to the batch of eggs sat upon by the fowl, and also to the brood of chickens hatched therefrom.

Cockerel—A young cock.

Crop—The bag or receptacle in which food is stored before digestion. Can be easily felt in any fowl after feeding.

Cushion—The mass of feathers over the tail end of a hen's back, covering the tail; chiefly developed in Cochins.

Deaf-ears—The folds of skin hanging from the true ears; same as ear lobes. They vary in color, being blue, white, cream-colored or red.

Dubbing—Cutting off the comb, wattles, etc., so as to leave the head smooth and clean.

Ear lobes—Same as deaf-ears.

Face—The bare skin around the eye.

Flights—The primary feathers of the wing, used in flying, but tucked under the wing out of sight when at rest.

Fluff—Soft, downy feathers about the thighs, chiefly developed in Asiatics.

Furnished—Assumed the full characters. When a cockerel has obtained full tail, comb, hackles, etc., as if adult, he is said to be furnished.

Gills—This term is often applied to the wattles, and sometimes more indefinitely to the whole region of the throat.

Hackles—The peculiar narrow feathers on the neck of fowls, also found in the saddle of the cock. In the latter case they are called "saddle" hackles or feathers (See saddle below). Hackles used alone always refer to the neck feathers.

Hen-feathered, or henny—Resembling a hen in the absence of sickles, or hackle feathers, and in plumage generally.

Hock—The knee or elbow joint of the leg.

Keel—Sometimes used to denote breastbone.

Leg—In a live fowl this is the scaly part, or shank. In the bird dressed for the table, on the contrary, the term refers to the joints above.

Leg feathers—The feathers projecting from the outside of the shanks, in some breeds, as Cochins.

Mossy—Confused or indistinct in the markings.

Pea comb—A triple comb, resembling three small combs in one, the middle being highest.

Pencilling—Small markings or stripes over a feather. These may run either straight across, as in Hamburgs, or in a crescentic form, as in Partridge Cochins.

Poult—A young turkey.

Primaries—The flight feathers of the wings, hidden when the wing is closed, being tucked under the visible wing composed of the "secondary" feathers. Usually the primaries contain the deepest color all over the body, except the tail; great importance is attached to their color by breeders.

Pullet—A young hen. The term is not properly applicable after Dec. 31st of the year in which a bird is hatched, though often used during the early months of the next year.

Rooster—An American term for a cock.

Saddle—The posterior part of the back, reaching the tail, in a cock, answering to the cushion in a hen; often, however, applied to both sexes, cushion being more restricted to a great development, as in Cochins; "saddle" may be applied to any breed.

Secondaries—The quill feathers of the wing which show when the bird is at rest.

Self-color—A uniform tint over the feathers.

Shaft—The stem or quill of a feather.

Shank—The scaly part of the leg.

Sickles—The top curved feathers of a cock's tail. Properly only applied to the top pair, but sometimes used for one or two pairs below, which can hardly be called tail coverts.

Spangling—The marking produced by each feather having one large spot or slash of some color different from the ground.

Spur—The sharp, offensive weapon on the heel of a cock.

Squirrel-tailed—The tail projecting in front of a perpendicular line over the back.

Stag—Another name for a young cock, chiefly used by game fanciers.

Strain—A race of fowls which, having been carefully bred by one breeder or his successors for years, has acquired individual character of its own which can be more or less relied upon.

Symmetry—Perfection of proportion; often confounded with carriage, but quite distinct, as a bird may be nearly perfect in proportion, and yet "carry" himself awkwardly.

Tail coverts—The soft, glossy, curved feathers at the sides of the bottom of the tail, usually the same color as the tail itself.

Tail feathers—The straight and stiff feathers of the tail only. The top pair are sometimes slightly curved, but they are nearly always, if not quite, straight, and are contained inside the sickles and tail coverts.

Thighs—The joint above the shanks, the first joint clothed with feathers. The same as the drumstick in dressed fowls.

Topknot—Same as crest.

Trio—A cock or cockerel and two hens or pullets.

Under-color—The color of the plumage seen when the surface has been lifted. It chiefly depends on the down seen at root of every feather.

Vulture hocks—Stiff projecting feathers at the hock joint. The feathers must be both stiff and projecting to be thus truly called and condemned.

Wattles—The red depending structures on each side of the base of the beak. Chiefly developed in the male sex.

Web—This term is indefinite, expressing a flat and thin structure. The web of a feather is the flat or plume portion; the web of the foot, the flat skin between the toes; of the wing, the triangular skin seen when the member is extended.

Wing bar—Any line of dark color across the middle of the wing, caused by the color or marking of the feathers known as the lower wing coverts.

Wing bow—The upper or shoulder part of wing.

Wing butts—The corners or ends of the wing. The upper ends are more properly called the shoulder butts, and are thus termed by game fanciers. The lower, similarly, are called the lower butts.

Wing coverts—The broad feathers covering the roots of the secondary quills.

CALENDAR OF POULTRY WORK.

January.—Make poultry houses as warm and dry as possible, stopping cracks and crevices, taking care to prevent drafts on the birds at night. Fowls should have a warm feed all through the cold weather, at least once a day. Feed cut bone two or three times a week. Sort the birds closely, and don't keep any surplus. Study the mating, so that no time will be lost at breeding season. When whole grain is fed at night, it is well to warm it in the oven. Plenty of grit is important. Hang up cabbages for green food. Feed some meat and cut bone twice a week. Keep the incubators running for early broilers. Keep brooders in repair.

February.—Protection against cold is important this month, but the fowls should have exercise in an open shed attached to the house. A curtain should be attached, to be let down stormy days. Warm mash for breakfast, green bone and meat should be continued. Mating should be finished by this time. Select only the vigorous birds. Weaklings, however well marked, are useless in the breeding pen. Feed plenty of bone and meat to the breeders, and make them exercise, in order to secure fertile eggs. Droppings should not be allowed to collect more than a day or two. Keep the floor covered with litter. This is the worst month for roup, which can be prevented by dry, warm houses, with no drafts upon the fowls, especially at night.

March.—Feeding is much the same as during the preceding month, but rather less whole corn should be given. Feed more wheat instead. If the breeding pens have been made up at least four weeks before, eggs may now be set for early chicks. Chicks hatched the last of March will not usually molt before winter, and will be the best winter layers. Large breeds should be hatched early, to secure laying pullets before winter. Small breeds will do well enough, hatched the last of April. See that the hens are set properly on the nests, carefully made, and guard against lice on sitting hens. Watch the hens, to be sure they attend to business. Fix up the brooders and coops for the chickens. Lath fences for the fowls can be nailed together indoors in stormy weather.

April.—Feed the laying hens plenty of egg-making food, such as meat and cut bone. The early chicks should have increasing attention. Feed them often, but only what they will eat up clean. Supply with fresh water, fresh charcoal, fine, coarse grit or fresh sand. A good food for young chickens consists of one pound corn meal, one-half pound middlings, one and one-half pounds ground meat, two ounces bone meal and a very little salt, mixed with milk or water, and baked, then fed in crumbs every two hours. After the first week, three or four times a day will be often enough to feed, except when finishing for market. Hens which prove good mothers may be given two broods of the same age, joining the broods at night.

May.—The early chicks should be pushed with plenty of wholesome food and a good variety. They should be given some soft feed each day. Give them as free a range as possible. Cracked corn should be fed with care to very young chicks. A ration of bones and meat once a week will be sufficient for chicks. Hatching may be continued for the smaller breeds, but the Asiatics and other large breeds should be all out before this month. Lice may give some trouble this month, and should be fought with vigor. Provide a dust bath. Rub fresh insect powder upon sitting hens. Whitewash and fumigate the houses. Kerosene the roosts. Don't give the chicks soured food.

June.—During the hot weather some kind of shade should be provided. It is almost as important as sunshine in winter. The food need not be as hearty as in cold weather. Green stuff must be abundant; bran, ground oats and wheat should be the staple food. Small breeds may be fed considerable corn. Early chickens should be pushed rapidly, and the surplus may be marketed at this time. Separate cockerels from pullets when finishing for market. Be sure that the water supply is abundant and clean.

July.—This is a trying month, on account of the heat. If there is no natural shade, make it by growing a crop, such as corn or sunflowers. Plenty of water is desirable. A little tincture of iron in the drinking water is an excellent tonic. Rusty nails will give some iron tonic. The old hens not needed for breeding should be sold. Move the small coops often and dig over the permanent runs.

August.—Some attention is needed to bring the hens through the molting season in good condition. Feed considerable lean meat, cut bone, wheat and oats, with a little linseed meal in the morning mash. Plenty of green food is necessary if the fowls are kept shut up. Continue a little iron tonic with the drinking water. Continue to sort out the larger chicks and market them. Don't sell those needed for breeding. Refuse apples and vegetables will be appreciated by the hens. Hens which get through molting quickest and in best condition are the most vigorous, and should be kept for breeders.

September.—Buildings should be cleaned thoroughly, whitewashed and made ready for cooler weather. The laying stock may be moved to winter quarters and pushed for egg production. Give a variety of grain diet and whatever green food can be had. Feed cut bones twice a week. Birds for exhibition should be made ready a week or two before sending to the show. Accustom them to being kept in the exhibition coop, and get them as tame as possible. Look them over carefully to see that they are in condition to appear their best. Feed waste vegetables and fruit to the hens.

October.—Cool weather will bring on disease, if care is not taken. The most common disease is roup, which is caused by dampness and draft in almost every case, unless caught from other fowls. Drafts which cause a current of air to blow over the fowls at night are especially dangerous. At the first signs of disease, separate the sick fowls from the well, place in a warm room, and feed carefully. The iron tonic in the drinking water is excellent. Lay in a stock of cheap vegetables for winter use.

November.—If not done before, the houses should be put in order for the winter. Even on cold days, the hens should be turned into the scratching shed for exercise. The great secret of eggs in November, is to make the hens work for their food. Plenty of litter should cover the entire floor of the scratching shed. Any kind of litter will do. The grain should be scattered over the litter. Hens that are not through molting at this time will be worthless, and might as well be sold, if kept merely for the value of the eggs. Use as much green food as possible, and feed boiled vegetables with the grain mash in the morning. November is a critical month, and if the pullets do not begin to shell out now, it will be a hard winter for their owner.

December.—Examine your own methods carefully, and see what can be improved. The skill of a poultry grower is shown, in securing eggs during cold weather. If the fowls don't lay, blame yourself and not the variety. There is real satisfaction and plenty of profit in December eggs. Everybody wants them and will pay a good price. There is no egg producer like cut bone and a little fresh meat fed to April-hatched pullets.

KEEPING EGGS.

Hundreds of rules have been given for putting up cheap eggs, to be kept until prices rise in late autumn and winter. The most careful experiments on record have been made by German scientists.

After eight months of preservation, 400 eggs, divided into 20 different parcels for that many methods of experiment, were examined, with heterogeneous results. Upon opening for use the eggs presented the following results, according to the parcels originally numbered: 1. Eggs put up for preservation in salt water were all bad; not rotten, but uneatable, the salt having penetrated into the eggs. 2. Wrapped in paper, 80 per cent bad. 3. Preserved in a solution of salicylic acid and glycerine, 80 per cent bad. 4. Rubbed with salt, 70 per cent bad. 5. Preserved in bran, 70 per cent bad. 6. Provided with a covering of paraffin, 70 per cent bad. 7. Varnished with a solution of glycerine and salicylic acid, 70 per cent bad. 8. Put in boiling water for 12 to 15 seconds, 50 per cent bad. 9. Treated with a solution of alum, 50 per cent bad. 10. Put in a solution of salicylic acid, 50 per cent bad. 11. Varnished with water glass, 40 per cent bad. 12. Varnished with collodion, 40 per cent bad. 13. Covered with lac (probably shellac varnish), 40 per cent bad. 14. Varnished with sward, 20 per cent bad. 15. Preserved in wood ashes, 20 per cent bad. 16. Treated with boric acid and water glass, 20 per cent bad. 17. Treated with manganate of potash, 20 per cent bad. 18. Varnished with vaseline, all good. 19. Preserved in lime water, all good. 20. Preserved in a solution of water glass, all good.

Water Glass is a soluble silicate of soda, and makes the shell air-tight. Use one part, by measure, of water glass to ten parts water. It appears to be the best of the methods. Before boiling eggs which have been kept by water glass, the shell should be pricked with a strong needle, to prevent bursting. Water glass may be ordered of druggists. Lime water ranks next to water glass. The main objection is the slightly musty flavor imparted by the lime. To pickle eggs, dissolve one pint of fresh slaked stone lime and a pint of salt in three gallons of water by boiling. Drain off, and it is ready for use. Put the eggs in carefully when fresh, so as not to crack the shells. Eggs pickled in this way will keep well, and are fully as good as fresh eggs for frying or boiling, but not quite so good for cooking purposes. Eggs may be kept in a lime solution in a butter firkin as well as a barrel. The keg may be kept in a cool place. It is best to put the eggs all in at a time, making a fresh solution of lime when fresh eggs are put in, so that the fine particles of the lime will coat the eggs and exclude the air.

National Butter, Cheese and Egg Association's Method. Take one bushel best stone lime, eight quarts of salt, twenty-five ten-quart pails of water. Slake the lime with a portion of the water; then add the balance of the water and the salt. Stir a few times and let it settle. Fill the cask or vat to a depth of eighteen inches, and put in a layer of eggs about a foot deep. Now pour over them some of the settlings that is a little milky in appearance. The object of this is to have the fine lime particles drawn into the pores of the shell to seal them. Continue this operation till the vessel is full. Put only fresh eggs in, if you would take good ones out. Eggs may also be preserved by the use of salicylic acid, which may be obtained of druggists. Dissolve a tablespoonful in a gallon of boiling water. Fill a stone jar or clean cask with eggs, and pour this solution over them after it has cooled. Keep the eggs covered with the solution, and cover the cask to keep out dust. If kept in a cool place, this preparation will be good for three months.

No metal of any kind should come in contact with the salicylic acid solution. Eggs preserved by either method must be used soon after being taken from the pickle.

Loomis Recipe.—To thirty gallons of soft water, add five pounds salt and thirteen pounds lime; stir it a little every hour or two for one day. Now take one-half pound borax, one-half pound cream tartar, one-half pound saltpeter, one and one-half ounces alum, pulverize and mix thoroughly, dissolve in two gallons of boiling water, and add to the other lot. Let stand till settled, pour off all the clear solution and put the eggs in that. I have tried this method and know it to be good.

Borax.—Eight ounces of borax, two ounces common salt, six ounces boracic acid, thoroughly pulverized, is an old recipe for preserving eggs that has been extensively advertised. The directions say: Put the above ingredients in a jar, stir thoroughly, and stand one week; then take one pound of the mixture and dissolve in five gallons of water; have the solution boiling hot, and dip a shallow wire basket filled with eggs into the boiling liquid so that the eggs will be covered, and out again as soon as possible. Pack the eggs thus treated in barrels or patent boxes, and turn packages upside down twice a week to prevent the yolk from settling to one side, and the eggs may be kept perfectly fresh for a reasonable length of time. The same liquid may be used over and over again until it is all absorbed. This recipe is for 100 dozen of eggs.

Lime Recipe.—My wife has just used in custards (which were very nice) the last of eggs put down sixteen months ago. I slaked one pound of lime slowly in one gallon of boiling water, and added a spoonful of salt. The eggs were put in a pork barrel (a butter firkin will not do), and the solution poured in until it covered them. They kept perfectly.—[J. S. R., Gloucester, Mass.

Lime and Brine.—It is a very easy matter to preserve eggs, by using a mixture of lime water and brine. I sell all my winter-laid eggs, except occasionally a thin-shelled one, and still have an abundance of hen fruit to use in the family whenever needed during the period of high prices. Equal quantities of salt and lime, and a small quantity of cream of tartar, are put into a water-tight barrel or vessel, and water is poured in until the mixture is of the right consistency. If the receptacle for the eggs and the preparation is not perfectly water-tight, it will be necessary to make a very thick, pasty mixture, but if water-tight a thin liquid will do. I use one-fourth pound of cream tartar to five pounds each of salt and lime. At the time of the lowest prices—in May—fresh eggs not more than three days old are put into the mixture. These eggs are used whenever prices are high until the next May. During ten years of experience I have put down thousands of eggs, and never had any spoil that were right at first.—[W. W. N., Litchfield County, Ct.

Another Recipe.—Lime, two quarts; salt, one quart; cream of tartar, three ounces; boiling water, eight gallons; stir well and let cool. It is immaterial whether you remove sediment or not, after about two weeks. Drop the eggs, as gathered (only the fresh ones), in the pickle, and keep covered from the light.

THE POULTRY YARD PROCESS.

Take one pint of salt and one quart of fresh lime, and slake with hot water. When slaked, add sufficient water to make four gallons. When well settled, pour off the liquid gently into a stone jar. Then with a dish place the eggs in, tipping the dish after it fills with the liquid, so they will roll out without cracking the shell, for if the shell is cracked the egg will spoil. Put the eggs in whenever you have them fresh. Keep them covered, in a cool place.

QUALITIES OF THE BREEDS.

The following tables are based on statements of many authorities and experts, bringing into compact form a large amount of descriptive data from various sources. The information is meant to represent the general average of the breeds under good care, excluding statements which apply only to greatly improved strains or to fowls exceptionally well managed. Moreover, in a flock that has not been improved by selection, many of the individuals will not come up to the normal average of the breed. Hence, the beginner cannot safely rely upon the yield and weight given, although the figures have often been exceeded.

In regard to cost of raising, Jacobs declares: "Fifty cents will more than pay the cost of raising any kind of fowls, not excepting turkeys and geese." By general purpose breeds are meant those which are equally good for production of meat or eggs. The meat breeds are those which are usually kept rather for market poultry than for eggs. The egg breeds are non-sitters and great layers, but less valuable for market poultry.

Authorities consulted in compiling these tables include government Bulletins 41, 51 and 64, reports of experiment stations of New York, Louisiana and Utah, published works of Wright, Beale, Jacobs, Boyer and Hunter, and direct inquiries of leading breeders of chickens, ducks, geese and turkeys. Whenever weights are mentioned in the Standard of Perfection, these are adopted in the tables.

INCUBATION PERIODS. (DAYS.)

	Shortest.	Average.	Longest.
Hen	19	21	24
Turkey	24	26	30
Duck	28	30	32
Goose	27	30	33
Pigeon	16	18	20
Pea hen	25	28	30
Guinea hen	20	23	25
Swan	40	42	45

FOR EGGS AND MEAT.

	Live Weight, Lbs.		Mos. at maturity.	Cost to Maturity, cts	Ann'al Cost of Keeping, cts	Age at Time of Laying, mos	Dressed Wt. at 3 mos.		Dressed Wt. at 12 mos.		Av Egg Yield p Yr..	Av Eggs Per Lb.
	Cock.	Hen.					M.	F.	M.	F.		
General Purpose Breeds.												
Barred Plymouth Rocks..	9½	7½	10	75	90	6	2½	1¾	6	5	115	8½
Wyandottes...	8½	6½	10	70	80	5½	2½	1¾	5	4	115	9
Java	10	8	9	75	90	6	2½	1¾	6	5	100	8½
Dominiques	8½	6½	7	60	75	6	2½	1½	5	4	100	10
Houdans	7	6	10	70	90	6	2½	1½	5	4	115	8
Langshans	10	7	12	75	90	6	3	2	7½	5½	120	8
Meat Breeds.												
Light Brahmas	12	9½	12	75	90	6½	3¼	2	9	7	115	8
Cochins	11	8½	12	75	90	6½	3	2	8	6	100	8½
Colored Dorkings	9½	7½	9	65	75	6	2½	1¾	7	5	90	9
Egg Breeds.												
Leghorns	5	4	7	40	75	4½	2	1½	3½	2½	125	10
Hamburgs	4½	3	7	40	75	4½	1¾	1½	3	2	115	11
Black Spanish	7	6	9	60	75	5	2½	1½	4	3	110	8
Minorcas	8	6½	9	65	75	5	2¾	1½	4	3	120	7
Andalusian	5	4	7	40	75	4½	2	1½	3½	2½	120	9
Miscellaneous Breeds.												
Indian Games	9	6½	10	75	90	5	2½	1¾	5	3½	130	9
Games, R. B. B.	7½	5	8	70	80	5	2½	1½	5	3½	95	10
Polish	5½	3½	7	50	75	5	2	1½	3½	2½	100	11
Common	4½	3½	9	50	75	5	2½	1¾	4	3	150	11
Ducks.												
Pekin	8	8	9	100	175	5	6	6	—	—	130	6
Rouen	9	8	12	110	185	6	5	5	—	—	100	5
Aylesbury	9	8	12	110	175	6	5	5	—	—	100	5
Cayuga	8	7½	9	100	110	5	6	6	—	—	110	5
Common	4	3½	6	100	150	5	5	5	—	—	100	6
Geese.												
Toulouse	22	20	36	200	150	6	10	10	—	—	40	3½
Embden	20	18	30	175	150	6	10	10	—	—	20	3½
African	18	16	30	175	150	6	10	10	—	—	50	3½
Turkeys.												
Bronze	32	22	24	200	120	6	4	3	16	25	40	6

POULTRY DICTIONARY AND CALENDAR. 349

GENERAL CHARACTERISTICS.

	Eggs, color.	Constitution.	Foragers.	As sitters.	As mother.	Meat.	Skin color.	Worst defect.	Strong points.
Gen'l purpose breeds.									
Barred P. Rock.	brown	hardy	good	fine	fair	good	yellow	dark pinfeathers	general purpose
Wyandotte.	brown	hardy	good	good	good	good	yellow	smallish eggs	quick growth
Java.	light brown	hardy	good	good	good	good	yellow	dark pinfeathers	general purpose
Dominique.	light brown	hardy	good	good	good	good	yellow	small eggs	general purpose
Houdan.	light	average	good	poor	poor	good	light	skin not yellow	flavor of meat
Meat breeds.									
Light Brahma.	d'k brown	hardy	fair	heavy	fair	yellow	yellow	slow to mature	size, meat, dark eggs
Cochin.	d'k brown	average	poor	clumsy	clumsy	coarse	yellow	lazy, broody	size, beauty
Langshan.	light brown	hardy	fair	fair	fair	light	light	skin not yellow	winter laying
Col. Dorking.	light	tender	good	good	good	fine	light	skin not yellow	flavor of meat
Egg breeds.									
Leghorn.	white	hardy	fine	non	non	poor	yellow	small body	number of eggs
Hamburg.	light	tender	good	non	non	poor	bluish	small egg	number of eggs
Black Spanish.	white	average	good	non	non	good	bluish	tender skin, dark	large eggs
Minorca.	white	hardy	good	non	poor	fair	light	skin light, big comb	large eggs
Misc. breeds.									
Indian Game.	light	tender	fair	fair	fair	fine	yellow	eggs few and small	breast meat
Game, R. B. B.	brown	hardy	good	fine	best	good	yellow	eggs few and small	style
Polish.	white	tender	poor	poor	poor	poor	white	tender	ornament
Andalusian.	light	hardy	good	non	poor	poor	light	skin not yellow	color, eggs
Common.	various	hardy	good	good	good	fair	various	uncertain	hardiness
Ducks.									
Pekin.	white	hardy	fair	poor	poor	fine	yellow	timid, noisy	quick growth, eggs
Rouen.	various	hardy	fair	poor	good	good	yellow	d'k feathers sm. eggs	general purpose
Aylesbury.	light	hardy	fair	fair	fair	fair	yellow	less compact	general purpose
Cayuga.	white	hardy	good	good	good	good	dark	dark feathers	general purpose
Common.	various	hardy	good	good	good	fair	various	less meaty	general purpose
Geese.									
Toulouse.	light	hardy	fair	good	good	fair	yellow	flesh coarse	compact shape
Embden.	light	average	fair	fair	fair	fine	yellow	poor layers	quality, weight
African.	white	hardy	good	fair	fair	fine	yellow	dark feathers	good layers, meat
Turkeys.									
Bronze.	light	tender	fine	fair	fair	fine	light	slow maturity	weight

INDEX.

	PAGE
Annex to poultry house	60
Bantam fowls	107
Barrel hens' nest	37
Blackhead	327
Breed—best for market	8
For broilers	10
For early roasters	9
For late roasters	9
Breeding and cross breeding	247
Breeds—characteristics	351
Facts about	350
Multiplication of	249
Popular	121
Breeds of Fowls:	
American	168
American Dominiques	172
American Javas	177
Asiatic	123
Black Cochin	131
Black Java (cut)	249
Black-red Game	144
Black Spanish	154
Brown Leghorns	160
Buff Cochins	131
Crevecoeur	165
Dark Brahmas	127
Duck-wing Game	140
European	136
French	161
Games	139
Hamburgs	145
Houdan	161
Langshans	131
Light Brahmas	123
Partridge Cochins	128
Plymouth Rocks	168
Polish	149
Silver-gray Dorkings	136
White Cochins	131
White-crested White Polish	150
White Dorkings	137
White Leghorns	156
White Wonders (cut)	267
Wyandottes	267
Breeds, qualities of	349
Brooders—care of	261
For chicks	62-75
Brooder house	75
Brooding pen for hens	52
Bumble-foot	186
Calendar of poultry work	339-342
Caponizing—how done	93
Instruments	95,96
Care of chicks	268-269
Care of ducks	270
Census of 1890	91

	PAGE
Charcoal and stimulants	106
Chicken coop—complete	54
Box	57
Barrel	58
Chicks—Brooders for early	62
Care of	54
Raising early	60
Cholera—	181,326
Mixture	333
Cleanliness	282
Cock, weight of	350
Cold latitudes, wintering fowls	113
Color of skin not affected by feed	8
Common sense	101
Constitution—compared	351
Of various breeds	351
Coops for turkeys	297,299,300
Crates, folding	43
Crook for catching fowls	117
Crops raised for poultry	109
Cross breeding—	247
Advantage of	100
Guide to	256
Systematic	253
Crosses—for eggs	259
Various	258-259
Defects of breeds	351
Dictionary, poultry	335
Disease, defence against	187
Diseases and pests	178,320
Blackhead of turkeys	327
Bumble-foot	186
Chicken-pox	181
Cholera, the	181,326
Cramp	320
Diarrhœa	323
Distemper	178
Egg-bound	186
Egg-eating	184
Feather-eating	185,323
Feathers, loss of	186
Gapes, the	185,322
Lice	329
Mites	329
Nest bug	330
Pip, the	185
Roup, the	178,317
Scabby legs	183,321
Tapeworms	324
Douglas mixture	333
Drinking fountain	281
Duck—house	220
Mothers	219
Raising	218,225
Ducks—American Wood	245

(350)

INDEX. 351

Ducks—Continued.
As layers....................220,226
Aylesbury 227
Need little water..............223
Pekin.............................226
Rouen............................230
Time of incubation............349
Whistling........................242
Egg—crate........................ 90
Bound............................186
Ladle............................ 89
Receipts and prices............ 92
Eggs—analysis of................287
Caudling........................ 48
Color of.........................351
Eating...........................184
Feeding for.....................273
For market...................... 86
Import and export of........... 91
In Great Britain and in the
 United States................. 91
Liming........................86-89
Market for...................... 91
Of various breeds..............350
Packing for winter........ 89, 342
Packing in barrels............. 87
Per pound.......................350
Record of.......................287
Selection for...................252
To secure in winter............115
Vat for pickling................ 90
Egg—testing..................... 47
Yield per year..................350
Excelsior meal bread...........266
Exercise........................277
Exports and imports of eggs.... 92
Fattening ration................ 11
Feather—bone................... 84
Eating......................185,323
Feathers—save the.............. 84
Loss of.........................185
Types of........................334
Feeding—Buffinton's rule for...275
Chicks..........................266
Economy in......................280
Felch's rule for................264
For eggs........................273
For growth......................261
Pen for chicks.................. 59
Feed trough—....................280
Cleanly......................... 41
Food, amount of.................282
Foods—analyses of...............286
Various.........................284
Foreign egg trade............... 92
Fowls—egg bound.................186
Egg-eating......................184
Feather-eating..................185
Green food for..................105
Losing feathers.................186
Management and food............ 10
Selecting and selling..........115
White-skinned preferred in
 Philadelphia, etc............. 8
Yellow-skinned preferred in
 New England................... 8
Gapes........................185,322

Game fowls at fairs.............144
Geese—Embden....................215
Plucking........................216
Sebastopol......................242
Time of incubation..............349
Toulouse origin.................215
Varieties of....................212
Goose-raising...................210
Green food......................105
Healthy fowls...................278
Hen, standard weight of........350
Hints, useful...................279
Incubation—artificial........... 65
Natural......................... 46
Periods.........................349
Incubators, direction for run-
 ning........................... 72
Hot water....................... 68
How to make..................... 69
Saw-dust packing................ 71
Self-regulators................. 68
Success and failure with....... 66
Thermometer for................. 74
Indian meal dough............... 11
Japanese Bantams................238
Keeping, cost of................350
Keeping eggs....................343
Borax method....................342
Lime and brine recipe..........346
Lime recipe.....................345
Loomis's recipe for keeping
 eggs...........................345
Waterglass......................343
Large birds, how to raise......119
Laying age, time of.............350
Lice on hens................189,329
Prevention of...............117,326
Louse eggs on feathers..........189
Males, importance of pure......122
Market for poultry and eggs.... 91
Marketing poultry...........80,270
Market law, New York........... 82
Mating—.........................248
Black and white breeds.........248
Buff Cochins....................251
Dark Brahmas....................250
Partridge Cochins...............251
Plymouth Rocks..................249
Wyandottes......................249
Maturity, time of...............350
Mistakes, common................282
Mites...........................329
Nest box—lock................... 39
Secure.......................... 50
With roller in front........... 40
Nest boxes—..................33-35
Pinned together................. 36
Sliding, through partition..... 34
Nest—of woven wire.............. 38
Bug.............................330
For egg-eating hens............. 37
In a barrel..................... 37
Tidy............................ 40
New York dressed poultry law... 82
Packing and shipping............270
Parrish food....................332
Parasites.......................189

	PAGE
Pasturing fowls	118
Pea-fowl—	235
Trained to stay at home	237
Perches, handy	31
Poultry—anatomy	248
Conveniences	31
Dressing and stuffing	81
Dressing, N. E. method	83
Ornamental	235
Raising	7
Special food crop	109
When to market	80
Poultry houses—	13
Building material for	25
C. H. Colburn's	21
Half under ground	25
Portable	27
Very cheap	13
Very complete	21
Warm	14
Poultry keeping—as a business	98
Money made by	99
Poultry management, hints	101
Poultryman's crook	117
Poultry yard, common sense in	101
Raising, cost of	349
Ration—for fattening	11
Salt in	104
Record of eggs	287
Rheumatism	320
Roosts, low	32
Roup	178, 317
Rules of I. K. Felch	247
Salt in the ration	104
Samuels on market breeds	8
Scabby legs	183, 321
Selection for eggs	252
Setting, time of	349
Shipping—	270
Crates, folding	43
Sitting box, secure	50
Sitting hens, care of	49

	PAGE
Skin, color of	351
Spring and summer care	279
Statistics of poultry trade	91-92
Stimulants, use of	106
Stone for poultry house	33
Tapeworms	324
Terms, explanation of	335-338
Theory and practice	247
Turkey—blackhead	327
Black (cut)	302
Breeding stock	292
Bronze	311, 313
Buff	294
Chicks	295
Coop	299
Culture, essay on	306
Incubation	293
Nests	203
Raising	193
Roosts	195
Turkeys—breed and care	291
Bronze	194
Care of	300-303
Early broods	204
Fattening	196
Feeding the chicks	206
Hints about	203
In Rhode Island	310-315
Loss of weight in dressing	208
Marking	303-306
On the farm	288
Setting the hens	205
Time of incubation	349
Wild, habits of	195
Water fountain—	42, 281
Pneumatic	41
Water fowls, ornamental	241
Weight of fowls at three mos	350
Weight of fowls at twelve mos	350
Wintering fowls in cold latitudes	113

www.ingramcontent.com/pod-product-compliance
Lightning Source LLC
Chambersburg PA
CBHW032354230426
43672CB00007B/696